THE SOCIAL WORK PRACTICUM:
A STUDENT GUIDE

DONALD COLLINS
BARBARA THOMLISON
RICHARD M. GRINNELL, Jr.

THE UNIVERSITY OF CALGARY

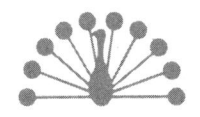

F. E. PEACOCK PUBLISHERS, INC. ▪ ITASCA, ILLINOIS

Copyright © 1992
F. E. Peacock Publishers, Inc.
All rights reserved.
Printed in the U.S.A.
Library of Congress Catalog Card Number 91:76457
ISBN 0-87581-359-3
2 3 4 5 6 7 8 9 10
1992 1993 1994 1995 1996

DEDICATED
TO ALL SOCIAL WORK
FIELD INSTRUCTORS,
FIELD LIAISONS,
PRACTICUM COORDINATORS,
AND THEIR STUDENTS

EXAMPLE OF THE INTERRELATIONS AMONG THE CONCEPTS AS PRESENTED IN THIS BOOK

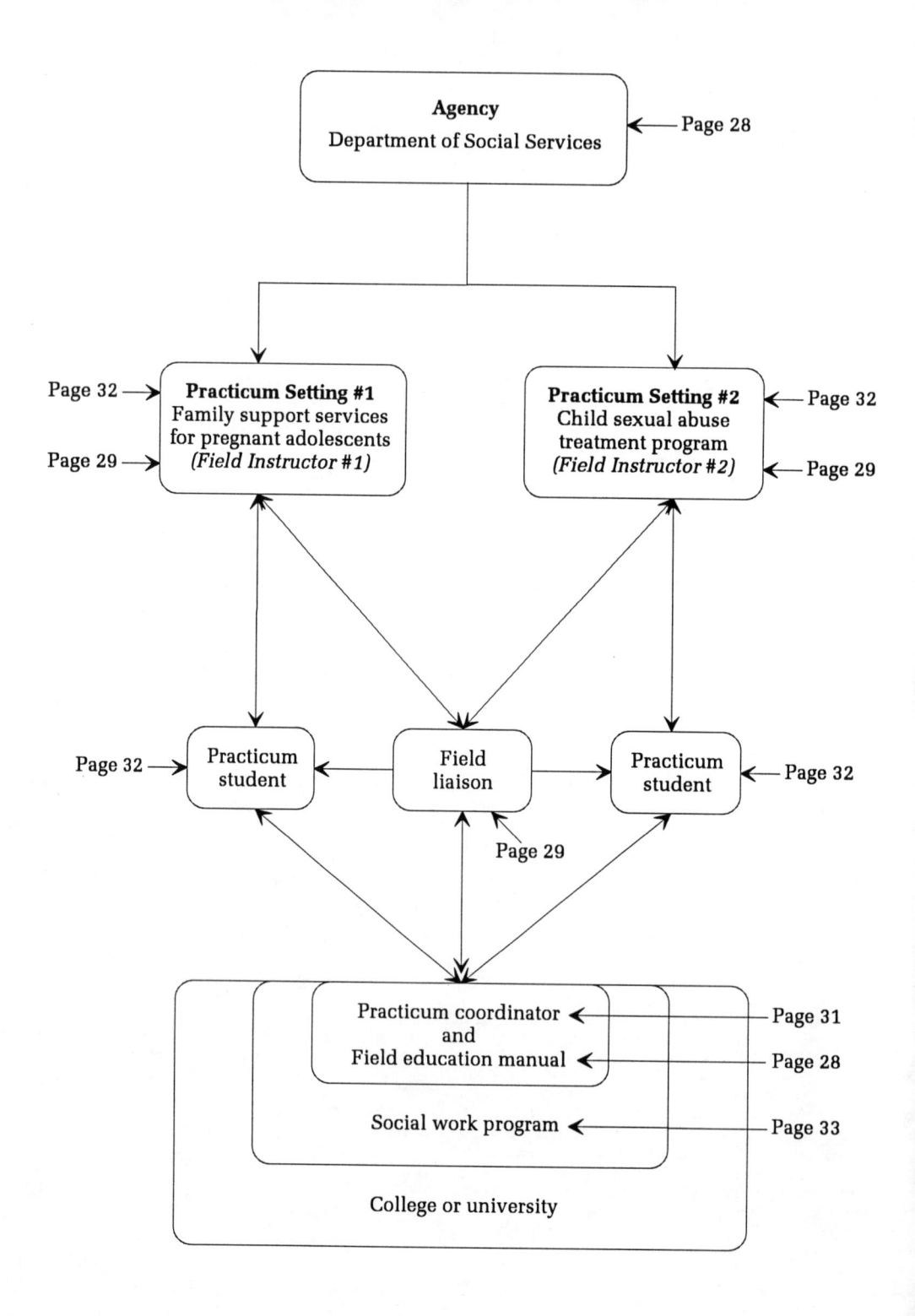

```
                    ┌─────────────────────────┐
                    │        Agency           │ ← Page 28
                    │ Department of Social    │
                    │      Services           │
                    └───────────┬─────────────┘
                                │
                 ┌──────────────┴──────────────┐
                 ▼                             ▼
Page 32 → ┌──────────────────────┐   ┌──────────────────────┐ ← Page 32
          │ Practicum Setting #1 │   │ Practicum Setting #2 │
          │Family support services│   │ Child sexual abuse   │
          │for pregnant adolescents│  │  treatment program   │
Page 29 → │ (Field Instructor #1)│   │ (Field Instructor #2)│ ← Page 29
          └──────────────────────┘   └──────────────────────┘
```

Page 32 → Practicum student ← Field liaison → Practicum student ← Page 32

Page 29 (Field liaison)

- Practicum coordinator ← Page 31
- and
- Field education manual ← Page 28
- Social work program ← Page 33
- College or university

Contents

PREFACE FOR INSTRUCTORS	xiii
PREFACE FOR STUDENTS	xvii
ACKNOWLEDGMENTS	xix
PART ONE: PRE-PRACTICUM	1
CHAPTER 1: WHY A PRACTICUM?	1
IS THE PRACTICUM AN APPRENTICESHIP?	1
☐ EXERCISE 1.1 GETTING TO KNOW THE PEOPLE INVOLVED IN FIELD EDUCATION	4
☐ EXERCISE 1.2 YOUR PRACTICUM GRADING PROCESS	6
☐ EXERCISE 1.3 FURTHER QUESTIONS TO BE ANSWERED	7
☐ EXERCISE 1.4 ANY MORE QUESTIONS?	8
☐ EXERCISE 1.5 OTHER STUDENTS' PERSPECTIVES ABOUT PRACTICUMS	10
☐ EXERCISE 1.6 FURTHER ISSUES THAT NEED TO BE EXPLORED	11
☐ EXERCISE 1.7 ADDITIONAL READINGS FOR THE PRACTICUM	12
CODE OF ETHICS	13
☐ EXERCISE 1.8 THE *CODE* AND YOU	27
☐ EXERCISE 1.9 DEFINING FIELD EDUCATION TERMS	28
SUMMARY	33
SELECTED REFERENCES	34

Chapter 2: Choosing a Practicum — 37

WHAT IS IN IT? — 37

- ☐ EXERCISE 2.1 — UNDERSTANDING YOUR VALUES — 38
- ☐ EXERCISE 2.2 — UNDERSTANDING SOCIAL WORK SERVICES — 40
- ☐ EXERCISE 2.3 — UNDERSTANDING SOCIAL SERVICES WITHIN YOUR COMMUNITY — 40
- ☐ EXERCISE 2.4 — PROCESS OF ETHICAL DECISION MAKING — 41
- ☐ EXERCISE 2.5 — LEARNING BY DOING — 41
- ☐ EXERCISE 2.6 — YOUR UNDERSTANDING OF THE SOCIAL WORK PROFESSION — 42
- ☐ EXERCISE 2.7 — INCREASING YOUR UNDERSTANDING OF THE SOCIAL WORK PROFESSION — 42
- ☐ EXERCISE 2.8 — SELF-AWARENESS AND POTENTIAL PRACTICUMS — 43
- ☐ EXERCISE 2.9 — YOUR PERSONAL QUALITIES FOR A PARTICULAR PRACTICUM — 47
- ☐ EXERCISE 2.10 — SELF-PROFILE — 48
- ☐ EXERCISE 2.11 — SOCIAL AND EMOTIONAL SUPPORT FROM YOUR SELF-PROFILE — 52
- ☐ EXERCISE 2.12 — CLIENT SYSTEMS WITH WHICH YOU ARE NOT SUITED TO WORK — 52
- ☐ EXERCISE 2.13 — FURTHER FEEDBACK FROM YOUR SELF-PROFILE — 53
- ☐ EXERCISE 2.14 — YOUR STUDENT PORTFOLIO — 54
- ☐ EXERCISE 2.15 — CHECKLIST FOR PRACTICUM SELECTION — 58
- ☐ EXERCISE 2.16 — RATING THE PRACTICUMS — 62
- ☐ EXERCISE 2.17 — PURPOSE OF THE PREPLACEMENT INTERVIEW — 64
- ☐ EXERCISE 2.18 — ROLE-PLAYING THE PREPLACEMENT INTERVIEW — 65
- ☐ EXERCISE 2.19 — INTERVIEW QUESTIONS FROM A FIELD INSTRUCTOR — 66
- ☐ EXERCISE 2.20 — PREPLACEMENT INTERVIEW QUESTIONS FOR A PRACTICUM STUDENT — 68
- ☐ EXERCISE 2.21 — IMPROVING YOUR PREPLACEMENT INTERVIEWING TECHNIQUES — 70
- ☐ EXERCISE 2.22 — THE PRACTICUM AND YOU — 71

WILL I LIKE IT? — 77

CAN I HAVE IT? — 80

- ☐ EXERCISE 2.23 — WRITING A THANK YOU LETTER — 81

SUMMARY — 83

SELECTED REFERENCES — 83

PART TWO: THE PRACTICUM	85
CHAPTER 3: SETTLING IN	85
TECHNIQUES TO SETTLING IN	85
MAKING FRIENDS AND INFLUENCING PEOPLE	87
EXPLORING YOUR PRACTICUM SETTING	88
☐ EXERCISE 3.1 GETTING TO KNOW YOUR PRACTICUM SETTING	89
YOUR TRUSTY JOURNAL	90
☐ EXERCISE 3.2 STARTING YOUR JOURNAL	90
☐ EXERCISE 3.3 INCREASING YOUR KNOWLEDGE OF YOUR PRACTICUM SETTING	91
LEARNING THE RULES AND REGULATIONS	96
FINDING OUT ABOUT YOUR AGENCY	96
☐ EXERCISE 3.4 GETTING TO KNOW YOUR AGENCY SETTING AS A SOCIAL SYSTEM	97
FINDING OUT ABOUT COMMUNITY RESOURCES	103
☐ EXERCISE 3.5 GETTING TO KNOW YOUR LOCAL COMMUNITY	103
☐ EXERCISE 3.6 INCREASING YOUR UNDERSTANDING OF YOUR COMMUNITY	107
MASTERING YOUR IMPATIENCE	108
☐ EXERCISE 3.7 PREPARING FOR YOUR FIRST SUPERVISORY CONFERENCE	108
SUMMARY	109
SELECTED REFERENCES	110
CHAPTER 4: THE LEARNING ENVIRONMENT	111
THE LEARNING CONTRACT	111
☐ EXERCISE 4.1 YOUR LEARNING CONTRACT	119
THE ACTORS	124
HOW TO LEARN BEST IN YOUR PRACTICUM	126
PRELIMINARY PRACTICUM EVALUATION	128
☐ EXERCISE 4.2 YOUR PRELIMINARY PRACTICUM EVALUATION	129
☐ EXERCISE 4.3 YOUR FIELD INSTRUCTOR'S PRELIMINARY EVALUATION OF YOU	130
☐ EXERCISE 4.4 YOUR DEVELOPING ABILITIES	131
☐ EXERCISE 4.5 RESPONDING TO FEEDBACK	132
SUMMARY	133

Contents

SELECTED REFERENCES ... 133

Chapter 5: Management ... 135

SUPERVISORY CONFERENCES ... 136

GROUP SUPERVISORY CONFERENCES ... 144

- EXERCISE 5.1 PLANNING FOR SUPERVISORY CONFERENCES ... 145
- EXERCISE 5.2 QUALITIES OF EFFECTIVE SUPERVISORY CONFERENCES ... 146
- EXERCISE 5.3 EVALUATING YOUR SUPERVISORY CONFERENCES ... 147
- EXERCISE 5.4 STEPS TO INCREASE THE EFFECTIVENESS OF SUPERVISORY CONFERENCES ... 149
- EXERCISE 5.5 USING FEEDBACK FROM SUPERVISORY CONFERENCES ... 150
- EXERCISE 5.6 KNOWING YOUR STRENGTHS ... 151

OTHER ASPECTS OF PRACTICUM MANAGEMENT ... 152

SUMMARY ... 153

SELECTED REFERENCES ... 154

Chapter 6: Documentation ... 155

YOUR JOURNAL ... 155

- EXERCISE 6.1 QUESTIONS TO PONDER ... 158

NOTES IN CLIENTS' FILES ... 160

NOTES ON SUPERVISORY CONFERENCES ... 161

PROCESS RECORDINGS ... 162

TAPED RECORDINGS ... 162

- EXERCISE 6.2 TYPES OF DOCUMENTATION WITHIN YOUR PRACTICUM ... 164
- EXERCISE 6.3 INCREASING THE USEFULNESS OF YOUR DOCUMENTATION ... 165
- EXERCISE 6.4 ADDITIONAL TYPES OF DOCUMENTATION AND RECORDING PROCEDURES ... 166

SUMMARY ... 167

SELECTED REFERENCES ... 168

Chapter 7: Mid-Term Evaluation ... 169

WHO IS AFFECTED? ... 169

THE EVALUATION CONFERENCE		174
☐ EXERCISE 7.1 COMPLETION OF YOUR MID-TERM EVALUATION		176
AN UNSATISFACTORY RATING		176
GRIEVANCE PROCEDURES		178
SUMMARY		179
SELECTED REFERENCES		180

CHAPTER 8: DILEMMAS — 181

CLIENT-RELATED ISSUES		181
☐ EXERCISE 8.1 CONFIDENTIALITY DILEMMAS WITHIN YOUR PRACTICUM SETTING		182
☐ EXERCISE 8.2 ETHICAL DILEMMAS WITHIN YOUR PRACTICUM SETTING		185
STUDENT-RELATED ISSUES		190
INSTRUCTOR-RELATED ISSUES		191
SUMMARY		194
SELECTED REFERENCES		195

CHAPTER 9: TERMINATION — 197

TERMINATING WITH YOUR CLIENTS		197
TERMINATING WITH YOUR FIELD INSTRUCTOR		198
☐ EXERCISE 9.1 EVALUATION OF YOUR FIELD INSTRUCTOR		205
TERMINATING WITH THE AGENCY		214
☐ EXERCISE 9.2 EVALUATION OF YOUR PRACTICUM SETTING		217
☐ EXERCISE 9.3 YOUR FINAL EVALUATION		223
PREPARING FOR YOUR NEXT PRACTICUM		224
☐ EXERCISE 9.4 GETTING READY FOR YOUR NEXT PRACTICUM SETTING		225
☐ EXERCISE 9.5 POSSIBILITIES OF FUTURE PRACTICUM SETTINGS		226
SUMMARY		227
SELECTED REFERENCES		228

APPENDIX A: PRACTICUM EVALUATION FORM ... 229
    INTRODUCTION ... 230
    LEARNING GOAL 1: FUNCTIONS EFFECTIVELY WITHIN A PROFESSIONAL CONTEXT ... 231
    LEARNING GOAL 2: FUNCTIONS EFFECTIVELY WITHIN AN ORGANIZATIONAL CONTEXT ... 239
    LEARNING GOAL 3: FUNCTIONS EFFECTIVELY UTILIZING KNOWLEDGE-DIRECTED PRACTICE SKILLS ... 244
    LEARNING GOAL 4: FUNCTIONS EFFECTIVELY WITHIN AN EVALUATIVE CONTEXT ... 260

INDEX ... 265

Preface for Instructors

SEVERAL EXCELLENT THEORETICALLY ORIENTED texts about field education have been written primarily for social work *faculty*. Building on the knowledge disseminated in these texts, this book is geared as an inexpensive, practical guide for social work *students* who are about to enter their first practicum. The major thrust of the book is centered around monitoring, quality improvement, and evaluation throughout the student's practicum experience.

GOALS

Keep the book's thrust in mind as you consider its four goals: to reinforce the concept that a practicum is a learning experience and not a work experience; to emphasize the necessity of integrating theoretical classroom learning with practicum learning; to encourage students to participate fully in their practicum experience; and to provide a guide to the triumphs and pitfalls along the way.

There are, however, three noteworthy goals that the book does *not* attempt to accomplish. First, the ideas, procedures, and suggestions contained in this book are not intended as a substitute for the program's field education manual and handouts. Rather, this book is to be used as a *supplement* or as a source book to complement a range of field education materials that practicum coordinators distribute to their practicum students. In fact, it could be used as a workbook for the integration seminar, or simply as a self-assisted working guide for students during their field education experience. Second, it *does not teach practice skills*. Many other books teach them with a depth and breadth that we could not hope to duplicate in this small volume. Finally, the book *contains little theory* and no issue is dealt with in-depth. Our intention is not to provide an exhaustive array of theories or issues to cover every unique practicum situation. Our aim is to skim the surface of what it is like to be in the first practicum—to put a toe in the water, so to speak, by providing beginning practicum students with a taste of what it might be like to swim.

BOOK'S ORGANIZATION

In addition to having perforated pages, the book is three-hole punched, so it can be inserted in a three-ring binder that the social work program provides or the student can buy at the local bookstore. The program's field education manual and handouts can then be added to the binder so a complete guide to the student's field educational experience is then self-contained and individualized not only for the student but for the practicum portion of the program as well.

As you can see from the table of contents, the book reflects the logical phases of the field education process. Tasks associated with monitoring, quality improvement, and evaluation are linked to the phases of field education and run throughout the book. Part One contains two chapters that are geared toward preplacement issues such as understanding the need and the selection of a practicum. Part Two, which contains seven chapters, reflects the actual practicum experience itself: settling in; creating, managing, and documenting the learning environment; participating in mid-term and final evaluations; solving various dilemmas; and using the first practicum as a foundation for a second one.

Some programs offer practicums through a block placement format while others prefer a concurrent arrangement. Some students, therefore, are taking social work classroom courses at the same time they are in the field, whereas others have completed most of their courses prior to their practicums. As a consequence, many students are at different phases of their total social work learning experience when they enter their practicums. In addition, some students make rapid progress through the learning phases while others move more slowly. This book provides students the opportunity to progress at their own pace by completing the book's exercises within the various phases as they become applicable. It is extremely flexible because it can be used in a 10- or 14-week time span in addition to a block or concurrent practicum arrangement.

We believe the learning that occurs during the practicum is unique. For many students, learning by doing is more effective than learning by reading. It is with this in mind that we have selected the exercises. Students and field instructors alike have found they serve to improve students' understanding of the text. In this way, students are learning by doing and are recognizing the need to integrate classroom and practicum learning. We encourage you to select the exercises, and their sequence, that you believe are most appropriate for helping students during their practicum supervisory conferences and integrative seminar experiences.

HOW TO USE THE BOOK

This book can be used within the three general phases of the field educational process. It can be used to guide agency and/or student practicum orientation procedures, guide student preplacement activities, and supplement the student's actual practicum experience.

Practicum Orientation

Orientation procedures to practicums vary considerably from one social work program to another. A series of tutorials or a workshop may be given (or meetings may be arranged) at which preplacement students, practice methods teachers, field liaisons, and field instructors use the book as a guide to introduce the entire field instruction process within their program. Whatever the preferred procedure, the text can be used selectively in the orientation to complement the information given by the program. In this way, an individualized orientation to the practicum is possible.

Preplacement

We suggest that students read Part One *before* they begin to plan for their practicums. The exercises in Part One focus on the work students need to do to ensure that the practicum they are selected for will match with their individual needs and learning goals. These exercises should therefore be completed by students *before* a practicum is finalized. The two chapters in Part One can be skimmed by students if the program assigns practicums to them rather than encouraging students to participate in the selection of a practicum.

During Practicum

During the first few days of the practicum, students should *briefly skim* Part Two. They then should thoroughly read the chapters, and complete selected exercises, as they go through the various phases within their practicums. Once students have begun their practicums, the book's content and exercises for Part Two may be used in four ways: as a reference (or guide) to self-directed learning, as a focal point or supplement to integrative field seminars, as a starting point for individual or group supervisory conferences, or to complement the practice methods course.

The book emphasizes the beginning and final phases of the field experience where understanding of the processes assumes a larger importance. In the middle phases, where the application of practice skills furthers the processes discussed in this book, students should select additional information sources particularly suited to assisting them with these skills.

The exercises in Part Two are to aid students with such tasks as organizing the learning contract, preparing for supervisory conferences, and participating in their mid-term and final evaluations. Throughout, emphasis is placed on the student's responsibility to create and manage a positive learning environment and to assume a proactive role in designing and managing a successful learning experience that is individual, goal oriented, and meets the highest standards of the profession.

A LOOK TOWARD THE FUTURE

The place of the practicum in social work education is continuing to develop in leaps and bounds. Students who understand what the practicum is intended to achieve and the issues associated with it will be in a better position to contribute to its growth, both immediately as students, and later as potential field instructors. If, at some future time, we prepare a second edition, your comments would be most appreciated. We would like to know, from your perspective, which parts were stimulating and useful in addition to those which you feel were downright useless.

We had a good time writing this book and we hope it shows. We used first and last names within the text to add a bit of pizazz; however, the names, characters, places, and incidents within this book are either the product of the authors' imaginations or are used fictitiously. Any resemblance to actual events, locales, or persons (living or dead) is entirely coincidental. We hope that the apparent levity with which we have treated the first social work practicum will be accepted in the same spirit as it is intended. Our intention is not to diminish the practicum experience; rather, it is to present it with humor, warmth, and humanness so that the student's first contact with it will be a positive one. After all, if wetting your big toe scares you, you will never learn to swim.

January 1992

Donald Collins
Barbara Thomlison
Richard M. Grinnell, Jr.

Preface for Students

EACH SOCIAL WORK PROGRAM IS unique in how it administers its practicums. We have designed this book to provide both you and your program with the opportunity to modify its contents in an effort to fit your specific learning needs and your program's practicum expectations as well. Your particular social work program will view different elements of the text and exercises as more or less essential during your total practicum experience. Our aim was to provide both you and your social work program with a sample of various practicum issues, some of which may only be of passing interest for you, while others will apply directly to you and your program. Whatever the case, carefully consider your program requirements and your learning interests or needs, then read the text and complete the exercises that are most relevant to not only your program but to you as well.

The book's underlying theme is evaluation. Tasks and exercises will assist you in the art of making sure that your activities result in a practicum in which you learn useful material that you can apply in actual practice situations. The emphasis on evaluation will differ in each social work program. Some programs require a formal preliminary and mid-term evaluation of your progress during your practicum while others do not. Some programs formally evaluate their field instructors while others do not. In addition, some programs formally evaluate your practicum setting through your practicum coordinator, your field liaison, you, or all three. Then there are programs that do not view evaluation quite this formally. Above all, evaluation assists in providing a continuing quality practicum not only for you but for future students as well.

You can use this book in four ways:

1. Use it as the main text or supplementary workbook for your integrative seminar course. Your integrative seminar instructor may require you to complete selected exercises for class discussion or for hand-in assignments.
2. Consider it as a supplementary or source book to other required field education

readings that your practicum coordinator may hand out. In this case, you can prepare in advance for your practicum by reading the book and completing selected exercises to help you experience a smooth transition into your practicum setting. The book can be used alone or in tandem with your field instructor as a source book, or stepping stone, for your supervisory conferences during your practicum.

3. Use it as a workbook from the initial practicum planning (Part One) through completion (Part Two), and as a guide to a second practicum. Some have suggested to us that it could even be considered as an aid in the preparation for your first social work job interview.
4. Use it as a self-instructional source book throughout your practicum if there are no required readings or exercises.

In any event, we hope that this book will be of some use to you in your first journey into uncharted territory. In this spirit, we offer this book to you—the future social work practitioner. We hope you will keep it on your bookshelf and refer to it from time to time as a reminder of your first practicum experience. If this book helps you to expand your practicum-related knowledge and skills in reference to becoming more effective with your future clients, our efforts will have been more than justified. If it also encourages you to become a field instructor in order to continue the pursuit of a stronger, better-knit practical base for social work practice, our task will be fully rewarded.

January 1992

Donald Collins
Barbara Thomlison
Richard M. Grinnell, Jr.

Acknowledgments

THE THREE OF US have been field instructors, field liaisons, integrative field seminar teachers, and practice methods teachers for longer than we wish to recall. We thank the countless number of social work students who we had the privilege of teaching (and learning from) as they have directly contributed to the conceptual development of this book. In addition to our students, special thanks go to the following 14 faculty who have read the initial manuscript in its entirety and had a great deal of input into the refinement of the final product:

Janet Black, Associate Director, Department of Social Work, California State University at Long Beach

John J. Conklin, Director of Field Education, School of Social Work, University of Connecticut

Geraldine Faria, Field Coordinator, Department of Social Work, University of Akron

Richard W. Greenlee, Department of Social Work, Ohio University

Reva Fine Holtzman, Director for the Center for Field Education, Hunter School of Social Work

Allie Callaway Kilpatrick, Director of Field Instruction, School of Social Work, University of Georgia

Ellen Sue Mesbur, Director, School of Social Work, Ryerson Polytechnical Institute

Sylvia Navari, Director of Field Education Program, Division of Social Work, California State University at Sacramento

Ginny T. Raymond, Assistant Professor, School of Social Work, University of Alabama

Gayla Rogers, Director of Field Education, Faculty of Social Work, The University of Calgary

Dean Schneck, Director of Field Education, School of Social Work, University of Wisconsin at Madison

Elaine Vayda, Director of Field Instruction, School of Social Work, York University, Atkinson College

Barbara Key Wickell, Director of Field Education, Jane Addams College of Social Work, University of Illinois

Linda R. Williams, Director of Field Education, Social Work Program, North Carolina State University

Within the limits of strict time frames and resources, we have strived to follow the suggestions offered by our colleagues; however, they should not be held responsible for our sins of omission or commission. We also wish to express our appreciation to Marj Andrukow, Irene Hoffart, Elsie Johnson, Judy Krysik, and Margaret Williams for their help in the preparation of the final manuscript. We also extend our sincere appreciation to Ray J. Thomlison, our dean, who provided the necessary academic milieu and encouragement to help us see this book to completion. We would be remiss not to mention that the people at F. E. Peacock Publishers have been more than supportive in our adventure into uncharted territory, and it is a privilege to publish under the Peacock banner.

The exercises have been extracted from numerous North American field education manuals over the past ten years. As you know (evidenced by the "course outline exchange" exhibit at the annual CSWE meetings), many of the manuals contain exercises that have been reproduced and modified from others and it is exceedingly difficult to locate their "original" sources. A few of the exercises in this book have been modified from the field education manuals from the following schools: School of Social Welfare, University of California at Berkeley; Faculty of Social Work, The University of Calgary; School of Social Work, Howard University; Department of Social Work, Tabor College; Social Work Program, Grambling State University; Department of Social Work, Morgan State University; Social Work Program, Northwestern College; Undergraduate Social Work Program, College of St. Francis; School of Social Work, University of Wisconsin at Madison; Department of Sociology and Social Work, Walla Walla College; School of Social Work, University of Texas at Austin; School of Social Work, University of Oklahoma; School of Social Work, University of Connecticut; Barry University School of Social Work, Barry University; School of Social Work, Arizona State University; Windsor School of Social Work, University of Windsor; School of Social Work, University of Victoria; The Maritime School of Social Work, Dalhousie University; Faculty of Social Work, Wilfrid Laurier University; Tri-College Social Work Program, Clarke College; Undergraduate Social Work Program, Salisbury State College; Department of Social Work, Atkinson College, York University; Social Work Program, Concordia College; Faculty of Social Work, University of Toronto; and Department of Social Work, University of Wyoming. We thank the National Association of Social Workers and the Canadian Association of Social Workers for providing permission for us to reprint their *Code of Ethics* contained in Figures 1.1 (pages 13–16) and 1.2 (pages 17–26), and Yaro Starak for Figures 4.1–4.4 (pages 115–118).

Part One: Pre-Practicum

CHAPTER 1

Why a Practicum?

IF YOU HIRE A lawyer to help you write your will, you will probably prefer one who has *practical* experience with will writing. It will not be enough that the lawyer can expound at length upon "will theory." You are not interested in wills in general. You just want someone to help you write one. In a similar way, a client seeking help from a social service agency does not care much if you can write a brilliant exposition on "problem solving with clients." Clients just want you to do *it*. They want you to know, in a very practical way, how to do *it*. If possible, they want you to have done *it* before.

The point of a *social work practicum*, sometimes referred to as a *social work field placement*, is to learn how to do *it*: how to apply theoretical social work material to a hands-on situation; how to cope with the practical limitations of a real-life environment; how to be useful to real people with real problems in a real setting that is less than ideal. For social workers, the importance of knowing and understanding how to help people cannot be overstated. An incompetent lawyer can write a poorly constructed will; an incompetent social worker can damage people's lives.

In the old days, before the industrial age invented classrooms, apprentices learned their trade by watching their masters practice. This apprenticeship system had certain advantages: practical work began at once and was ongoing; instruction was given individually or in small groups; mistakes and triumphs were noticed quickly; and feedback, often in the form of shouts and thumps, was relevant and fast. There were also disadvantages, however, which we will now explore.

IS THE PRACTICUM AN APPRENTICESHIP?

Apprentices sometimes had little say about which master would teach them. If they had an incompetent master, they may not have been able to recognize (or rise above) the incompetence because they had no alternative sources of information. Without general information, they may not have been able to see their own profession as part of a larger whole, a necessary cog in the wheel of a social system.

Your social work practicum is a form of apprenticeship. However, because of the disadvantages just mentioned, your program does not merely say, "Find a job in the social work field and get some *practical* experience." Instead, practicums are carefully designed to incorporate the advantages of the apprenticeship system while minimizing the disadvantages. Let us look more closely at what this means.

The Profession and the Teacher

The first disadvantage to be minimized is that the apprentice might have little say about which master should do the teaching. Since you are now enrolled in a social work program you have already, to some extent, selected a field. You have decided, if only tentatively, that you want to practice social work; you do not want to practice dentistry or law.

Like dentistry and law, social work is a large and diverse field. As you know from your previous social work practice classes, some social workers work with individuals. Some work only with individuals who have a problem in a specific area—abusing their children, for example, or having too intimate an acquaintanceship with the criminal justice system. Some social workers are more comfortable working with groups. Some social workers work with families, some with communities, some with organizations; some do research and some write books. Some social workers do all of the above.

Social workers work in environments that range from their own offices to small two-person agencies to business offices to large and complex organizations, hospitals, schools, courts, and many others. They are known as counselors, psychotherapists, clinical social workers, family therapists, group workers, community workers, researchers, program planners, or policy analysts.

The Practicum Coordinator. Because the choice of potential practicums is so enormous and so potentially confusing, your social work program has tried to narrow it down a little. Most programs have some form of an office of field education, or the equivalent, where everything to do with social work practicums is administered and managed. Depending on the size of the social work program, this office can be staffed by several persons and a hive of humming computers or it may be a single person, working from a small inconspicuous room. Whatever the situation, this person is usually known as the *field education coordinator, field coordinator, director of field,* or *practicum coordinator* and has two main tasks.

The first task is to locate and secure good practicums. Practicums are usually located in a social service agency (or a specific program within an agency). The task involves ensuring that there are enough practicums to accommodate all the social work students, that the practicums are sufficiently varied to afford a meaningful choice, and that each practicum offered provides a real *learning* experience. Some agencies are unable to find the time to accommodate students. The practicum settings selected by the practicum coordinator are reputable social work agencies whose social work staff have the time, the interest, the knowledge, and the skills to provide social work students with good practical learning environments.

The second task of the practicum coordinator is to disseminate to you the information about the selected practicum opportunities within your local community. The vital match between you and the practicum finally selected is not made only by the practicum coordinator. Neither is it made only by the agency where the practicum takes place, although agency personnel obviously have a say in which social work students they finally accept.

The selection also rests with you, the student, who must make an intelligent match by comparing information about available practicum opportunities with information about yourself. The art of selecting, and being selected by, a suitable agency where you can do your practicum will be discussed later on in this book. For the time being, it is enough to say that your program has tackled the problem of incompetent masters.

Alternate Sources of Information

The second disadvantage of the apprenticeship system is that the apprentice does not have enough information from other sources to evaluate and improve upon the skills taught by the master. You go to classes. You are taught the knowledge and skills that you are supposed to apply in your practicum. There is, in every good practicum experience, a direct relationship between the practical experience gained in your practicum and the theoretical knowledge learned in the classroom. Furthermore, the practical experience is usually set at a level that students find challenging but not overwhelming. There are four primary sources of information that you can draw on to improve your practical helping skills: your field instructor, your field liaison, the practicum, and the integrative seminar.

Your Field Instructor. All this is easier said than done. Practice that is challenging to one student might be overwhelming to another, and downright boring to yet a third. Look around at your classmates. They come from a variety of backgrounds. Some have recently graduated from high school. Some have worked in the field for years and returned to school for a degree. Some are mature students with a great deal of life experience but no social work experience. Others are knowledgeable in one particular social work area but know little of other areas. You will have a field instructor in your practicum who must take all of these variables into account.

Field instructors are traditionally professional social workers employed by the agencies where the practicums are located. They communicate with the social work program via the field liaison (to be discussed). Often they are responsible for assigning and evaluating your progress and are responsible for the ongoing day-to-day instruction. Field instructors have a formidable task.

First, the field instructor must satisfy your social work program that its practicum standards are being met; second, she must match your skills, qualities, and potential with the various tasks to be accomplished within the agency; third, she must protect the agency's clients from errors that could be made by beginning students; fourth, she must ensure smooth relationships between you, the social workers, and other staff within the agency; and fifth, she must find the time to do all this. Field instructors are very dedicated people and without them we, as professionals, would flounder. Field instructors provide the practical backbone to social work education.

The field instructor's challenges are not yet over. Your program's standards include the integration between practicum and classroom learning, but most field instructors never go to the students' classrooms. Possibly, it has been some time since she was in any classroom, and social work, like life, moves on. Ideas change; expectations change; accepted techniques and methods of presentation change. It is quite possible that your field instructor will not know what theoretical material she is supposed to integrate with your practicum. Just as you prepare, your field instructor prepares by reading about the roles and responsibilities she must assume. Your social work program may have orientation procedures in place to prepare field instructors for these roles and responsibilities.

Your field instructor may wish to complete Exercise 1.1 below, which is related to the roles of key field education persons, in her own way or with you when you are ready. Her challenge is to accurately identify and weigh all the necessary factors so that your practicum has the essential qualities to be successful.

Your Field Liaison. The structure and design of your practicum has allowed for the possibility that your field instructor is not kept fully informed on what is going on in your program. The person known as a field liaison, who is usually a faculty member in your program, is responsible for the liaison between your program, your field instructor, and you. Becoming absolutely familiar with the roles, functions, and expectations of your field liaison is the purpose of Exercises 1.1 and 1.2. Their main function is to link your program with your practicum, to assist in building the bridge between theory and practice, and to help solve any problems that may arise. There is another important member of the field education team who can assist with the communication, the bridge building, and the problem solving. This is *you*. It is after all, *your* learning experience, *your* future, the beginning of *your* professional life. It is your practicum experience which you will never forget.

**EXERCISE 1.1
GETTING TO KNOW THE PEOPLE
INVOLVED IN FIELD EDUCATION**

For you to understand and get prepared for your practicum, you will find it useful to do some background reading and reflection about how your practicum fits into your social work program. This important preparatory activity will assist you to understand the expectations and responsibilities associated with your future practicum.

Read your social work program's field education manual (if it has one). List the roles and responsibilities for yourself, your field instructor, your field liaison, and the practicum coordinator in the spaces provided on the following page. Mark the items where the roles and responsibilities are the same and different by highlighting in two different colors.

Chapter 1 / Why a Practicum?

Yourself	Roles	Responsibilities

Field Instructor	Roles	Responsibilities

Field Liaison	Roles	Responsibilities

Practicum Coordinator	Roles	Responsibilities

EXERCISE 1.2
YOUR PRACTICUM GRADING PROCESS

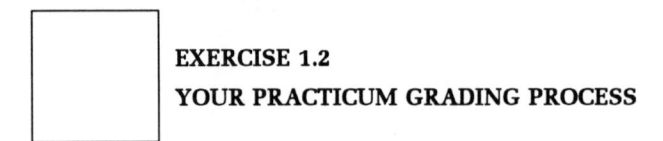

Describe below the process of finalizing your mid-term practicum grade (if you have one) and final practicum grade. Who is responsible for your mid-term and/or final grade submission? What is the grading format (e.g., pass/fail, letter grade)?

The Practicum. The practicum is a required core course in the social work curriculum. Accredited social work programs are required to have their students spend a minimum number of hours in a supervised practice setting under a qualified field instructor; however, many programs require more than the minimum. Depending on your particular program, you may have two independent practicum experiences in the last part of your program. These hours may be taken as a "block" placement, in which you go to the practicum setting daily for a period of about 14 to 15 weeks. As we stated in the preface for instructors, sometimes the two 14- or 15-week block periods follow each other, back to back, and sometimes they are alternated with a period in the classroom, depending on the particular program.

A second possibility is that you may take your practicum in a concurrent format. This means that you go to your practicum for part of the week and continue to take classroom courses during the other part of the week. Either way, the same total number of hours are spent in the practicum. Preference for one format has nothing to do with hours; rather, it is concerned with the advantages and disadvantages of a total immersion as compared with a split situation. For example, a student who exists half in school and half in the practicum setting, not to mention the third half which goes home occasionally, might feel torn between the demands of classroom course work and the demands of the practicum.

It might be tempting to skip class to accommodate a new client or to spend the day in the agency's washroom to finish an overdue term paper. On the other hand, it may be easier to integrate your practicum experience with your classroom courses when both are occurring simultaneously. If you are taking a class on group work, for example, it may be helpful if you are also coleading a client group.

Some programs use the block format and others the concurrent format. Some use one format for the undergraduate program and the other for the graduate program. Most tailor the format to the needs and resources of the local agencies and the social work program. A majority of social work programs ensure that practicums and classroom courses are integrated by providing an *integrative seminar* sometimes called a *practicum tutorial*.

The Integrative Seminar. The integrative seminar is a required practicum-related class and provides an opportunity for students to discuss their practicum experiences with other students. The seminar may be taught by the field liaison, the field instructor, or another instructor. It may take place at the university or in the agency, but its purpose is always the same: to help students integrate practicum practice issues with theory.

To a certain extent, elective social work courses can also serve this integrative function. If your practicum setting is concerned with foster care, for example, you may wish to choose an elective that gives you as much information as possible about foster care in the child welfare system. The point is, the practicum is a core component in your overall learning. It may be the most important part in your social work program. The field instructor evaluates your progress in a different manner than your other classroom instructors. Exercises 1.1, 1.2, and 1.3 can assist your understanding of the evaluation process used in your practicum course. The practicum is indeed a unique course in reference to how students are evaluated.

**EXERCISE 1.3
FURTHER QUESTIONS
TO BE ANSWERED**

After reading your program's field education manual, list four questions that you have about planning for (and obtaining) a practicum at this time.

1.

2.

3.

4.

EXERCISE 1.4
ANY MORE QUESTIONS?

In a small group with other preplacement students, discuss your understanding and questions (Exercises 1.1–1.3) of what the practicum experience is all about. Summarize the group discussion and note any remaining questions that you may have at this time.

Summary:

Further questions:

Social Work as Part of a Larger Whole

The third disadvantage of the apprenticeship system is that apprentices sometimes do not understand how their particular trade fits into the social system as a whole; that is, they do not understand *why* they are doing *what* they are doing. The purpose of some tasks is fairly self-evident. If garbage collectors fail to collect, garbage, rats, and germs will grow fruitful and multiply. If physicians fail to heal, some people will suffer unnecessary pain and others will die. The task of the social worker, however, is not quite so clear-cut as it may seem. The social work profession exists to provide humane and effective social services to individuals, families, groups, communities, and society so that people's social functioning may be enhanced and the quality of life improved.

There is nothing wrong with this. Obviously, the enhancement of social functioning and the improvement of the quality of life are desirable goals. On the other hand, it is a comment on our society that the enhancing and improving needs to be done by *professionals*. What happened to Aunt Dorothy? To Grandpa? To the idea that if your roof leaks you mend it, if your fence falls down you rebuild it, and if your child has a problem you help solve it?

Like dentists and lawyers, social workers also live in an age of specialization where professionals categorize, subdivide, and do battle over their respective turfs. Mrs. Puccio's weak heart, for example, is looked at first by her family doctor who then sends her to a doctor who specializes in weak hearts. Mrs. Puccio's depression, helped along by the malfunctioning weak heart, falls to the social worker.

Mrs. Puccio's older mother, whom she can no longer care for because she is depressed, is looked after by the gerontologist and the nursing home staff. Mrs. Puccio's children are taken into care by child welfare services. Her husband, who has had an ongoing problem with drinking, is being treated in an alcohol detoxification program.

Specialization is not necessarily bad. Like everything else, it has its brighter and darker sides, and certainly Mrs. Puccio, her husband, mother, and children have to be cared for somehow. The point is that specialization in social work may hold more potential dangers than specialization in other fields. If you hire a specialist to mend your roof, for example, you may be depriving yourself of the sense of accomplishment that comes from fixing it yourself. More likely, however, you will just be depriving yourself of lost hours, wasted money, and a broken leg.

To hire a specialist to mend your life is a different matter. Now you stand to lose such things as your sense of control, your self-esteem, and your identity as a functioning, competent adult. Social work as a profession is well aware of these dangers and phrases such as "self-determination" and "helping others to help themselves" occur over and over again in social work books.

The practicum is an opportunity to learn to help. It is also an opportunity to learn when *not* to help—when *not* to take children out of their homes, when *not* to move Mrs. Puccio's mother from her evil-smelling bedroom to an antiseptic nursing home, when *not* to take a juvenile back to court for breaking the terms of probation.

All of these "nots" involve ethical choices. For example, do you have the right to move Mrs. Puccio's mother to "safety" against her wishes? Does your agency have the right? Does our society have the right? Who makes these decisions?

**EXERCISE 1.5
OTHER STUDENTS' PERSPECTIVES
ABOUT PRACTICUMS**

Contact another social work student who has completed or is about to complete a practicum. Find out from the student's perspective if the roles and responsibilities of your field instructor, your field liaison, and the practicum coordinator work in the way your program's field education manual suggests (Exercise 1.1). Ask how the student regards the grading process and if he or she has any suggestions about planning and obtaining a practicum. Write a summary of your discussion below.

**EXERCISE 1.6
FURTHER ISSUES THAT
NEED TO BE EXPLORED**

Refer back to your questions and notes in the previous five exercises. If any questions or concerns remain unanswered, rewrite and highlight them below. Beside each item, write the name of a person, and his or her role, who you believe might assist you to clarify or answer your questions. Take steps to contact the people on your list.

Questions: *Names:*   *Roles:*

**EXERCISE 1.7
ADDITIONAL READINGS
FOR THE PRACTICUM**

Check with your practicum coordinator for additional reading beyond your program's field education manual. Many articles on field education will provide a helpful overview of the skills and information necessary for successful student practicum learning. Additional reading will expand your knowledge and understanding of what to expect from this learning experience. Some books and articles are listed at the end of each chapter in this book. After reading, record the book(s) or article(s) and the theme or issue(s) addressed. In what way might this information be helpful in the preparation for your practicum? Use the space below for your response.

CODE OF ETHICS

The National Association of Social Workers formulated a *Code of Ethics* to help social workers make difficult decisions. The *Code* was adopted by the Delegate Assembly of the National Association of Social Workers in 1979 and came into effect July 1, 1980 (see Figure 1.1 on pages 13–16). The Canadian Association of Social Workers formulated its *Code of Ethics* in 1983 (see Figure 1.2 on pages 17–26). The *Code* that is relevant to your social work program should be read, re-read, and followed. Nevertheless, you may come across situations where the *Code* will not help you, where you will have to make your own professional judgments based on your knowledge and experience of the place of social work in society.

FIGURE 1.1

NATIONAL ASSOCIATION OF SOCIAL WORKERS
CODE OF ETHICS

I. THE SOCIAL WORKER'S CONDUCT AND COMPORTMENT AS A SOCIAL WORKER

A. Propriety—The social worker should maintain high standards of personal conduct in the capacity or identity as social worker.

1. The private conduct of the social worker is a personal matter to the same degree as is any other person's, except when such conduct compromises the fulfillment of professional responsibilities.

2. The social worker should not participate in, condone, or be associated with dishonesty, fraud, deceit, or misrepresentation.

3. The social worker should distinguish clearly between statements and actions made as a private individual and as a representative of the social work profession or an organization or group.

B. Competence and Professional Development—The social worker should strive to become and remain proficient in professional practice and the performance of professional functions.

1. The social worker should accept responsibility or employment only on the basis of existing competence or the intention to acquire the necessary competence.

2. The social worker should not misrepresent professional qualifications, education, experience, or affiliations.

C. Service—The social worker should regard as primary the service obligation of the social work profession.

1. The social worker should retain ultimate responsibility for the quality and extent of the service that individual assumes, assigns, or performs.

2. The social worker should act to prevent practices that are inhumane or discriminatory against any person or group of persons.

D. Integrity—The social worker should act in accordance with the highest standards of professional integrity and impartiality.

1. The social worker should be alert to and resist the influences and pressures that interfere with the exercise of professional discretion and impartial judgment required for the performance of professional functions.

2. The social worker should not exploit professional relationships for personal gain.

E. Scholarship and Research—The social worker engaged in study and research should be guided by the conventions of scholarly inquiry.

1. The social worker engaged in research should consider carefully its possible consequences for human beings.

2. The social worker engaged in research should ascertain that the consent of participants in the research is voluntary and informed without any implied deprivation or penalty for refusal to participate, and with due regard for participants' privacy and dignity.

3. The social worker engaged in research should protect participants from unwarrant-

ed physical or mental discomfort, distress, harm, danger, or deprivation.

4. The social worker who engages in the evaluation of services or cases should discuss them only for professional purposes and only with persons directly and professionally concerned with them.

5. Information obtained about participants in research should be treated as confidential.

6. The social worker should take credit only for work actually done in connection with scholarly and research endeavors and credit contributions made by others.

II. THE SOCIAL WORKER'S ETHICAL RESPONSIBILITY TO CLIENTS

F. Primacy of Clients' Interests—The social worker's primary responsibility is to clients.

1. The social worker should serve clients with devotion, loyalty, determination, and the maximum application of professional skill and competence.

2. The social worker should not exploit relationships with clients for personal advantage, or solicit the clients of one's agency for private practice.

3. The social worker should not practice, condone, facilitate, or collaborate with any form of discrimination on the basis of race, color, sex, sexual orientation, age, religion, national origin, marital status, political belief, mental or physical handicap, or any other preference or personal characteristic, condition, or status.

4. The social worker should avoid relationships or commitments that conflict with the interests of clients.

5. The social worker should under no circumstances engage in sexual activities with clients.

6. The social worker should provide clients with accurate and complete information regarding the extent and nature of the services available to them.

7. The social worker should apprise clients of their risks, rights, opportunities, and obligations associated with social service to them.

8. The social worker should seek advice and counsel of colleagues and supervisors whenever such consultation is in the best interest of clients.

9. The social worker should terminate service to clients, and professional relationships with them, when such service and relationships are no longer required or no longer serve the clients' needs or interests.

10. The social worker should withdraw services precipitously only under unusual circumstances, giving careful consideration to all factors in the situation and taking care to minimize possible adverse effects.

11. The social worker who anticipates the termination or interruption of service to clients should notify clients promptly and seek the transfer, referral, or continuation of services in relation to the clients' needs and preferences.

G. Rights and Prerogatives of Clients— The social worker should make every effort to foster maximum self-determination on the part of clients.

1. When the social worker must act on behalf of a client who has been adjudged legally incompetent, the social worker should safeguard the interests and rights of that client.

2. When another individual has been legally authorized to act on behalf of a client, the social worker should deal with that person always with the client's best interest in mind.

3. The social worker should not engage in any action that violates or diminishes the civil or legal rights of clients.

H. Confidentiality and Privacy—The social worker should respect the privacy of clients and hold in confidence all information obtained in the course of professional service.

1. The social worker should share with others confidences revealed by clients, without their consent, only for compelling professional reasons.

2. The social worker should inform clients fully about the limits of confidentiality in a given situation, the purposes for which information is obtained, and how it may be used.

3. The social worker should afford clients reasonable access to any official social work records concerning them.

4. When providing clients with access to records, the social worker should take due care to protect the confidences of others contained in those records.

5. The social worker should obtain informed consent of clients before taping, recording or permitting third party observation of their activities.

I. Fees—When setting fees, the social worker should ensure that they are fair, reasonable, considerate, and commensurate with the service performed and with due regard for the clients' ability to pay.

1. The social worker should not divide a fee or accept or give anything of value for receiving or making a referral.

III. THE SOCIAL WORKER'S ETHICAL RESPONSIBILITY TO COLLEAGUES

J. Respect, Fairness, and Courtesy—The social worker should treat colleagues with respect, courtesy, fairness, and good faith.

1. The social worker should cooperate with colleagues to promote professional interests and concerns.
2. The social worker should respect confidences shared by colleagues in the course of their professional relationships and transactions.
3. The social worker should create and maintain conditions of practice that facilitate ethical and competent professional performance by colleagues.
4. The social worker should treat with respect, and represent accurately and fairly, the qualifications, views, and findings of colleagues and use appropriate channels to express judgments on these matters.
5. The social worker who replaces or is replaced by a colleague in professional practice should act with consideration for the interest, character, and reputation of that colleague.
6. The social worker should not exploit a dispute between a colleague and employers to obtain a position or otherwise advance the social worker's interest.
7. The social worker should seek arbitration or mediation when conflicts with colleagues require resolution for compelling professional reasons.
8. The social worker should extend to colleagues of other professions the same respect and cooperation that is extended to social work colleagues.
9. The social worker who serves as an employer, supervisor, or mentor to colleagues should make orderly and explicit arrangements regarding the conditions of their continuing professional relationship.
10. The social worker who has the responsibility for employing and evaluating the performance of other staff members should fulfill such responsibility in a fair, considerate, and equitable manner, on the basis of clearly enunciated criteria.
11. The social worker who has the responsibility for evaluating the performance of employees, supervisees, or students should share evaluations with them.

K. Dealing with Colleagues' Clients—The social worker has the responsibility to relate to the clients of colleagues with full professional consideration.

1. The social worker should not solicit the clients of colleagues.
2. The social worker should not assume professional responsibility for the clients of another agency or a colleague without appropriate communication with that agency or colleague.
3. The social worker who serves the clients of colleagues, during a temporary absence or emergency, should serve those clients with the same consideration as that afforded any client.

IV. THE SOCIAL WORKER'S ETHICAL RESPONSIBILITY TO EMPLOYERS AND EMPLOYING ORGANIZATIONS

L. Commitments to Employing Organization—The social worker should adhere to commitments made to the employing organization.

1. The social worker should work to improve the employing agency's policies and procedures, and the efficiency and effectiveness of its services.
2. The social worker should not accept employment or arrange student field placements in an organization which is currently under public sanction by NASW for violating personnel standards, or imposing limitations on or penalties for professional actions on behalf of clients.
3. The social worker should act to prevent and eliminate discrimination in the employing organization's work assignments and in its employment policies and practices.
4. The social worker should use with scrupulous regard, and only for the purpose for which they are intended, the resources of the employing organization.

V. THE SOCIAL WORKER'S ETHICAL RESPONSIBILITY TO THE SOCIAL WORK PROFESSION

M. Maintaining the Integrity of the Profession—The social worker should uphold and advance the values, ethics, knowledge, and mission of the profession.

1. The social worker should protect and enhance the dignity and integrity of the profession and should be responsible and vigorous in discussion and criticism of the profession.

2. The social worker should take action through appropriate channels against unethical conduct by any other member of the profession.

3. The social worker should act to prevent the unauthorized and unqualified practice of social work.

4. The social worker should make no misrepresentation in advertising as to qualifications, competence, service, or results to be achieved.

N. Community Service—The social worker should assist the profession in making social services available to the general public.

1. The social worker should contribute time and professional expertise to activities that promote respect for the utility, the integrity, and the competence of the social work profession.

2. The social worker should support the formulation, development, enactment, and implementation of social policies of concern to the profession.

O. Development of Knowledge—The social worker should take responsibility for identifying, developing, and fully utilizing knowledge for professional practice.

1. The social worker should base practice upon recognized knowledge relevant to social work.

2. The social worker should critically examine, and keep current with, emerging knowledge relevant to social work.

3. The social worker should contribute to the knowledge base of social work and share research knowledge and practice wisdom with colleagues.

VI. THE SOCIAL WORKER'S ETHICAL RESPONSIBILITY TO SOCIETY

P. Promoting the General Welfare—The social worker should promote the general welfare of society.

1. The social worker should act to prevent and eliminate discrimination against any person or group on the basis of race, color, sex, sexual orientation, age, religion, national origin, marital status, political belief, mental or physical handicap, or any other preference or personal characteristic, condition, or status.

2. The social worker should act to ensure that all persons have access to the resources, services, and opportunities which they require.

3. The social worker should act to expand choice and opportunity for all persons, with special regard for disadvantaged or oppressed groups and persons.

4. The social worker should promote conditions that encourage respect for the diversity of cultures which constitute American society.

5. The social worker should provide appropriate professional services in public emergencies.

6. The social worker should advocate changes in policy and legislation to improve social conditions and to promote social justice.

7. The social worker should encourage informed participation by the public in shaping social policies and institutions.

FIGURE 1.2

CANADIAN ASSOCIATION OF SOCIAL WORKERS
CODE OF ETHICS

INTRODUCTION

Social workers are engaged in planning, developing, implementing, evaluating and changing social policies, services and programs that affect individuals, families, social groups, organizations and communities. They practise in many functional fields, use a variety of methods, work in a wide range of organizational settings, and provide a spectrum of psychosocial services to diverse population groups. Therefore, the basic principles of ethical conduct are necessarily broad and quite general. The purpose of a detailed Code of Ethics, outlining the professional attributes and conduct expected of the social worker, is to provide a practical guide for professional behavior and the maintenance of a reasonable standard of practice within a given cultural context.

The Preamble identifies the philosophy, purpose and accountability of the profession in general terms. The Declaration sets out in code form the ethical attitudes expected of the social worker regardless of educational or experiential preparation, role classification, field of practice location, methods of practice, place of work or population focus. The Commentary is a more detailed statement of the reasonable standard of practice expected from the social worker's commitment to the Declaration. The Code of Ethics is presented with full knowledge that specific conduct will be further guided by professional judgments and situational circumstances. However, in all instances the social worker is expected to practise competently and to refrain from conduct unbecoming to a professional.

Certain terms used in the Code require definition as follows:

Client means the person(s) on whose behalf a social worker provides or undertakes to provide professional services.

Workplace means any place of employment, public, private or self-employment of persons who ordinarily are recognized as social workers regardless of classification or job title.

Profession of social work refers to social workers collectively.

Social worker means an individual who is duly authorized to practise social work, including students in post-secondary social work education programs.

Regulatory body means the body charged under the laws of a particular jurisdiction with the duty of governing the profession of social work or the body voluntarily recognized in a particular jurisdiction by professional social workers as having the duty to govern the profession of social work.

Standards of practice means the standard of care ordinarily expected of a competent social worker. It means that the public can be assured that a social worker has the training, the talent and the diligence to provide them with professional social work services.

Conduct unbecoming means the behavior or conduct that does not meet standard of care requirements, which is subject to discipline.

Malpractice and negligence means behavior that is included as "conduct unbecoming" which relates to practice behavior within the parameters of the professional relationship that falls below the standard of practice and results in or aggravates an injury to a client. It includes behavior which results in assault, deceit, fraudulent misrepresentations, defamation of character, breach of contract, violation of human rights, malicious prosecution, false imprisonment or criminal conviction.

Person includes individuals, families, social groups, public and private organizations, associations and recognized community entities.

PREAMBLE

Philosophy:

The profession of social work is founded on humanitarian and egalitarian ideals. Social workers believe in the intrinsic worth and dignity of every human being and are committed to the values of acceptance, self-determination and respect of individuality. They believe in the obligation of all people, individually and collectively, to provide resources, services and opportunities for the overall benefit of humanity.

Social workers are dedicated to the welfare and self-realization of human beings; to the development and disciplined use of scientific knowledge regarding human and societal behaviours; to the development of resources to meet individual, group, national and international needs and aspirations; and to the achievement of social justice for all.

Social workers are pledged to serve without discrimination on any grounds of race, ethnicity, language, religion, marital status, gender, sexual orientation, age, abilities, economic status, political affiliation or national ancestry.

Purpose:

Social work is a profession committed to the goal of effecting social changes in society and the ways in which individuals develop within their society for the benefit of both. Advancement toward this purpose is achieved through the complementarity of social reform and therapeutic approaches premised in the belief that social conditions of humanity can be bettered.

The practice of social work has a primary focus on patterns of psychosocial relationships between people and the socio-economic resources, services and opportunities of their respective societies. The functions of social work include helping people to develop individual and collective social problem-solving skills; enhancing self-determination and the adaptive and developmental capacities of people; advocating, promoting and acting to obtain a socially just distribution of societal resources; and facilitating social connections between people and their societal resources.

Accountability:

Social workers are accountable to the people they serve, to their profession and to society. This accountability is achieved by adherence to the philosophy, purpose and standard of practice determined by the profession.

Failure to fulfill the obligation of this Code of Ethics may result in disciplinary procedures and appropriate consequences under the statutory or non-statutory authority of a recognized regulatory body.

SOCIAL WORKER DECLARATION

As a member of the profession of social work I commit myself to fulfill to the best of my ability the following obligations:

1. I will regard the well-being of the persons I serve as my primary professional obligation.

2. I will fulfill my obligations and responsibilities with integrity.

3. I will be competent in the performance of the services and functions I undertake on behalf of the persons I serve.

4. I will act in a conscientious, diligent and efficient manner.

5. I will respect the intrinsic worth of persons I serve in my professional relationships with them.

6. I will protect the confidentiality of all professionally acquired information. I will disclose such information only when properly authorized or when obligated legally or professionally to do so.

7. I will ensure that outside interests do not jeopardize my professional judgment, independence or competence.

8. I will work for the creation and maintenance of workplace conditions and policies that are consistent with the standard of practice set by this Code.

9. I will act to promote excellence in the social work profession.

10. I will act to effect social change for the overall benefit of humanity.

COMMENTARY

Primary Professional Obligation

1. I will regard the well-being of the persons I serve as my primary professional obligation.

Commentary

1.1 This declaration is fundamental and self-explanatory. All subsequent declarations are intended to aid the social worker in maintaining a reasonable standard of practice.

1.2 The social worker will be able to apply the practice values of acceptance, self-determination and individuality without being discriminatory on any grounds of race, ethnicity, language, religion, marital status, gender, sexual orientation, age, abilities, socioeconomic status, political affiliation or national ancestry.

1.3 Client (persons served) shall mean the individuals, families, social groups, organizations and communities who have contractual agreements (written or unwritten) with the social worker for the purpose of trying to achieve a specified psychosocial outcome(s).

Integrity

2. I will fulfill my obligations and responsibilities with integrity.

Commentary

2.1 The social worker will possess reasonable moral principles especially in relation to truth and fair dealing and have personal qualities of honesty and sincerity.

2.2 Integrity is the foundation of social work practice and therefore underlies each ethical declaration.

2.3 The social worker will identify and describe education, training, experience, professional affiliations, competence, nature of service, and actions in an honest and accurate manner.

2.3.1 Educational degrees will be cited only when they have been received from an accredited institution of higher education.

2.3.2 No person shall claim formal social work education/training solely by attending a lecture, demonstration, conference, panel discussion, workshop, seminar or other similar teaching presentation, unless such activities are designated by a recognized unit of an institution of higher education as a formal part of its social work education program.

2.3.3 The social worker will not make a false, misleading or exaggerated claim of efficacy regarding past or anticipated achievement, with respect to clients, scholarly pursuits or contributions to society.

2.3.4 The social worker will take reasonable care to distinguish between public statements and actions made as a private citizen and as a representative of the social work profession, workplace organization or specific membership group.

2.4 If a conflict arises in professional practice, the standards declared in this Code take precedence. Conflicts of interest may occur because of demands from the general public, workplace, organizations or clients. In all cases, if the declarations of this Code would be compromised, the social worker must act in a manner consistent with the standard of practice set by this Code.

2.5 The social worker is expected to observe the declarations of this Code in spirit as well as to the letter. Therefore, it is expected that a social worker will report to the appropriate regulatory body any instance involving or appearing to involve a breach of conduct set out in this Code. In all cases a report should be made in good faith, without malice or prejudice.

2.6 The social worker's private life is a personal matter to the same degree as it is for any other citizen, except as it may compromise the fulfillment of professional responsibilities, or reduce the public trust in social work and social workers. If the behavior would likely constitute conduct unbecoming a professional social worker, the regulatory body will consider a complaint and take appropriate action.

2.7 It is noted that this Code is not meant to imply a standard of perfection. Even though some practice behaviours might be actionable under law, the consequences of same would not necessarily constitute a failure to maintain the standard set by this Code. However, evidence of gross neglect in a particular matter or a pattern of neglect or mistakes may be evidence of such failure regardless of civil or criminal liability.

Competence and Quality of Service

3. I will be competent in the performance of the services and functions I undertake on behalf of the persons I serve.

4. I will act in a conscientious, diligent and efficient manner.

Commentary

3.1 Competence goes beyond formal qualifications. The social worker will make reasonable and continuous efforts to upgrade and use effectively the values, knowledge and skills of professional practice.

3.2 The social worker will not undertake a matter of professional practice unless there is an honest belief in the competence to handle it. If sufficient ability cannot be attained without undue delay, risk or expense to the client, the social worker should either decline to act or obtain the client's consent to consult or collaborate with, or refer to, a social worker or other professional who is competent on that matter.

The above is not to be construed to mean that a social worker, when lacking specialized ability, will decline to make a reasonable response to a request for help or to work cooperatively with others when there is no one with the required competence available to those requesting the help.

3.3 The social worker will recognize that sufficient ability for a particular task may require advice from or collaboration with (experts in) other professional disciplines and will seek client agreement to work in these collaborative situations.

3.4 The social worker will recognize that personal problems and conflicts may interfere with professional effectiveness. Reasonable health and well-being will be maintained by the social worker as a recognized component of competent practice. If personal problems occur, reasonable care will be taken by the social worker to determine whether professional activities should be suspended, terminated or limited.

3.5 The social worker will provide a quality of service which is at least equal to the standard of practice one would expect to receive in a like situation.

3.6 The social worker will have adequate knowledge and abilities to meet standard of practice requirements:

3.6.1 Knowledge and understanding of human development and functioning; cultural and environmental factors affecting human life and the patterns of social interactions contributing to the interdependence of human behavior.

3.6.2 Knowledge of social institutions, social welfare and social work as a distinct professional discipline.

3.6.3 Knowledge of interpersonal communications, including forms of, message patterns and interviewing processes.

3.6.4 Knowledge of social work intervention methods, individual and social change strategies, and social networks and resources.

3.6.5 Knowledge of formal organizations, including structures, goals, power relations, teamwork and administration.

3.6.6 Knowledge of social policy and relevant law, including administrative and legal processes.

3.6.7 Knowledge of professional ethics.

3.6.8 Knowledge of the limited reasons for terminating services: loss of a client's confidence; prolonged failure of services to benefit the client; further intervention unnecessary; service offered or requested is unethical or criminal in nature.

3.6.9 Ability to use interpersonal interviewing skills to provide clear explanations of professional and workplace roles; to establish the expectation of mutual participation in the change process; to clarify the need to gather sufficient and appropriate information for understanding and assessment; to determine competence to consent; to implement the requirement of informed consent; to determine what must be disclosed to clients with respect to assessments, the nature of the helping process, alternative modes of intervention and innovative intervention possibilities.

3.6.10 Ability to facilitate termination of services or referral to others in an orderly manner with a minimum amount of expense and other inconvenience to the client.

3.6.11 Ability to keep clients informed of all relevant commitments and possible implications of their situation.

3.6.12 Ability to notify a client within a reasonable interval when unable to meet a request.

3.6.13 Ability to make a prompt and reasonable report when required.

3.6.14 Ability to keep appointments with clients and answer all verbal and written communications in a reasonable time.

3.6.15 Ability to arrange adequate coverage of work in times of absence.

3.6.16 Ability to constructively contribute to the retention of support staff and to the maintenance of workplace facilities.

3.6.17 Ability to respond reasonably to client dissatisfaction, early and directly.

3.6.18 Ability to use consultation and supervision in the management of the professional relationship and the application of practice methods.

Social Worker-Client Relationship

5. I will respect the intrinsic worth of persons I serve in my professional relationships with them.

Commentary

5.1 The social worker will respect the intrinsic worth of clients and act to ensure through reasonable advocacy and other intervention activities that dignity, individuality and rights of persons are safeguarded.

5.2 The social worker will be trustworthy and possess the necessary values to demonstrate primary respect for the intrinsic worth of individuals.

5.3 The central focus of practice, within a professional relationship, will be based on voluntary (and under some circumstances, involuntary) mutual agreements between the social worker and client. The social worker will maintain a reasonable level of objective self-awareness in order to appropriately manage personal needs, feelings, values and limitations in the context of a professional relationship, the planned change process and the intended outcomes. This means the social worker may need to reasonably self-disclose to the client. This is advisable in order to appropriately manage (these personal needs and beliefs in the context of) social work practice.

5.4 The social worker will respect client motivation, capacity and opportunity for change at all times during the planned change process and use this knowledge appropriately to facilitate the attainment of intended outcomes.

5.5 The social worker's professional relationship with voluntary and involuntary clients will be developed on the principle of mutuality. This means that the helping process, where feasible, will involve shared control responsibilities between the client and the social worker toward the achievement of agreed to or acknowledged outcome goals. In the case of the involuntary client, mutual agreements may not exist at the outset of the relationship but the social worker's reasonable adherence to this principle is expected. Where the client is defined by statutory legislation, or where the rights of the community and others to protection are paramount and may be harmed by adherence to the principle, the latter may need to be modified or disregarded. The social worker will take care to reasonably manage all parameters of authority involved in social control responsibilities and act to protect clients from undue influence and abusive use of power or expert position. When it is apparent that clients, voluntary or involuntary, have misunderstood the achieved or intended interdependence of the professional relationship, the social worker will explain and renegotiate so that the client is fully advised of and encouraged to participate in an atmosphere of mutuality.

5.6 The social worker will act to ensure that the difference between professional and personal relationships with clients is explicitly understood and respected, and that the social worker's behavior is appropriate to this difference. Sexual intimacy with a client is unethical.

5.7 The social worker will not exploit relationships with clients, supervisors, students, employees or research participants sexually or otherwise. The social worker will not condone nor engage in sexual harassment.

Confidential Information

6. I will protect the confidentiality of all professionally acquired information. I will disclose such information only when properly authorized or obligated legally or professionally to do so.

Commentary

Confidentiality means that information received or observed about a client by a social worker will be held in confidence and disclosed only when the social worker is properly authorized or obligated legally or professionally to do so. This also means that professionally acquired information may be treated as privileged communication and ordinarily only the client has the right to waive privilege.

Maintaining confidentiality of privileged communication means that information about clients does not have to be transmitted in any oral, written or recorded form. Such information, for example, does not have to be disclosed to a supervisor, written into a workplace record, stored in a computer or microfilm data base, held on an audio or videotape or discussed orally. The right of privileged communication is respected by the social worker in the practice of social work notwithstanding that this right is not ordinarily granted in law.

The disclosure of confidential information in social work practice involves the obligation to share information professionally with others in the workplace of the social worker as part of a reasonable service to the client. Social workers recognize the need to obtain permission from clients before releasing information about them to sources outside their workplace and to inform clients at the outset of their relationship that some information acquired may be shared with the officers and personnel of the agency who maintain the case record and who have a reasonable need for the information in the performance of their duties.

6.1 The social worker will take reasonable care to keep confidential all information learned and observations made regarding clients served. This requirement of confidentiality also applies to supervisory, administrative and other indirect service personnel who work with employees, students, community groups and others.

6.2 The social worker will respect the inner workings and difficulties of a workplace setting; however, where there are circumstances which are contrary to the best interests of the client, the social worker has a responsibility to seek reasonable changes in those circumstances.

6.3 The social worker, in a workplace setting, may disclose information to persons who, by virtue of their responsibilities, have an identified need to know. Such persons may include other social workers, supervisors, administrators, members of other disciplines, volunteers (and their parent organization), agency support staff, computer and data processing personnel, consultants, agency legal counsel, persons involved with peer review and accountability mechanisms, accrediting and licensing authorities, third party funding resources and researchers.

6.3.1 Workplace settings should have confidentiality policies which spell out clearly who does and does not have access to what kinds of information and why the information is needed, especially information of an identifying nature. Those employees having even limited access to confidential information should receive formal orientation on the principles of confidentiality and related personnel policies when first hired.

6.4 Receiving information

6.4.1 Clients will be the primary source of information about themselves and their problems. Exceptions to this occur when the client is incapable of giving reliable information or when corroborative reporting is required as in the preparation of a community study, the assessment of mental illness or the investigation of criminal behavior (probation, parole, corrections, forensic work).

6.4.2 The social worker has the obligation to ensure that the client understands what is being asked, why, and to what purpose the information will be used. Generally, persons seeking social services go to an agency, not an individual social worker; therefore, in addition to ensuring that the client understands professional practice policies on confidentiality, the social worker should reasonably ascertain that the client also understands the confidentiality policies and practices of the workplace setting.

6.4.3 Where information is required by law, the social worker will help the client understand the consequences, if any, of refusing to provide the required information.

6.4.4 When information is required from other sources, the social worker will make a reasonable effort to explain this to the client, decide with the client what other sources are to be used and seek agreement on the method of obtaining the needed information.

6.4.5 The social worker will take reasonable care to safeguard personal papers or other property belonging to the client if they need to be held for safekeeping.

6.5 Recording information

6.5.1 The social worker will ensure that all information recorded is either relevant to the solution of the client(s) problems or is needed for others within the workplace setting who have a need to know the information in the performance of their duties.

6.5.2 The social worker will make reasonable efforts to avoid recording information that would be against the best interests of the client should the case record be subpoenaed or seen by the client, and will promote the adoption of workplace procedures concerning the kind of information which does not belong in case records.

6.5.3 The social worker will include preliminary assessments, intervention plans and social change strategies as part of a permanent record only for purposes of monitoring implementation of, progress toward, and response(s) to planned interventions.

6.5.4 The social worker must obtain informed consent or be reasonably satisfied of the client's incompetence to consent when it is proposed to use any electronic method of recording actual work being done with the client.

6.6 Accessibility to records

6.6.1 The case record itself is the property of the self-employed social worker or the employer of social workers and is, unless otherwise dictated by statute, the responsibility of the social worker or employer and subject to their control.

6.6.2 The social worker will respect the client's general right to know and will allow reasonable periodic opportunity to check the accuracy of all information that is recorded as fact and contained in the permanent case record of an agency. In circumstances where client access to information contained in the record is dictated by statute, the law prescribes what access may or may not be permitted.

6.6.3 The client's general access to information contained in the case record may be refused for just and reasonable causes: for example, when the work involves different members of a family, group or community and unrestricted access to the agency record could mean divulging personal confidences of others or when recorded language could be misunderstood and prejudicial to one of the members. In such instances the social worker will only allow individuals to check the accuracy of information pertaining to themselves.

6.7 Disclosure

6.7.1 The social worker will not disclose the identity of persons who have sought a social work service or disclose sources of information about clients unless compelled legally or professionally to do so.

6.7.2 The obligation to maintain confidentiality continues indefinitely after the social worker has ceased contact with persons served.

6.7.3 The social worker will avoid unnecessary conversation regarding clients and their affairs, as matters overheard by persons without an official need to know may prove to be detrimental to the overall well-being of those being served.

6.7.4 The social worker may divulge confidential information with informed consent of the client, preferably expressed in writing.

6.7.5 The social worker will transfer information to another agency or individual, only with the informed consent of the client or guardian of the client and then only with reasonable assurance that the receiving agency provides the same guarantee of confidentiality and respect for the right of privileged communication as provided by the sending agency.

6.7.6 Disclosure of confidential information required by law or the policies of the workplace will be explained to the client, where reasonably possible, before such disclosure is made.

6.7.7 The social worker in practice with groups and communities of people will notify the participants of the likelihood that aspects of their private lives may be revealed in the course of their work together, and therefore require a commitment from each member to respect the privileged and confidential nature of the communication between and among members of the client group(s).

6.7.8 The social worker in practice with families must safeguard the rights to privilege and confidentiality of information acquired concerning individuals in the couple or in the family. Disclosure of information that one client has requested be kept confidential from his or her partner will not be made without the informed consent of the person providing the confidential information. When one person provides consent to the release of confidential records or information, the social worker may release only information about the consenting person and must protect the confidentiality of all information derived from the non-consenting person(s).

6.7.9 Disclosure of information by the social worker may be justified to defend oneself, colleagues or employees against formal allegations of conduct unbecoming a professional, including malpractice and negligence, or to collect fees. However, such disclosure must occur only to the extent necessary for such purposes.

6.7.10 Disclosure of information necessary to prevent a crime, to prevent clients doing harm to themselves or to others is justified. Such disclosure should be made with reasonable care and with the client's knowledge, unless informing the client would impede the due process of law or violate the duty to warn others. The discharge of this duty requires the social worker to take steps including, but not limited to, warning the intended victim or others who would likely apprise the victim of the danger, notifying the police, or taking whatever other steps are reasonably necessary under the circumstances.

6.7.11 When disclosure is required by order of a court, the social worker should not divulge more information than is reasonably required and should where possible notify the client of this requirement. In cases in which a subpoena is served to obtain confidential information about a client, the social worker should attempt to protect the client's right to privileged communication. When such privilege is not clearly recognized, the social worker should obtain legal counsel and assert the claim of privilege that belongs to a client.

6.7.12 The social worker must take

reasonable care to thoroughly disguise confidential information when using it for teaching, public education, accountability and research purposes. When a client is presented to a scientific gathering, the social worker must obtain prior consent and prior confirmation that the confidentiality of the presentation is understood and accepted by the audience. The social worker may present a client or former client to a public gathering or to the news media only if that client is fully informed of the loss of confidentiality, is competent to consent, and consents in writing without coercion.

6.8 Retention and disposition of information

6.8.1 The social worker will promote the adoption of policies and procedures concerning retention and disposition that will physically safeguard case records and personnel files against any anticipated threats or hazards to their security or integrity which would result in substantial harm, embarrassment, inconvenience or unfairness to any individual on whom information is maintained.

6.8.2 The social worker will not use case records and personnel files and the information contained in them for any purpose that is not consistent with the standard of practice set by this Code.

6.8.3 Where the social worker's documentation becomes part of the workplace's permanent record, retention or destruction of such records must be done in accordance with workplace policies which are consistent with the standard of practice set by this Code.

Outside Interests and the Practice of Social Work

7. I will ensure that outside interests do not jeopardize my professional judgment, independence or competence.

Commentary

7.1 When participating in outside interests, the capacity in which the social worker is acting must be made clear.

7.2 The commitment to professional values does not exclude the social worker from participating in outside interests such as politics, another profession, occupation or business enterprise. The term "outside interests" covers the widest possible range and includes activities which may or may not overlap with the practice of social work.

7.3 Ethical considerations will usually not arise from outside interests unless the conduct is unbecoming and brings the social worker or the profession into disrepute, impairs competence or constitutes malpractice.

7.4 Whenever an outside interest might influence the social worker's judgment, the nature of the conflict should be disclosed and explained to the client and to the employer.

Responsibility to the Workplace

8. I will work for the creation and maintenance of workplace conditions and policies that are consistent with the standard of practice set by this Code.

Commentary

8.1 The social worker is accountable and responsible to the employer for the efficient performance of duties.

8.2 At times the responsibilities to the employer and the client may be in conflict and the social worker will bring this situation to the attention of the employer. In some instances it may be necessary to consult and enlist the support of professional colleagues and associations in an attempt to safeguard client rights and promote changes in the procedures of the agency which will be consistent with the values and obligations of this Code. It may be required of the social worker to subordinate the employer's interests to the interests of the client. If these alternatives fail it may be necessary in extreme circumstances for the social worker to resign from that employment. In such cases the social worker should inform the regulatory authority governing the practice of social work.

8.3 The social worker who has the responsibility for employing and evaluating the performance of other staff members will fulfill such responsibility in a fair, considerate and equitable manner on the basis of a clearly enunciated criteria.

8.4 The social worker who has the responsibility for evaluating the performance of employees, supervisees or students will share evaluations with them.

8.5 The social worker will make reasonable efforts to prevent and eliminate discrimination in the employing organization's work assignments and in its employment policies and practices.

8.6 The social worker will use with

scrupulous regard, and only for the purposes for which they are intended, the resources of the employing organization.

8.7 The social worker who is responsible for the administration and supervision of personnel will make reasonable efforts to promote written policies and procedures concerning the confidentiality of personnel records which will protect data on personnel as fully as possible under current ethical and legal guidelines.

8.8 As a teacher, the social worker will promote the adoption of reasonable policies and procedures in the workplace and academic institutions concerning confidentiality guidelines for students who take recorded material from the field into the classroom.

8.9 As a teacher, the social worker is aware that personal values may affect the selection and presentation of instructional materials. When dealing with topics that give conflicting ideas, styles and perspectives, the social worker will make reasonable efforts to recognize and respect the diverse critical and analytical attitudes that students may have toward such materials.

8.10 As a teacher, the social worker will take reasonable actions to ensure that statements in course outlines are accurate and not misleading, particularly in terms of subject matter to be covered, basis for evaluating progress and the nature of course experiences.

8.11 As a teacher, the social worker assigned to teach practicum/field practice courses will assume responsibility and accountability for the services provided by a student.

8.12 Responsibility for the total operation of private practice will be assumed by the self-employed social worker.

8.13 The self-employed social worker will disclose to the client at the outset of their relationship the fee schedule and charge fees that are reasonable and reflect the customary charges of other practitioners of similar standing in the locality in like matters and circumstances.

8.14 The self-employed social worker may properly make social work services available by charging a reduced fee or no fee at all to a client(s) who would have difficulty in paying the fee.

8.15 The self-employed social worker who is also employed in an agency or organization shall communicate fully and completely all intentions and activities to the employer. A detailed written agreement between the employer and the self-employed social worker should be completed with regard to such things as use of office space and other facilities. Reasonable caution must be taken to ensure that there is a clear distinction between referrals to the employing organization and to the private practitioner.

8.16 The self-employed social worker will carry adequate malpractice, defamation and premises liability insurance.

8.17 The self-employed social worker and client will agree to an initial contract, preferably in writing. Conditions of the contract should be clear and explicit with respect to fees, length, frequency and location of meetings, penalties for appointments missed or cancelled without adequate notice, and vacation coverage during an absence.

8.18 The self-employed social worker's bill will reflect only services actually rendered and reasonable penalties for appointments missed or cancelled without adequate notice from the client.

Responsibility to the Profession

9. I will act to promote excellence in the social work profession.

Commentary

9.1 The social worker will contribute reasonable time and professional expertise to activities that promote respect for the utility, the integrity and the competence of the social work profession.

9.2 The social worker will protect and enhance the dignity and integrity of the profession and will be responsible and vigorous in discussion and criticism of the profession.

9.3 The social worker will take reasonable action against unethical conduct by any other member of the profession.

9.4 The social worker will make reasonable efforts to prevent the unauthorized and unqualified practice of social work.

9.5 The social worker will treat with respect and represent accurately and fairly the qualifications, views and findings of colleagues, and use appropriate channels to express judgments on these matters, confining such comments to matters of fact and matters of their own knowledge.

9.6 The social worker will not solicit the clients of colleagues.

9.7 The social worker will not assume professional responsibility for the clients of another agency or a colleague without appropriate communication with that agency or colleague and consent of the client.

9.8 The social worker who serves the clients of colleagues during a temporary absence or emergency will serve those clients with the same consideration as that afforded any client.

9.9 The social worker who replaces or is replaced by a colleague in professional practice will act with consideration for the interest, character and reputation of that colleague.

9.10 The social worker will not exploit a dispute between a colleague and employer to obtain a position or otherwise advance the social worker's own interests.

9.11 The social worker will seek arbitration or mediation when conflicts with colleagues require resolution for compelling professional reasons.

9.12 The social worker will extend to colleagues of other professions reasonable respect and cooperation.

9.13 The social worker engaged in research will ascertain that the consent of participants in the research is voluntary and informed, without any implied deprivations or penalty for refusal to participate, and with due regard for participants' privacy and dignity.

9.14 The social worker engaged in research will take reasonable actions to protect participants from unwarranted physical or mental discomfort, distress, harm, danger or deprivation.

9.15 The social worker will take credit only for work actually done in connection with scholarly and research endeavours, and will credit contributions by others.

9.16 The social worker is responsible for participation in reasonable periodic continuing education activities and is committed to a lifetime of learning.

Responsibility to Society

10. I will act to effect social change for the overall benefit of humanity.

Commentary

10.1 The social worker will take reasonable actions to prevent and eliminate discrimination against any person or group on the basis of race, ethnicity, language, religion, marital status, gender, sexual orientation, age, abilities, socioeconomic status, political affiliation, national ancestry or any other preference or personal characteristic, condition or status.

10.2 The social worker will make reasonable efforts to advocate for the equitable distribution of societal resources and act to ensure that all persons have reasonable access to the resources, services and opportunities which they require.

10.3 The social worker will take reasonable actions to expand choice and opportunity for all persons, with special regard to disadvantaged or oppressed groups and persons.

10.4 The social worker will make reasonable efforts to promote conditions that encourage respect for the diversity of cultures which constitute society.

10.5 The social worker will provide reasonable professional services in public emergencies.

10.6 The social worker will make reasonable efforts to advocate for changes in policy and legislation to improve social conditions and to promote social justice.

10.7 The social worker will make reasonable efforts to encourage informed participation by the public in shaping social policies and institutions.

EXERCISE 1.8
THE *CODE* AND YOU

Read the American *Code of Ethics* contained in Figure 1.1 (pages 13–16) or the Canadian *Code of Ethics* contained in Figure 1.2 (pages 17–26). Discuss the *Code* with other preplacement students. Discuss the ethical dilemmas your group members feel they may encounter in a social work practicum. Use the space below to summarize your discussion.

EXERCISE 1.9

DEFINING FIELD EDUCATION TERMS

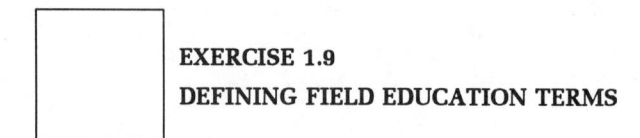

Exercise 1.9 is for your use in comparing our definitions of the various terms that have been used in reference to field education with the terms your program uses. Many of the terms used to refer to the social work field education process are different from one social work program to another. Although the terms may be used interchangeably, each program has unique terms and concepts that are necessary for you to know. Working definitions of the terms as used in the book are presented for you on pages 28–33.

Following each of the book's definitions, write the definition commonly used in *your* social work program. Information for your definitions may be found in your program's field education manual. Be prepared to discuss the definitions at your practicum orientation session.

Agency:

>The place where your practicum setting is located. Some agencies have several practicum settings for social work students.

>Your program's definition:

Field Education Manual:

>The document that outlines the field education process and requirements for social work students, field instructors, field liaisons, and the practicum coordinator.

>Your program's definition:

Field Instructor:

The social worker to whom students are assigned during the practicum. This person instructs, monitors, and usually evaluates the student's acquisition of professional skills, knowledge, and values. This social worker is usually employed by the agency where the practicum setting is located. Also referred to as a field supervisor or practicum instructor.

Your program's definition:

Field Liaison:

Usually a faculty-based person who is the link between your field instructor and your program's practicum coordinator. This person is usually responsible for the assignment of your final grade based on discussions with your field instructor. Also referred to as a faculty-field liaison or a faculty liaison.

Your program's definition:

Field Placement: See practicum on page 31.

Your program's definition:

Part One / Pre-Practicum

Field Supervisor: See field instructor on page 29.

    Your program's definition:

Integrative Seminar:

    A required course that provides an opportunity for you to discuss your practicum issues and experiences and related classroom courses with other practicum students. Also referred to as an integrative field seminar and integration seminar.

    Your program's definition:

Practice Methods Course:

    A required course that provides the theoretical knowledge, concepts, and skills to understand the problem-solving process and activities with different client systems.

    Your program's definition:

Practicum:

A required course in which you are enrolled. The practicum provides opportunities for you to apply the knowledge and skills learned in the classroom, especially from your practice methods course with different client systems. Also referred to as a field placement or fieldwork. A practicum occurs in a practicum setting.

Your program's definition:

Practicum Coordinator:

Usually a faculty person who is responsible for developing, monitoring, and administering a wide range of practicum opportunities for students enrolled in the social work program. Also referred to as director of field, fieldwork director, field coordinator, fieldwork coordinator, field placement coordinator, and so on.

Your program's definition:

Practicum Instructor: See field instructor on page 29.

Your program's definition:

Practicum Setting:

The place where you will work with actual client systems. The setting is usually located within an agency. Sometimes a practicum setting is one of many social programs within an agency. If an agency has only one social program, then the agency becomes the practicum setting.

Your program's definition:

Practicum Student:

A student enrolled in a practicum.

Your program's definition:

Preplacement Student:

A social work student who is planning for a practicum course or is about to begin a practicum. A preplacement student may conduct selective preplacement interviews with potential practicum settings.

Your program's definition:

Social Work Program:

The department, school, faculty, or program that offers a BSW, MSW, DSW, or PhD in social work/welfare.

Your program's definition:

Supervisory Conference:

Educationally focused supervisory meetings with you and your field instructor. They are usually held on a regular basis within your practicum setting. Supervisory conferences may be supplemented with group meetings with other staff and students. Also referred to as supervisory sessions. These conferences will be discussed fully in Chapter 5.

Your program's definition:

SUMMARY

The practicum is an opportunity to apply theoretical knowledge to practice situations in a purposeful way. At one level, applying knowledge may involve remembering the theory behind engaging a client in treatment or terminating an interview. At a different level, applying knowledge means applying the total knowledge and understanding acquired throughout your lifetime in order to evaluate what you are doing, what your agency is doing, and what the individual and societal consequences are likely to be.

Knowing what your agency is doing is an important part of fitting your own activities into the broader frame of social work. Agencies—their types, goals, structures, and dynamics—will be discussed later in this book. For now, it is enough to say that one of the goals of your practicum experience is to first examine your role within the agency and the agency's role within the social service delivery system and society in general. When you have done this, you will have a better understanding of whether you want to be a social worker, why you want to be a social worker, and what kind of social worker you want to be.

The practicum is a form of apprenticeship that has been carefully designed to incorporate all the advantages of the apprenticeship system while minimizing the disadvantages. It is a core course where the planned integration between practice and theory can occur.

Four key players are needed to make the practicum effective: the practicum coordinator who identifies suitable practicums and is responsible for the overall coordination and administration; your field instructor who is usually employed by the agency where your practicum takes place and supervises you; your field liaison who is usually a faculty member of your program and links the program with the field instructor; and, most importantly, you—the student.

The integrative seminar is a required course generally taken every week while you are placed in a practicum. Its purpose is to integrate practice issues with practice theory by allowing students to discuss their practice experiences with others. Preparation in the form of reading and discussion is critical to achieving integration.

In the next chapter we will look at how to select, and be selected by, a suitable agency in which to complete your practicum.

SELECTED REFERENCES

Bogo, M., & Vayda, E. (1986). *The practice of field instruction in social work.* Toronto, ON, Canada: University of Toronto Press.

Brownstein, C., Smith, H.Y., & Faria, G. (1991). The liaison role: A three phase study of the schools, the field, the faculty. In D. Schneck, B. Grossman, & U. Glassman (Eds.), *Field education in social work: Contemporary issues and trends* (pp. 237–248). Dubuque, IA: Kendall/Hunt.

Cherrey R.L., Wertkin, R.A., & Davis, E. (1991). Differences in undergraduate and graduate practicums: Elitism, racism, and classism? In D. Schneck, B. Grossman, & U. Glassman (Eds.), *Field education in social work: Contemporary issues and trends* (pp. 261–270). Dubuque, IA: Kendall/Hunt.

Collins, D., & Bogo, M. (1986). Competency-based field instruction: Bridging the gap between laboratory and field learning. *Clinical Supervisor, 4,* 39–52.

Fellin, P.A. (1982). Responsibilities of the school. In B.W. Sheafor & L.E. Jenkins (Eds.), *Quality of field instruction in social work* (pp. 101–116). White Plains, NY: Longman.

George, A. (1982). A history of social work field instruction. In B. W. Sheafor & L. E. Jenkins (Eds.), *Quality field instruction in social work* (pp. 37–59). White Plains, NY: Longman.

Gitterman, A. (1975). The faculty field instructor in social work education. In Council on Social Work Education (Ed.), *The dynamics of field instruction: Learning through doing* (pp. 31–39). Silver Spring, MD: Author.

Green, S.H. (1972). Educational assessments of student learning through practice in field instruction. *Social Work Education Reporter, 20,* 48–54.

Hamilton, N., & Else, J. (1983). *Designing field education: Philosophy, structure and process.* Springfield, IL: Charles C. Thomas.

Hartman, C., & Wills, R.M. (1991). The gatekeepers role in social work: A survey. In D. Schneck, B. Grossman, & U. Glassman (Eds.), *Field education in social work: Contemporary issues and trends* (pp. 310–319). Dubuque, IA: Kendall/Hunt.

Hartung Hagen, B. J. (1989). The practicum instructor: A study of role expectations. In M. Raskin (Ed.), *Empirical studies in field instruction* (pp. 219–236). New York: Haworth.

Hawthorne, L., & Fine Holtzman, R. (1991). Directors of field education: Critical role dilemmas. In D. Schneck, B. Grossman, & U. Glassman (Eds.), *Field education in social work: Contemporary issues and trends* (pp. 320–328). Dubuque, IA: Kendall/Hunt.

Jenkins, L.E., & Sheafor, B.W. (1982). (Eds.). *Quality field instruction in social work.* White Plains, NY: Longman.

Jenkins, L.E., & Sheafor, B.W. (1982). An overview of social work field instruction. In B. W. Sheafor & L. E. Jenkins (Eds.), *Quality field instruction in social work* (pp. 3–20). White Plains, NY: Longman.

Jones, E.F. (1984). Square peg, round hole: The dilemma of the undergraduate social work field coordinator. *Journal of Education for Social Work, 20,* 45–50.

Kilpatrick, A.C. (1991). Differences and commonalities in BSW and MSW field instruction: In search of continuity. In D. Schneck, B. Grossman, & U. Glassman (Eds.), *Field education in social work: Contemporary issues and trends* (pp. 167–176). Dubuque, IA: Kendall/Hunt.

Lacerte, J., & Ray, J. (1991). Recognizing the educational contributions of field instructors. In D. Schneck, B. Grossman, & U. Glassman (Eds.), *Field education in social work: Contemporary issues and trends* (pp. 217–225). Dubuque, IA: Kendall/Hunt.

Larsen, J. (1980). Competency-based and task-centered practicum instruction. *Journal of Education for Social Work, 16,* 87–94.

Levy, C. (1965). A conceptual framework for field instruction in social work education. *Child Welfare, 44,* 447–452.

Martin, M.L. (1991). Employment setting as practicum site: A field instruction dilemma. In D. Schneck, B. Grossman, & U. Glassman (Eds.), *Field education in social work: Contemporary issues and trends* (pp. 288–294). Dubuque, IA: Kendall/Hunt.

Mesbur, E.S. (1991). Overview of baccalaureate field education: Objectives and outcomes. In D. Schneck, B. Grossman, & U. Glassman (Eds.), *Field education in social work: Contemporary issues and trends* (pp. 155–166). Dubuque, IA: Kendall/Hunt.

Mesbur, E.S., & Glassman, U. (1991). From commitment to curriculum: The humanistic foundations for field instruction. In D. Schneck, B. Grossman, & U. Glassman (Eds.), *Field education in social work: Contemporary issues and trends* (pp. 47–58). Dubuque, IA: Kendall/Hunt.

Norberg, W., & Schneck, D. (1991). A dual matrix structure for field education. In D. Schneck, B. Grossman, & U. Glassman (Eds.), *Field education in social work: Contemporary issues and trends* (pp. 96–121). Dubuque, IA: Kendall/Hunt.

Raskin, M. (Ed.). (1989). *Empirical studies in field instruction.* New York: Haworth.

Raskin, M. (1989). Field placement decisions: Art, science or guesswork? In M. Raskin (Ed.), *Empirical studies in field instruction* (pp. 105–122). New York: Haworth.

Rogers, G., & McDonald, L. (1989). Field supervisors: Is a social work degree necessary? *Canadian Social Work Review, 6,* 203–221.

Rosenblum, A. F., & Raphael, F. B. (1983). The role and function of the faculty-field liaison. *Journal of Education for Social Work, 19,* 67–73.

Schneck, D. (1991). Integration of learning in field education: Elusive goal and educational imperative. In D. Schneck, B. Grossman, & U. Glassman (Eds.), *Field education in social work: Contemporary issues and trends* (pp. 67–77). Dubuque, IA: Kendall/Hunt.

Schneck, D. (1991). Arbiter of change in field education: The critical role for faculty. In D. Schneck, B. Grossman, & U. Glassman (Eds.), *Field education in social work: Contemporary issues and trends* (pp. 233–236). Dubuque, IA: Kendall/Hunt.

Schneck, D. (1991). The leadership opportunity in fieldwork for responding to change. In D. Schneck, B. Grossman, & U. Glassman (Eds.), *Field education in social work: Contemporary issues and trends* (pp. 78–79). Dubuque, IA: Kendall/Hunt.

Schneck, D. (1991). Ideal and reality in field education. In D. Schneck, B. Grossman, & U. Glassman (Eds.), *Field education in social work: Contemporary issues and trends* (pp. 17–35). Dubuque, IA: Kendall/Hunt.

Sheafor, B.W., & Jenkins, L.E. (Eds.). (1982). *Quality field instruction in social work*. New York: Longman.

Sheafor, B.W., & Jenkins, L.E. (1981). Issues that affect the development of a field instruction curriculum. *Journal of Education for Social Work, 17,* 12–20.

Skolnik, L. (1989). Field instruction in the 1980s—Realities, issues and problem-solving strategies. In M. Raskin (Ed.), *Empirical studies in field instruction* (pp. 47–76). New York: Haworth.

Smith, S.L., & Baker, D.R. (1989). The relationship between educational background of field instructors and the quality of supervision. In M. Raskin (Ed.), *Empirical studies in field instruction* (pp. 257–270). New York: Haworth.

Thomlison, B., & Watt, S. (1980). Trends and issues in the field preparation of social work manpower: A summary report. *Canadian Journal of Social Work Education, 6,* 137–158.

Thyer, B., Williams, M., Love, J.P., Sowers-Hong, K.M. (1989). The MSW supervisory requirements in field instruction: Does it make a difference? In M. Raskin (Ed.), *Empirical studies in field instruction* (pp. 249–256). New York: Haworth.

Urbanowski, M.L., & Dwyer, M.M. (1988). *Learning through field instruction*. Milwaukee, WI: Family Service of America.

Walden, T., & Brown, L. (1985). The integration seminar: A vehicle for joining theory and practice. *Journal of Education for Social Work, 21,* 13–19.

Waldfogel, D. (1983). Supervision of students and practitioners. In A. Rosenblatt & D. Waldfogel (Eds.), *Handbook of clinical social work* (pp. 319–344). San Francisco: Jossey-Bass.

Wayne, J. (1989). A comparison of beliefs about student supervision between micro and macro practitioners. In M. Raskin (Ed.), *Empirical studies in field instruction* (pp. 271–298). New York: Haworth.

Wayne, J., Skolnik, L., & Raskin, M. (1989). Field instruction in the United States and Canada: A comparison of studies. In M. Raskin (Ed.), *Empirical studies in field instruction* (pp. 77–88). New York: Haworth.

Wijnberg, M.H., & Schwartz, M.C. (1977). Models of student supervision: The apprentice, growth, and role systems models. *Journal of Education for Social Work, 13,* 107–113.

CHAPTER 2

Choosing a Practicum

CHILDREN WHO WHEEDLE CANDY bars out of their parents on shopping trips are subject to definite limitations. Because of the dual specters of tooth decay and budget deficits, they are allowed to choose *one* bar from those in the cheaper range. They are given a certain time to muse and ponder but, once the selection is made, their parents will glare if they want to change their minds. When the selection is paid for, they are then obliged to eat it. Never mind if they didn't realize it had peanuts. A parent, increasingly harassed, may hiss forbiddingly, "You picked it. You eat it. And if I hear any more whining about it, there will be no candy at all the next time we come to the store."

Choosing your practicum is similar. The choices, though many and tempting, are limited. The time allowed for selection is also limited. The matter of knowing about the peanuts is very much your responsibility, and it is also a reality that the selection, once made, must be lived with unless the circumstances are exceptional. If the choice is to be the right one for the individual, in terms of candy bars or practicums, there are three basic questions that must be addressed: What is in it? Will I like it? Can I have it?

WHAT IS IN IT?

If you were thinking of taking a job with a social service agency, there would be certain things you would want to know. For example, whom does it serve? Elderly persons? Adolescents in trouble with the law? Pregnant teenagers? In what ways does it serve them? Through individual, group, or family counseling? Through in-home services? Financial assistance? Residential placements? What are its goals? Obtaining an agency pamphlet will provide you answers to some of these questions. A visit to the agency can provide an additional perspective.

Is it a large institution or a two-person office? Is it on the bus route? Does its philosophical and value positions agree with yours? Do you get a corner office or a corner in the basement? Are the social workers generally supportive of one another or is there an ongoing battle between several factions? Does it have a stable funding base? Is it well regarded in the community?

Before you learn about available practicum settings, you must have a sound understanding of your values in relation to the values of the social work profession. Exercises 2.1 through 2.13 can help you with this beginning process of finding the best practicum for you from a vast array that exist. In short, the next 13 exercises will help you explore your values and how to choose a practicum with these values in mind.

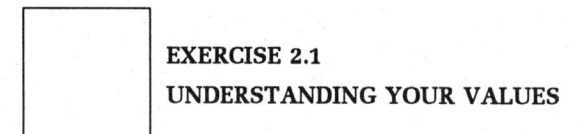

EXERCISE 2.1
UNDERSTANDING YOUR VALUES

Understanding your values goes hand in hand with understanding the values, ethics, and functions of the profession of social work. It is also an important preparation activity in the process of selecting a practicum and being selected for a practicum. This self-knowledge can be helpful in understanding the ways various practicum settings may affect and influence your practice. In addition, this knowledge can assist in determining what kinds of practicum settings you will fit into best. Record your responses in the spaces provided.

1. What do you believe is the role of a professional social worker?

2. What do you believe is meant by social work values and ethics? Why do you believe they are important to the practice of social work? How do you think they will influence your behavior in your future practicum setting?

3. Discuss what you believe are the key ethical principles and responsibilities that form the basis of the profession of social work. Why do you think they are important to professional social workers? Discuss in detail.

4. In your opinion, in what ways or situations might your values and ethics differ or depart from professional social work practice?

EXERCISE 2.2
UNDERSTANDING SOCIAL WORK SERVICES

List four different kinds (or areas) of social work services. Rank your list according to the kind of social work service that most interests you at this time.

1.

2.

3.

4.

EXERCISE 2.3
UNDERSTANDING SOCIAL SERVICES WITHIN YOUR COMMUNITY

Name at least four social service organizations in your community and their functions.

Organizations: *Functions:*

1.

2.

3.

4.

**EXERCISE 2.4
PROCESS OF ETHICAL
DECISION MAKING**

Consider your responses in Exercises 2.1–2.3. With a group of preplacement students, discuss practice circumstances in which client, student, and agency values might conflict with ethical decision making. Describe below what you believe is the process of responsible ethical decision making during your practicum.

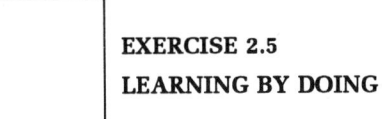

**EXERCISE 2.5
LEARNING BY DOING**

Describe the new learning that emerged from the discussion about the profession of social work, values, agencies, and services in Exercise 2.4. Also record any new aspects you learned about yourself below.

EXERCISE 2.6
YOUR UNDERSTANDING OF THE SOCIAL WORK PROFESSION

Consider your responses to Exercises 2.1 and 2.2 and use the scale below to rate your understanding of the profession of social work and the services provided by social service agencies. A rating of 1 indicates no understanding and a rating of 4 indicates a great deal of understanding about the six items listed. Be fair and honest about your level of understanding. Sum your responses. A score of 20–24 indicates high understanding of the effect of ethics and values.

1. I understand the role of professional social work.   1   2   3   4

2. I understand why I am in social work.   1   2   3   4

3. I understand the values and ethics of the profession of social work.   1   2   3   4

4. I understand the various settings that employ social workers.   1   2   3   4

5. I understand the function of a social service agency.   1   2   3   4

6. I understand responsible ethical decision making.   1   2   3   4

Total _____

EXERCISE 2.7
INCREASING YOUR UNDERSTANDING OF THE SOCIAL WORK PROFESSION

After completing Exercise 2.6, list the steps you can take before selecting your practicum to increase your understanding of the profession of social work, social work ethics, social work values, and social work services.

1.

2.

3.

**EXERCISE 2.8
SELF-AWARENESS AND
POTENTIAL PRACTICUMS**

Now that you have spent some time exploring the values of the profession, it will also be helpful to explore similar issues about yourself. Developing self-awareness is part of the process of developing as a professional social worker and becoming an effective practitioner. Understanding yourself, your personal and social resources, will help you begin to recognize those practicum settings where you can best assist clients.

1. If you were to describe yourself to someone else, what characteristics would *you* be sure to include? Why?

2. If people who know you quite well were to describe you, what characteristics would *they* include? Why?

3. Is there a difference in the two lists of characteristics (1 and 2)? How do you account for that difference?

4. Rate your comfort level (1 being least comfortable, 4 being most comfortable) in relating to others who are

of the opposite gender	1	2	3	4
physically disabled	1	2	3	4
developmentally delayed	1	2	3	4
a visible minority or whose ethnic background differs from yours	1	2	3	4
of sexual orientation which differs from yours	1	2	3	4

5. Comment on your comfort level with people who are different from you and how this might affect your choice of a practicum setting.

6. Considering your value system, what situations or types of clients might create a value conflict for you? Why?

7. How might the possible value conflicts affect your choice of a practicum setting? Do you believe you should avoid those situations and/or clients or confront the conflicts? Explain why or why not.

8. Considering your personal history, what situations or types of clients do you feel you could overidentify with? Why?

9. How might possible overidentification affect your choice of a practicum? Would your personal history make you more or less suitable for certain practicum settings or certain populations? Why or why not?

10. How do you typically respond when you are in a stressful or anxious situation? Be specific in your response.

11. What helps you cope in stressful situations?

12. How do you typically respond when others are in a crisis or in a stressful and anxious situation? Be specific in your response.

13. How can you use your responses in 10-12 to help you choose a practicum setting?

EXERCISE 2.9
YOUR PERSONAL QUALITIES
FOR A PARTICULAR PRACTICUM

Imagine you are going to be placed in *one* of the social work agencies you listed in Exercise 2.3 on page 40. Review your responses to Exercise 2.8 on pages 43–46 and identify the personal values, resources, and qualities that you think are most important for a student social worker to have in that particular practicum setting. Identify the personal values, resources, and qualities you believe would be least important for a student to have in that particular practicum setting.

Name of potential practicum
setting identified in Exercise 2.3: _____

Most important qualities:

Least important qualities:

In what types of practicum settings do you believe some of your personal qualities to be more important than others? Identify those types of client problems for which your personal qualities might best be suited. Identify those types of client problems that your personal qualities would not be suited for.

Best suited for:

Least suited for:

EXERCISE 2.10
SELF-PROFILE

Organizing personal descriptive information is another step in the selection and preparation process for the kind of practicum setting and client problem areas you wish to work with. This information will help you decide which practicum setting best fits your attributes and circumstances. Record your responses in the spaces provided.

Attributes

1. Age:

2. Gender:

3. Work and volunteer experiences:

4. Ethnic background:

Family and Social System

5. Describe your physical appearance:

6. Describe your family and members of your household:

7. Describe your immediate or primary social system:

8. Languages spoken:

9. Describe your community or neighborhood:

Personal Resources

10. Describe your primary personal characteristics, or personal style:

11. Describe your personal strengths or qualities that contribute to your ability as a professional social worker:

12. Describe your personal qualities that may detract from your ability as a professional social worker:

13. Describe how much structure you need to work effectively—a great deal, some, or very little:

14. Describe how important the various methods of learning are to you such as doing, thinking, reading, listening, or observing:

15. Describe your speaking and writing abilities:

16. Describe your organizational ability:

17. Describe any additional abilities that you believe are important to include in your profile:

EXERCISE 2.11
SOCIAL AND EMOTIONAL SUPPORT
FROM YOUR SELF-PROFILE

Mark those items in Exercise 2.10 that are sources of social and emotional support to you. Now mark those items in Exercise 2.10 that are positive qualities or abilities that would contribute to work with a particular client group. Summarize your perceived abilities below.

EXERCISE 2.12
CLIENT SYSTEMS WITH WHICH
YOU ARE NOT SUITED TO WORK

Identify the type of client problem areas you feel you are *not* suited to work with. Why do you feel this way?

**EXERCISE 2.13
FURTHER FEEDBACK FROM
YOUR SELF-PROFILE**

Find one other social work preplacement student and discuss your self-profile (Exercise 2.10). Ask for feedback from the student regarding his or her observations of your potential matches with client problem areas. List the issues that emerged from your discussion below.

Exercises 2.1–2.13 are important because they can help you understand what the various practicum settings consist of and whether, like the candy bar, you will like a setting, like most of it, or like it so much you want more. After completing these exercises, you will have more knowledge of what is beyond the exteriors of practicum settings and whether your values and qualities are potentially suited for each of the practicum settings you are considering. What is included then, in finding out the content of the practicum?

Finding Out What Is in It

There are four basic sources of information you can use to find out about practicum settings: your social work program, printed material, word of mouth, and preplacement interviews.

The Social Work Program. Your program, via the practicum coordinator, can answer some of your questions. For example, do all the practicum settings from which you can choose have good reputations? All of them, while chronically short of funds, will have been in existence for a reasonable time and are probably not in danger of imminent collapse. The list of available practicum settings will probably include some general information on what each agency does and the nature of its clientele. From this list, you can eliminate places where you would *not* like to be placed.

If you develop sympathy pains when you are within ten yards of a sick person, you may wish to eliminate hospitals. The following exercises in this chapter will take you another step toward the process of narrowing down the potential list of practicum settings. Although this can be an exciting part of your planning, do not get caught up in the glamour of potential practicum settings and their social workers and lose sight of functional aspects of your own abilities and limitations regarding "goodness of fit." These exercises require considerable thought and time, so that you get the most out of this learning process.

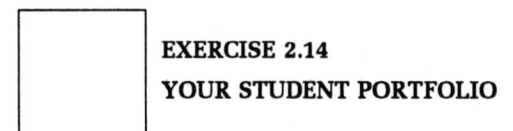

EXERCISE 2.14
YOUR STUDENT PORTFOLIO

Complete the student portfolio that follows. It contains information needed to make a decision about selecting and be selected for a practicum. The form can be given to your practicum coordinator or field liaison and potential field instructors.

1. Name:

2. Career goals:

    Short term:

    Long term:

3. Type of service (or setting) preferred:

4. Type of agency (or problem area the agency addresses) that would *not* be appropriate due to personal/religious beliefs:

5. Previous paid social work experience (specify):

6. Previous volunteer social work experience (specify):

7. Personal views about the social work profession:

8. Educational preparation:

   Languages spoken:

   Previous degrees:

   Social work courses taken:

9. Strengths, abilities, and personal resources to offer:

10. Special social work interests:

11. Other pertinent comments or information:

12. References:

EXERCISE 2.15
CHECKLIST FOR PRACTICUM SELECTION

Each practicum setting has different assets and learning opportunities available for students. It is important for you to compare and contrast the learning opportunities in relation to your own learning needs. Complete this checklist of some factors to consider when selecting a practicum. Check off and comment on the resources and learning opportunities available in each practicum setting during or after the preplacement interview. Complete a separate checklist for each practicum setting. This exercise is to be used in conjunction with Exercise 2.22 on pages 71–74.

(Priority Rank Number _____)

1. Name of agency:

2. Area of specialty:

3. Name of field instructor:

4. Availability of practice opportunities and experiences in the following areas:

Individual	____	Policy	____
Group	____	Program Planning	____
Marital	____	Staff Development	____
Family	____	Research	____
Community	____	Evaluation	____

5. Philosophy of service:

   Agency centered ____

   Family centered ____

   Community based ____

   Other ____

6. Theoretical orientation—generalist or specialist:

7. Previous placement history with practicum students:

8. Resources available:

   Number of professional staff:

   Number of different disciplines:

   Availability of support staff:

   Workload of professional social workers:

   Workload of field instructor:

   Professional qualifications of field instructor:

Years of experience as a field instructor:

Nature of social work role in agency:

Roles of students:

Audio equipment:

One-way mirror:

Video equipment:

Library facilities:

Parking, telephone for students, office space:

Interviewing space:

Staff shortages:

Morale of staff:

Hours of service:

Overtime expected:

Anticipated expenses:

Other notes:

EXERCISE 2.16

RATING THE PRACTICUMS

After completing Exercise 2.15 for each preplacement practicum visit, rank order each potential practicum in terms of its desirability (or match) with your learning or educational needs. This exercise is to be used in conjunction with Exercise 2.22.

1. First choice: _____

2. Second choice: _____

3. Third choice: _____

4. Fourth choice: _____

The Orientation Meeting. Many social work programs also hold an orientation meeting or workshop for students and field instructors. *Attend this meeting.* It may be the only chance you have to hear about possible practicum settings. This opportunity to hear about them should also provide you with an overview of the major social resources offered in your community. A sound knowledge of available services is useful when you want to suggest sources of assistance to clients with pregnant daughters, elderly fathers, handicapped infants, and so forth.

Printed Material. Once you have developed a short list, you can answer other questions by obtaining and reading printed material about each potential practicum from every possible source. Pamphlets normally outline clients served, services offered, and the agency's general philosophy and goals. Agency manuals, like your program's field education manual, may present useful organizational charts and more complete information about the history of the agency, its philosophies, goals, and activities, its clientele, its size, and which geographical area it serves.

Another invaluable resource when you are looking for information about client populations and problems your potential practicum deals with is the library. University libraries tend to be ignored by students until every other avenue of enquiry has been explored. This is partly because it is always easier to ask someone than to read something. Card catalogues can help you. Librarians can help you. Computer searches can help you if they are available in your particular library.

But the time to get them to help you is *now*, not in a moment of dreadful stress when you have to have whatever by tomorrow. Take a guided tour of the library if one is offered. If not, go through it by yourself, finding out where the books and journals on social work and related disciplines are kept. Pretend you need to find something. Practice. Explore the microfiche. Familiarize yourself with the computer. If you can actually bring yourself to do this, you will be one of the visible minority and intensely grateful for your foresight later on.

Word of Mouth. Tales about agencies related by other students provide valuable information and are, at the same time, dangerous. Fascinating tidbits will come to light about the relationships between departments and people. Enthusiasms will abound; horror stories will be told with gusto. Some of the information will be true and some will not. Some will be irrelevant and some will be true from the point of view of the teller.

Remember that other students are not you. They do not have the same background as you or the same personal characteristics or the same educational objectives. They relate to people differently. They have different priorities, preferences, and prejudices. Your informant, for example, might object on principle to a field instructor who puts her feet on the desk and talks through her sandwich. You, on the other hand, indifferent to sandwiches and feet, might admire the way she counsels troubled pregnant adolescents.

Prejudgment, on the basis of another student's opinions, might lose you a good opportunity or it might cause you to apply for a practicum setting that will not really suit you. Store all the information you receive in your mental files but be prepared to form your own opinions based on your own perceptions. If possible, it may be a good idea to visit the practicum setting yourself to gain a first-hand impression. However, be sure that you have first received permission to do so by your program's practicum coordinator.

Preplacement Interviews. The fourth way to obtain information about a potential practicum is through the preplacement interview. In many ways, this will be similar to an employment interview. It is quite possible, in fact, that your selected agency *might* employ you at a later date if you enjoy the practicum experience and all goes well. One of the advantages of accepting students, from an agency's point of view, is that potential employees can be previewed without the commitment to hire. The student, of course, has the chance to decide whether this particular agency would make a good employer.

Right now, however, you are not going to be employed by the agency. You are going to be a student there. This raises several additional questions. Do the agency's social workers want social work students? Are they prepared for students? Do they believe that students should (1) do nothing but make the coffee, (2) do everything that no one else has time for, (3) fill in as required for staff who are ill or on vacation, or (4) do satisfying work of their own in a learning environment? In other words, can the agency offer you a range of educationally focused *learning* opportunities (as distinct from *working* opportunities) which are challenging and will focus on your learning needs? Will the field instructor have time to instruct you? Is she qualified to instruct you? Is the agency presently undergoing any crisis that will interfere with your learning? What kind of assignments or projects will you be expected to undertake? Will you be located in the same service area as your field instructor or will you be in a different building?

These are all important questions, and trying to keep them all in your mind is not easy. Exercises 2.17 through 2.22 are designed to enhance your ability to handle the preplacement interview. Time spent on preparing to obtain information from the preplacement interview may be the most important factor in your coming to a decision. Repeating Exercises 2.17 through 2.22 may be some of the most important activities you can do at this time.

EXERCISE 2.17
PURPOSE OF THE
PREPLACEMENT INTERVIEW

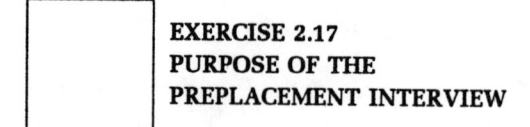

The preplacement interview is extremely important in the process of being selected as a practicum student. The manner in which you present yourself, including your physical presentation, will influence your chance of being chosen. The exercises you completed earlier in this book will prepare you for possible questions during the preplacement interview. Review your responses prior to this interview to ensure a confident presentation.

To further prepare for your preplacement interview, outline what you feel is the purpose of the preplacement interview and what you intend to communicate about yourself. Record your comments below.

**EXERCISE 2.18
ROLE-PLAYING THE
PREPLACEMENT INTERVIEW**

To further enhance your presentation, a rehearsal of the preplacement interview offers the opportunity to test a variety of approaches and responses.

In groups of three, role-play a 15-minute preplacement interview. Take turns in the roles of practicum student, field instructor, and neutral observer. Use video equipment if it is available. When the interview is complete, discuss your feelings about the role and your understanding of the other roles. As the neutral observer, evaluate the role performance by providing immediate feedback to the players. Suggest ways the student player can improve. Record the feedback you received in the student role. How can you use this feedback in your preplacement interview? Record your ideas below.

**EXERCISE 2.19
INTERVIEW QUESTIONS FROM
A FIELD INSTRUCTOR**

Below are 13 preplacement interview questions that a potential field instructor may ask. Remember to review prior exercises for possible responses that you could provide. Write some of your responses in the spaces provided.

1. May I see your student portfolio (Exercise 2.14)?

2. Why are you interested in a practicum in this setting?

3. What do you believe qualifies you for this practicum?

4. What do you believe you will contribute to this agency?

5. Tell me about any social work-related volunteer or employment experience you may have.

6. Describe your educational goals.

7. What social work courses do you like best/least and why?

8. What is your grade point average?

9. What would you like to be doing five years from now?

10. If you had complete freedom to choose any practicum setting, which would you choose? Why?

11. How do you believe you fit the requirements of this practicum setting?

12. What do you feel are your greatest strengths and limitations?

13. What kinds of people appeal most/least to you as potential clients?

EXERCISE 2.20
PREPLACEMENT INTERVIEW QUESTIONS FOR A PRACTICUM STUDENT

Below are 12 questions that you might ask a potential field instructor during the preplacement interview. Record the field instructor's possible responses in the spaces provided.

1. Would you like me to introduce myself by showing you my portfolio (Exercise 2.14)?

2. Did the portfolio raise any questions about my interests and abilities that I can answer for you?

3. Please describe for me my learning opportunities in this practicum setting.

4. Please show me where social work students fit into the overall structure of the organization.

5. What do you consider to be ideal experiences for students in this practicum setting?

6. What is the largest single problem or issue facing the organization that I should know about? How would this affect my learning?

7. What have been some of the best outcomes produced by social work students in this organization?

8. Please tell me about the primary client system with which I would be working.

9. What kinds of results would you like to see me produce as a practicum student?

10. May I talk with other social workers and staff about their functions and responsibilities?

11. Is there anything else I can tell you about my qualifications, abilities, or interests?

12. Other questions:

EXERCISE 2.21
IMPROVING YOUR PREPLACEMENT INTERVIEWING TECHNIQUES

After completing Exercises 2.19 and 2.20, role-play another 15-minute preplacement interview using the same roles of student, potential field instructor, and neutral observer with a different group of students. Take turns in the different roles and provide feedback to the players. Record feedback comments in the space provided. What steps have you taken to improve your abilities to deal with the preplacement interview?

EXERCISE 2.22
THE PRACTICUM AND YOU

After completing each preplacement interview, assess your fit with the particular practicum setting by completing the following 11 questions. Rate the items on a scale of 1 to 10, where the rating of 1 indicates an extremely poor fit and a rating of 10 indicates an extremely good fit. Make additional comments in the spaces provided. This exercise is to be used in conjunction with Exercises 2.15 and 2.16.

Name of potential practicum setting: _____

1. Assess the degree of the practicum setting's ability to have you as a social work student.

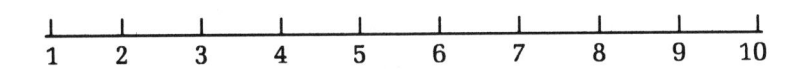

    1 2 3 4 5 6 7 8 9 10

    Comments:

2. Assess the degree of the practicum setting's willingness to have you as a social work student.

    1 2 3 4 5 6 7 8 9 10

    Comments:

Part One / Pre-Practicum

3. Assess the degree of the field instructor's ability to respond to your learning needs.

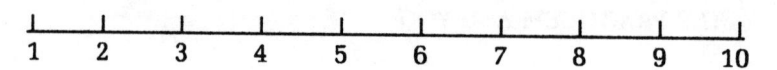

```
1  2  3  4  5  6  7  8  9  10
```

Comments:

4. Assess the degree of the field instructor's willingness to respond to your learning needs.

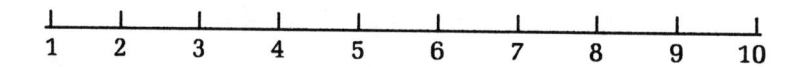

```
1  2  3  4  5  6  7  8  9  10
```

Comments:

5. Assess the degree of the practicum setting's ability to provide you with an adequate number of learning opportunities.

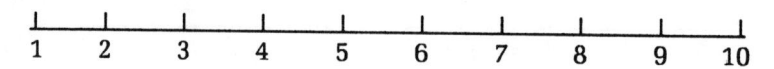

```
1  2  3  4  5  6  7  8  9  10
```

Comments:

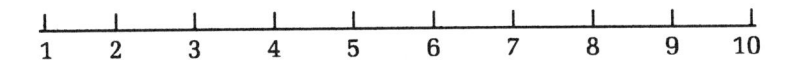

6. Assess the degree the practicum setting will provide you with an adequate quality of learning opportunities.

   |___|___|___|___|___|___|___|___|___|
   1   2   3   4   5   6   7   8   9   10

   Comments:

7. Assess the degree to which you will be adequately and reasonably challenged in the practicum setting.

   |___|___|___|___|___|___|___|___|___|
   1   2   3   4   5   6   7   8   9   10

   Comments:

8. Assess the degree as to whether your learning assignments will allow you to handle a case from initial contact through to termination.

   |___|___|___|___|___|___|___|___|___|
   1   2   3   4   5   6   7   8   9   10

   Comments:

9. Assess the degree to which the practicum setting will encourage you to work toward the enhancement of resources for clients within the agency and community.

   |___|___|___|___|___|___|___|___|___|
   1   2   3   4   5   6   7   8   9   10

   Comments:

10. Assess the degree as to whether establishing working relationships with other programs, units, and agency staff is encouraged.

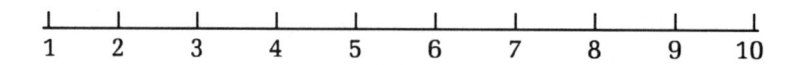

    |___|___|___|___|___|___|___|___|___|
    1   2   3   4   5   6   7   8   9   10

    Comments:

11. Assess the degree to which you could seek help for managing personal feelings associated with certain types of clients.

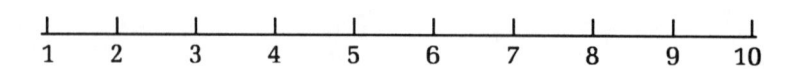

    |___|___|___|___|___|___|___|___|___|
    1   2   3   4   5   6   7   8   9   10

    Comments:

Field Instructor Qualifications

Your social work program has already answered the question about field instructor qualifications by listing the practicum setting. You can assume that your field instructor has adequate paper qualifications and is experienced in her own field. It is also probable that she has good teaching skills, but that does not mean that she will be good at teaching *you*.

Your learning style may be different from her teaching style. There may be personality clashes, stresses around ethnicity, value disagreements about client issues, or other factors. Fortunately, it is seldom that a compromise between field instructor and student cannot be made, but a mutual ease from the beginning is certainly an advantage.

Projected Tasks

You learn about your field instructor at the same time that you learn the answers to your other questions. For example, when you ask what kind of tasks you will be expected to undertake, your field instructor might outline for you not only specific projects but also your role as a student and the way that your role integrates with the normal activities of the agency. If she does this, you will know that there is to be something more in a practicum than just reading client files.

You will also know that your field instructor has thought a great deal about having a student; she is prepared for a student and she has done the initial work of planning what you will do and how you will fit within the agency's organization. It may be that she has planned for two or three students and has a number of educational opportunities in mind from which you can choose. In this case, you can indicate a preference—an enthusiasm is even better—but nothing will be finalized until you have been officially accepted by the field instructor and have had a chance to discuss this with your practicum coordinator. Always remember that your practicum coordinator has the final say about your final practicum selection.

Projected Location within the Agency

The next question to come up may be that of location within the agency. In a small agency, you might be located in the only office, with your field instructor. It is also probable that the person who interviews you at your preplacement interview will be the person who will be your field instructor.

In large organizations such as hospitals, however, students commonly spend much of their time in departments other than the social work department—pediatrics or geriatrics, for example. In this case, you may be interviewed by one person and assigned to a different field instructor later. It is a good idea to ask who your field instructor will be, what position she holds in the organization, and whether you and she will be located in the same department. Try, if possible, to meet with her and with other staff members.

There are advantages and disadvantages to having your field instructor nearby. On the plus side, she will be there to sort out minor issues before they can turn into major ones and she may be in a position to give you frequent, hands-on feedback. On the minus side, you will probably be allowed less self-direction and you may not develop as much confidence in your own independent abilities.

Similarly, there are advantages and disadvantages to being located in a different department. In large organizations there are often tensions between departments and you may run the risk of becoming embroiled in territorial and personal disputes. For example, there may be a particular service to patients that social workers believe should be performed by social workers, psychologists believe should be performed by psychologists, and nurses believe should be performed by nurses. Such a situation is more than an organizational problem.

Whatever your opinion on the subject, your place as a student is to smile benignly and refuse to become involved in other people's disputes. If you feel yourself becoming involved anyway, *talk with your field instructor*. If your instructor, herself embroiled, is unable to handle the matter, *talk with your field liaison*. Provided that you avoid embroilment through your own canny wiles or the advice of your field instructor, such episodes provide a wonderful opportunity to watch political maneuvering at work.

You should not let this worst-case scenario of possible embroilment dissuade you from taking a practicum in a larger agency. Being placed in another department and working with people from different disciplines will give you a chance to see how the disciplines mesh, how the various rumblings are resolved before they erupt into conflict, and how people with different goals and loyalties manage to work together.

If you are placed in a different department, be alert to the possibility that the lines of authority may be unclear or confused. Your work may be observed not only by your own field instructor but also by other members of the interdisciplinary team. Comments may float back. Approval of the physician may prove to be an important factor even though the physician's name does not appear anywhere in the official lines of social work authority. This comparison between formal and informal hierarchical structures is a fascinating study that will serve you well in years to come.

All in all, being placed in a different department has more potential benefits and more potential complexities than occupying the only desk in the agency's office. The prospect may excite you, or it may leave you indifferent, but it is certainly a matter to be explored during the course of your preplacement interview.

Crises the Agency May Be Facing

All agencies, like all people, face crises from time to time. These crises are commonly related to funding or labor disputes and may not affect your practicum in any way. Occasionally, however, an agency crisis may mean that your field instructor has less time for you and temporarily has less interest in your learning than she does in the resolution of the crisis. Again, there are advantages and disadvantages to such a situation.

You get to watch the crisis unfold—a worthwhile experience in itself. You can catch a glimpse of the multitude of personal, professional, and political factors that affect an agency's functioning in the real world and are not taught to you in your social work program. On the other hand, your formal learning objectives may not be met to the same degree as they otherwise would have been.

The exploration of a possible agency crisis during your preplacement practicum interview is a subtle matter. You do not want in any way to appear critical of your practicum setting or the agency in which it is housed; such criticism will be resented if it is unjustified and probably resented even more if there is an element of truth in it. If the crisis is common knowledge, for example if it involves a cut in funding or a looming strike which has been reported in the newspaper, you might make a sympathetic comment. If it has come to you through the grapevine, even more subtlety is required.

Toward the end of the interview, when rapport with the interviewer has been established, you might ask what are the major issues or problems facing the potential practicum setting that you should know about. Responses may vary from a defensive "*we* don't have any problems" to a humorous evasion to a frank discussion of pertinent issues. Do not expect all of the agency's problems to be displayed for your inspection. The interviewer should, however, be prepared to discuss with you any problem that might relate to you as a practicum student. Frankness in this regard is a positive sign that issues arising later will be discussed openly.

WILL I LIKE IT?

When you buy a candy bar, you will choose one with peanuts only if you like them. The same system applies to selecting a practicum. The problem, of course, is that your practicum has more ingredients to be considered. The first ingredient is philosophy.

Philosophy

A fit between your own values and those of your practicum setting is vital. For example, if you believe in your soul that abortion is wrong, you should not work in a setting where abortion is offered as an option to pregnant teens. If you are pro-choice, however, a practicum setting whose mission is opposed to abortion would also not be a good fit for you. If you are a moderate feminist, you should not choose a practicum setting whose views are radical, and so on. You should definitely not enter a setting whose views differ from your own in the hope of converting the agency staff.

Structure

Another point to be considered is structure. Large organizations tend to be more highly structured than smaller ones. The codes of dress and behavior tend to be more rigid. Correct procedures are defined and must be followed. Schedules, forms, and notices abound. The two points to think about here are, first, do you *like* structure and, second, do you *need* structure.

Some people feel more comfortable and achieve more readily when guidelines are clear and discipline is imposed from within; others prefer a feet-on-the-table, sandwich-in-hand approach. If you are a feet-on-the-table person, are you also a leave-it-until-tomorrow person who needs structure to perform? Be honest with yourself from the beginning. If you settle happily into a relatively unstructured setting and do little because no one is making you do it, trouble is just around the corner. On the other hand, if you have a lot of self-discipline but just prefer blue jeans, a less structured setting might suit you very well.

Agency Clientele

The type of client the agency serves will obviously affect your decision. Inspect your preferences with regard to older people, younger people, handicapped people, destitute people, pregnant people, and so forth. Even more importantly, *inspect your prejudices*. You may think that social workers are not supposed to have prejudices but this is a myth and an illusion. Social workers are supposed to *recognize* their prejudices and make sure that said prejudices do not adversely affect their work with clients.

For example, you may harbor a secret loathing for persons who sexually abuse children, or you may think that homosexuality is against nature, or you may believe that people who have attempted suicide have committed a mortal sin. If these are your secret beliefs, it is far better to admit them to yourself and avoid possible situations in which they might become problematic. If you wish you felt differently, you might attempt self-change but this is a long-term process. It is not a good idea, for example, to seek a practicum setting that works with sexual offenders in the hope that closer contact with them will help you change your views.

Sometimes people become social workers because of some traumatic event in their lives. Review your life. Be very sure that you are not choosing a particular field or type of client problem in order to resolve your own difficulties through contact with your clients. In the first place, this is not ethical since your personal problems will cloud your clients' issues. In the second place, it will not work. Examine your feelings and motives carefully—be certain that you do not do it.

Theoretical Orientation of the Agency

Some agencies specialize in a certain type of service. One may deal only with sexual abuse, for example, or another only with runaway youths. Other agencies provide a generalist service to people with a range of problems. Obviously, your choice will depend on whether you want to acquire general experience in a variety of problem situations or develop focused practice skills in one area. Other factors also need to be considered.

If you want to emphasize group work, for example, you will want to be sure that the setting you choose runs groups. Some agencies believe that group work is the most efficient and effective form of help and make it their primary focus, even though they also offer individual, couple, and family counseling. Other agencies, serving the same type of client, may believe that individual counseling is generally more beneficial and offer group work almost as an aside. Practicums, however, should offer as many opportunities as possible for students to work with all sizes of client systems such as families, groups, individuals, and communities.

If you have an interest in a particular practice mode—family therapy, say—find out whether the agency looks on family therapy as a major focus, a minor focus, or does not offer it at all. In a specialist agency, you may find that the focus depends on some philosophical position with regard to the special problem area. For example (to put it simplistically), some sexual abuse treatment agencies believe that sexual abuse results from individual pathology on the part of the offender. They therefore offer individual and group therapies to facilitate individual change and add family therapy if the family wishes to reunite.

Other agencies believe that sexual abuse is a symptom of a more general familial dysfunction. Their prime focus, therefore, is on family counseling with a view to changing the family system. At this point, you will probably not have definite opinions on such issues, but it is still a good idea to explore the opinions of agency staff so that you will understand how their value systems affect the services they offer to clients.

Perhaps your interest is not as a generalist social worker at all but centers around research, evaluation, social policy, or program planning. In this case, you may be unable to find a practicum setting that specializes in your interest area, but you can select one that is active in it to a greater extent. For example, some agencies include research among their activities and some do not. All agencies do some form of program planning and evaluation but they vary greatly in the enthusiasm they bring to these tasks.

If you are interested in these areas, the very words *evaluation*, *research*, and *planning* uttered by you in the course of your preplacement interview will bring an immediate response. A reluctant or guarded response will tell you that the agency's interest is low. On the other hand, interest may be high but the agency staff may be facing the common problem of having too much to do in too little time. In this case, your interviewer will make it plain to you that your input along the lines of research and evaluation will be appreciated.

Agency Resources

The term *agency resources* covers a wide spectrum, from field instructor qualifications to parking space for students. In general, it refers to everything the agency provides that will help to build a good learning environment. Exercise 2.15 will help you identify agency resources. Consider access, for example. The question, "is it on the bus route?" may sound frivolous, but in fact "getting there" can be a major consideration for staff members, clients, and social work students.

Then, there is the matter of leaving, perhaps on a regular basis, to make home visits to clients. If home visits are encouraged, or even required as part of your practicum duties, you may need a car. Do you have a car or access to one? If you do, can you afford to use it given that the agency's mileage allowance may only cover paid employees? Who will pay for the doughnut you bought for Mr. Jackson the first time you met him in the coffee shop?

What about overtime? A number of your home visits may have to be made in the evening. How many evenings on the average? Is overtime rare, routine, expected, or required? Are you allowed to come in later in the morning if you worked the evening before? Will you ever be asked to work nights? Is shift work involved?

Next on the list is the question of physical resources. Will you have a telephone? If you have to interview clients, will these interviews take place in the six-foot area around your desk or is there a separate interviewing room? If there is a separate room, is it provided with audio equipment for taping? Video equipment? Will you have time to try the equipment to get comfortable with it? Is there a one-way mirror so that you can observe other staff members at work and have them observe you? Is there a library? Agency libraries, often small, specialized, and close at hand, can be a valuable source of information. Is there a cafeteria? Can you smoke in it? If you cannot smoke in it or anywhere else in the building, what do you say to

Mr. Jackson who is a chain smoker, particularly during a crisis, and needs to "smoke up a storm" before he can talk?

An agency's resources are a lot to cover in one interview, and you do not want to dwell on doughnuts to the exclusion of more vital pieces of information. The best idea is to select from the plethora of seemingly trivial things only those that are important to you.

CAN I HAVE IT?

The preplacement interview will decide not only whether you want the practicum but whether it wants you. Normal considerations such as punctuality, good grooming, and appropriate dress most definitely apply. Be five minutes early. Smile in a way that is cheery but not idiotic. Shake hands firmly, somewhere between the damp-fish droop and the all-in wrestle. Demonstrate controlled enthusiasm, contained energy, and pertinent humor. Be attentive yet outgoing. Do not fidget.

If you can do all those things, the practicum setting is probably already yours. Still, you should sound intelligent and, to sound intelligent, you need to be prepared. You should already have gathered and absorbed as much information as possible about the agency and the practicum setting, and you should have a list of questions at hand. Next you must consider the questions that you will likely be asked.

You can control the direction of these questions to a certain extent by preparing your student portfolio. A guide to the student portfolio is presented in Exercise 2.14. It is much like a résumé, setting out your educational achievements, your social work interests and experience, and your volunteer experience, with references at the end. The major difference between a portfolio and a résumé is that, at this point, you will probably not have much work experience to offer. You have few acquired skills but you do have a great deal of learning potential, and it is on this learning potential that your portfolio should focus.

What are your career goals? In what ways can this practicum, as compared with other practicums, help you achieve those goals? You may want to point out, for example, that your long-term career goal is sexual abuse treatment and this agency has an excellent reputation for serving sexual offenders. Furthermore, one of your short-term career goals is to learn how to facilitate groups and this agency uses group therapy extensively in its offender treatment program. If you say all this, you will have demonstrated in one fell swoop, first, that you know something about the practicum setting, second, that you know where you want to go in social work and, third, that you have integrated your learning goals with the agency's service goals.

If you can back up these statements by saying that as a volunteer you acted as a special friend to a woman who is a survivor of sexual abuse, you will have added experience to the list of your triumphs. The point is integration. It is not enough to know what you want and what the agency does. You have to link them. You have to demonstrate in your preplacement interview that you have linked them.

Before you finally decide on a practicum, you will probably have a number of preplacement interviews. You can rate the potential practicums using Exercises 2.15, 2.16, and 2.22 to help in your decision-making process. If you are not placed with a particular practicum setting, either because you decided against it or because the practicum was not available to you, you should not merely move this agency to the back of your mind. Instead, you should write a letter. Writing a letter of appreciation after an unsuccessful interview will set you apart from the herd.

EXERCISE 2.23
WRITING A THANK YOU LETTER

After the completion of each preplacement practicum interview write a letter thanking the person who interviewed you. Such a letter can place you in good standing, especially if there is considerable competition for a particular practicum setting. At any rate, the public relations accorded such a letter cannot be underestimated for both you and your social work program.

By writing a letter you will be remembered. You will have begun, in the small world of social work, to have built a reputation for consideration and politeness. After graduation, when you are looking for work, this beginning reputation can make a big difference.

An example of the kind of letter you might write after an unsuccessful preplacement interview can be found in Figure 2.1 on the following page. Of course, if you have obtained the practicum, your letter will be different. You can then briefly summarize the agreement that has been reached with regard to dates, times, tasks, and conditions of work and add thanks for the interview and hopes for the future as appropriate.

Be sure to check with the practicum coordinator that your letter is suitable. Do not assume that you have the practicum until you have received official *written confirmation* from your practicum coordinator. If you are sufficiently confident, you might outline the letter in advance so that it can be sent without delay.

FIGURE 2.1
EXAMPLE OF A STUDENT LETTER

July 7, 1992

Ms Marianne Bernard, MSW   (person's name)
Clinical Supervisor   (person's position)
Family Support Program   (practicum setting)
Human Resources Department   (agency's name)
Grande Phoenix, Arizona   (location)

Dear Ms Bernard:

I greatly enjoyed our discussion today regarding your current initiatives in the use of family support services for adolescent pregnancy.

Although we agreed that as a practicum setting the Family Support Program would not be able to fully meet my learning objectives at this time, I would like to let you know that I was most impressed with the quality of work being done by your staff.

Perhaps my abilities and the available learning opportunities at your program will be fitting for my next practicum.

Thank you for the consideration you showed me today. I hope that we will have the opportunity to meet again.

Sincerely,

Josee Stanford
Social Work Student

SUMMARY

There are several logical steps in the selection of a practicum:

1. Identify career interests and goals.
2. Identify practicum preferences from the list provided by the practicum coordinator (or your field liaison).
3. Gather information about the preferred practicum settings and refine the list.
4. Complete your student portfolio; refine the list still more.
5. Submit the refined list to the appropriate person.
6. Coordinate and attend preplacement practicum interviews.
7. Rank potential practicums and submit the ranked list to the appropriate person.
8. Receive written notification of your practicum by the appropriate person.
9. Write after-interview letter.
10. Begin practicum.

During the first two steps, you determine your career interests and what the various practicum settings can offer in light of what you want. Factors to be considered about the agency are included in Exercise 2.15.

The third step in identifying a practicum involves taking an honest look at yourself. You should not only identify your own strengths, weaknesses, skills, needs, and so forth, but you should try to match them with your career goals and what the practicum setting has to offer. Factors to be considered about yourself are included in Exercises 2.10 through to 2.13.

The preplacement interview itself, step 6, is an opportunity for you to present your portfolio. Since you will probably be asked questions about the material it contains, this is your chance to display your knowledge of the practicum setting by linking your learning objectives and personal characteristics to the services provided by the agency. The preplacement interview also gives you a chance to meet agency staff and discover those things that were not included in your printed information. Questions to be ready for during the interview are included in Exercise 2.19. Questions that you might ask during the interview are included in Exercise 2.20.

When all your preplacement interviews are over, you will be in a position to decide which practicum you would really prefer. Even if your first choice is available to you, a polite letter to *all* of the others concerned is in order.

We will now turn to settling into your practicum, the first chapter in Part Two of this book.

SELECTED REFERENCES

Brownstein, C. (1989). Practicum issues: A placement planning model. In M. Raskin (Ed.), *Empirical studies in field instruction* (pp. 93–104). New York: Haworth.

Campbell R.P. (1989). Practice orientation of students in field instruction. In M. Raskin (Ed.), *Empirical studies in field instruction* (pp. 137–160). New York: Haworth.

Conklin, J.J., & Borecki, M.C. (1991). Field education units revisited: A model for the 1990's. In D. Schneck, B. Grossman, & U. Glassman (Eds.), *Field education in social work: Contemporary issues and trends* (pp. 122–130). Dubuque, IA: Kendall/Hunt.

Fine Holtzman, R., & Raskin, M. (1989). Why field placements fail: Study results. In M. Raskin (Ed.), *Empirical studies in field instruction* (pp. 77-88). New York: Haworth.

Fortune, A.E., Feathers, C.E., Rook, S.R., Scrimenti, R.M., Smollen, P., Stemerman, B., & Tucker, E.L. (1989). Student satisfaction with field placement. In M. Raskin (Ed.), *Empirical studies in field instruction* (pp. 359-381). New York: Haworth.

Gantt, A., Pinsky, S., Rosenberg, E., & Rock, B. (1991). The practice research center: A field/class model to teach research, practice and values. In D. Schneck, B. Grossman, & U. Glassman (Eds.), *Field education in social work: Contemporary issues and trends* (pp. 149-154). Dubuque, IA: Kendall/Hunt.

Gordon, W.E., & Gordon, M.S. (1989). George Warren Brown's field instruction research project: An experimental design tested by empirical data. In M. Raskin (Ed.), *Empirical studies in field instruction* (pp. 15-28). New York: Haworth.

Grossman, B. (1980). Teaching research in the field practicum. *Social Work, 25*, 36-39.

Grossman, B., & Barth, R.P. (1991). Evaluating a delayed entry model of first year field work. In D. Schneck, B. Grossman, & U. Glassman (Eds.), *Field education in social work: Contemporary issues and trends* (pp. 131-140). Dubuque, IA: Kendall/Hunt.

Hamilton, N., & Else, J. (1983). *Designing field education: Philosophy, structure and process*. Springfield, IL: Charles C. Thomas.

Lammert, M.H., & Hagen, J.E. (1975). A model for community-oriented field experience. In Council on Social Work Education (Ed.), *The dynamics of field instruction: Learning through doing* (pp. 66-67). New York: Author.

Larsen, J. (1980). Competency-based and task-centered practicum instruction. *Journal of Education for Social Work, 16*, 87-94.

Martin, M.L. (1991). Employment setting as practicum site: A field instruction dilemma. In D. Schneck, B. Grossman, & U. Glassman (Eds.), *Field education in social work: Contemporary issues and trends* (pp. 288-294). Dubuque, IA: Kendall/Hunt.

May, L.I., & Kilpatrick, A.C. (1989). Stress of self-awareness in clinical practice: Are students prepared? In M. Raskin (Ed.), *Empirical studies in field instruction* (pp. 303-320). New York: Haworth.

McClelland, R.W. (1991). Innovation in field education. In D. Schneck, B. Grossman, & U. Glassman (Eds.), *Field education in social work: Contemporary issues and trends* (pp. 177-184). Dubuque, IA: Kendall/Hunt.

Mesbur, E.S. (1991). Overview of baccalaureate field education: Objectives and outcomes. In D. Schneck, B. Grossman, & U. Glassman (Eds.), *Field education in social work: Contemporary issues and trends* (pp. 155-166). Dubuque, IA: Kendall/Hunt.

Mesbur, E.S., & Glassman, U. (1991). From commitment to curriculum: The humanistic foundations for field instruction. In D. Schneck, B. Grossman, & U. Glassman (Eds.), *Field education in social work: Contemporary issues and trends* (pp. 47-58). Dubuque, IA: Kendall/Hunt.

Raskin, M. (1989). Field placement decisions: Art, science or guesswork? In M. Raskin (Ed.), *Empirical studies in field instruction* (pp. 105-122). New York: Haworth.

Schneck, D. (1991). Ideal and reality in field education. In D. Schneck, B. Grossman, & U. Glassman (Eds.), *Field education in social work: Contemporary issues and trends* (pp. 17-35). Dubuque, IA: Kendall/Hunt.

Part Two: The Practicum

CHAPTER 3

Settling In

No MATTER HOW CAREFULLY you plan for the first day at your practicum, some essential details will only occur to you the night before. For example, lunch. Will you be reduced to accepting half a sandwich and a carrot from your field instructor's brown bag if you do not take a lunch? Or, if you do take it, will you be able to hide it successfully when you discover that everyone else eats at The Food Fair next door? Then, there is stationery and documentation. Should you go armed with a notebook and pen or should you assume that these will be provided? Should you take all of the material you have collected about the practicum setting, none of it, or some selected bits? Should you take your student portfolio? Information about your social work program and courses? Will you look silly if you carry a briefcase or unprofessional if you do not?

TECHNIQUES TO SETTLING IN

Though these questions are trivial, they can induce extreme panic and cause you to arrive with lines of strain already engraved. The lines will deepen to grooves as your first day proceeds. The impression of carefree competence you meant to present will be gone, and worry over the mess you may have made will make the next day even worse. This wretched spiral can be avoided by the use of three basic techniques: common sense, compromise, and the practice of humility.

Common Sense

Common sense is a much underrated virtue that is essential to social workers and sometimes ignored by social work programs. For example, if your practicum setting has a cafeteria, or is two doors down from The Food Fair, you do not need to take a lunch. If it is miles from the nearest habitation, bringing a lunch is probably in order. In a similar way, the dilemma about briefcases can readily be resolved. First, do you have one? Second, do you have anything to put in it if you do have one? Third, is your practicum setting a stern and formal place where briefcases are valued, or is it a more relaxed affair whose forte is the plastic bag?

All this is not as silly as it sounds. The day-to-day problems you will encounter in your practicum are rarely of earth-shattering dimensions. They are usually *small* vexations that you do not quite know how to handle. Nowhere is the exact procedure written down, no one has told you what to do, and your field instructor is in a meeting. Even if she were not in a meeting, you would not want to bother her with anything so trivial but, at the same time, you are temporarily stuck.

If you make the wrong decision, nations will not fall; however, your sense of your own competence may be eroded. Continued erosion, in the long term, does more extensive damage than a number of explosions. It is therefore important that you learn early not to agonize over trifles. Apply your common sense, which is just as well developed as everyone else's common sense, make a decision that seems sensible, and continue with other tasks.

Compromise

Compromise is another useful tool in avoiding erosion. For example, you do not want to appear unprepared for your first day, but neither do you want to look as if you are moving from your dorm or apartment. Take a few things. Leave the impressive textbook on research methodology and statistics; leave that bit from your program's field education manual about appeal procedures after being asked to leave the agency. Take the agency's address, letters if there were any, documents given to you by your practicum coordinator, your Social Security number, which you are sure to need for something, and a pen and notebook just in case. If you find that you have forgotten some vital piece of paper, you will have to practice humility, which brings us to the next section.

The Practice of Humility

Practicing humility is not the same thing as degrading yourself. In fact, it is quite the opposite. Practicing humility means understanding that you are a beginning student in a new practicum setting. You do not yet know where the washrooms are and it is all right not to know—for now, at any rate. There will continue to be, throughout your practicum, a host of other things that you do not know and cannot do.

It is very easy to be overwhelmed by the sheer weight of your perceived insufficiencies—to decide that you are incompetent as a social worker, unworthy as a person, and, as Homer Simpson says, "not too bright to boot." This decision will probably be based on an information overload and a number of little errors. You were introduced to four new people at a meeting and got Joan confused with Jane. You earned a raised eyebrow from your field instructor when you asked a question that was answered already in a client's file you were required to have read.

If you make a mistake, you should certainly analyze it and try not to repeat it. But remember also that you are a student. You are allowed to make a mistake, to not know what to do, to ask "stupid" questions. If you cannot admit this to yourself, and thus make allowances for yourself, you are failing to practice humility. Just remember the phrase, "The Mother of all Battles."

MAKING FRIENDS AND INFLUENCING PEOPLE

Your next task after arriving at the agency in a reasonably stressless state will be to meet unfamiliar people. You hope you will win their instant approval with *your* knowledge, wisdom, and charm. In fact, you are far more likely to win their approval if you show an appreciation for *their* knowledge, wisdom, and charm.

At first, you may feel threatened by them. They know more than you; they are more experienced than you; they are professional staff while you are a social work student. Very possibly they too are feeling threatened. You have bubbled eagerly into their lives, filled to the brim with new knowledge, new techniques, new theories, ready to pounce on their inadequacies, bursting to question their smallest acts, with all the weight of your social work program behind you.

In fact, new techniques and theories may be advantageous to the agency; one of the reasons students are welcomed is because they bring updated information from the social work program to the practicum setting. Nevertheless, from a few staff members' point of view, anything that challenges the established way of doing things may contain a hint of threat.

Observing Others

Your beginning task, therefore, is to make it clear that you are not a threat; you are an earnest seeker of staff members' knowledge, wisdom, and truth. Introduce yourself as a social work student, tell them what social work program you are from, answer their questions as best you can, and then be quiet and listen. Observe. Remember. Link names to faces and personal mannerisms. Link faces to positions, roles, and departments. Try to identify people whose names are mentioned in conversations. Notice who sits with whom, who talks to whom, who avoids whom, whose opinion is respected, who says least or most.

Observation of this kind will not only help you to know your colleagues more quickly; it will also help you to understand the personal and political nuances of the system in which you must function. Such awareness is very important for social workers. Your job on behalf of your clients will often involve knowing who provides what social service, where to go for information, and how to use the system for your clients' benefit. You must therefore know the system—its traps and its tigers, its fairy godmothers and its hidden pots of gold.

You will not learn all this during your first coffee break. One of the ongoing tasks of your practicum—and, indeed, of your social work career—is to develop an awareness of your immediate environment. If you can do this, you will avoid becoming a cynical, burned-out grump who secretly believes that the social service delivery system is rotten, all social workers are only concerned with their own careers, and all clients are selfish, grasping, and lazy.

You will also avoid becoming a person who believes that the system was designed by God, all social workers play harps, and all clients are blameless victims of society. Instead, you will develop into a competent and balanced social worker who can ride the tiger's tail to reach the pot of gold.

With any luck, you will be introduced to people gradually. This will give you time to write down your impressions in your trusty journal (to be discussed shortly) so that Joan, once met, will be forever branded into your memory. If Joan happens to be a member of the support staff, remember that the work performed by her is at least as important as the work performed by social workers; and, without the secretary, the entire organization would probably come to a halt. Members of the support staff can also be a student's best allies.

Finding Support Systems

If there are other students in your practicum setting, they are worthy of your particular attention. They will be your support system—people in the same position as yourself with whom you can share your mutual miseries, hopes, and uncertainties. At the beginning, it may *seem* that they know more than you or that they are more competent and better liked.

Perhaps this is even true. There will always be people who know more than you about something or other, whose personalities are brighter, whose intellects are more acute. Remember, though, that scientists who are not Einsteins still make contributions to science; writers who are not Shakespeares still make contributions to literature; and social workers who are not Perlmans still provide useful services to clients.

In all likelihood, the other social work students in your practicum setting are as confused and nervous as you are. If by some miracle they are not, you must remember that a practicum is not a competition. Your learning is based on your own goals, your social work program's learning requirements, and your strengths and needs. It will not take place at the same rate or in the same way as someone else's learning, and it is not expected to. You cannot enter a race with other social work students when all of you are running in different directions. Some field instructors will evaluate you on your improvement and give recognition to your personal circumstances; others will treat your performance in the practicum the same as it is treated in a classroom.

EXPLORING YOUR PRACTICUM SETTING

By now you will have found out where the washrooms are. You will also, before too long, locate your desk, your field instructor's office, the photocopying machine, the stationery shelf, and the cold drink dispenser, along with other sundries such as the library and parking lot. Some large organizations provide guided tours or maps to aid the wandering public. Whatever your route to discovery, pretend that you are not a social work student but a client seeking help from the agency. The intent of Exercise 3.1 is to help you examine your first impressions of your new practicum setting.

**EXERCISE 3.1
GETTING TO KNOW YOUR
PRACTICUM SETTING**

Now that you are in your practicum, it is important to learn as much as possible about its environment. This will not only help you become comfortable with the agency as a system, but it will also serve as the first assignment or activity you will be evaluated on by your field instructor.

First impressions can be very powerful and affect us in many ways. How did you experience your first day in your practicum? Consider the physical appearances of your practicum setting and agency, their sights, sounds, and smells and their impact on you. Record your brief initial impressions in the space provided below.

How welcome do you feel, how comfortable, how intimidated? If you feel comfortable, is your comfort due to the color scheme, the furniture, the art work, the layout? If you feel intimidated, what is it about the place that makes it intimidating? What has been done to make the most of a tiny space, to compensate for a much-scuffed floor, to brighten a beige expanse of institutional walls?

Social workers definitely are not experts in interior design but they should have some sense of the relationship between mood and environment. If you have no natural talent for expressing welcome with pink geraniums, this is your chance to see how other people do it. What turns a room into a good play therapy room, a safe room for anxious clients, a warm room for children, an encouraging room, a relaxing room? Are conversations audible through the walls? Will drapes reduce the morgue-like echo? What are the different effects of natural light, ceiling light, and shaded lamps? Your exploration of the setting should teach you a good deal more than the precise location of the coffee pot and washrooms.

YOUR TRUSTY JOURNAL

During the first few days at your practicum, you will be given more information than you can possibly digest. The rules, titles, faces, and impressions will soon fade into a dusty haze. People whose names you have forgotten will expect recognition. Meetings will take place in rooms you cannot find. To some extent this is inevitable, but you can lessen the impact by writing things down. Start a journal. Even if you are not a "journal person" and have never kept a diary in your life, now is the time to begin. Exercise 3.2 below gets you started.

Your journal can serve a number of purposes. At first, it may be a mixture of a wailing wall, a list of questions to ask your field instructor, and notes on vital facts you have to remember. Many things will emerge from your initial questions or those generated from Exercise 3.3 on pages 91–95. A little later, appointments will creep in: colleagues you will have to see, telephone calls you will have to make, sessions you will have to observe, and clients you will have to see. Make it a habit to document these things. If you make or receive a telephone call, note who you talked to, about what, when, and for how long. Also note what you promised to do as a result of the call, for whom and by when.

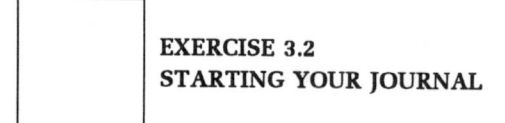

**EXERCISE 3.2
STARTING YOUR JOURNAL**

Get a notebook that will serve as a daily journal or log for your practicum experience. The purpose of the journal is to keep track of questions, thoughts, feelings, ideas, and facts about you, your practicum setting, your agency, your clients, and the processes occurring during your time in the practicum. Keep your journal up-to-date by regularly recording in it. It will become an invaluable source of data and learning as you proceed with your practicum. It may be very important when it comes time for your mid-term and final evaluations.

EXERCISE 3.3
INCREASING YOUR KNOWLEDGE
OF YOUR PRACTICUM SETTING

Getting started and oriented to your practicum setting is not easy. It can be awkward when everyone except you seems to know what to do. Because the duration of practicums is short, there is relatively little time to have the luxury of easing yourself into the setting. You have already analyzed the initial impact of the setting on you (Exercise 3.1). This exercise is a list of possible activities to increase your knowledge of your practicum setting and agency, and help you feel more at ease as a member of the organization.

Over the next few days carry out the following 13 activities to increase your knowledge of your practicum setting and the community in which it functions. These activities will help you get started and gain legitimacy within the setting. Record your responses in the spaces provided. Add to your list any other activities unique to the understanding of your particular practicum setting.

1. Use your journal to develop a list of questions for your supervisory conferences (to be discussed in Chapter 5). What questions do you have about the practicum setting's services, the agency as an organization, or the community it serves? List these questions below.

2. Planning for your time is critical. Review your journal and anticipate some "blank spots" in time management. Check with your field instructor for further ideas to enhance learning opportunities. Describe some of your ideas below.

3. Orientation to your practicum setting and agency is also considered critical to your learning. Read all of the material you can find about their services. What information is disseminated to clients? What information is disseminated to staff? Pamphlets, booklets, reports, or manuals are good sources of information. Identify each piece of information you read. Use these readings to generate questions for future supervisory conferences.

4. Provide extra copies of your student portfolio (developed in Exercise 2.14). Give your field instructor written permission to share it with other colleagues. You may also use this to introduce yourself to other departments, staff, or other professionals. Introducing yourself provides an opportunity for you to ask questions of other staff about their roles, responsibilities, and their previous contact with social work students. What did you learn? What new questions emerged? Record your comments here.

5. Collect course material, course outlines, and your favorite handouts from class. Share them with your practicum colleagues when they ask about your social work program.

6. If the practicum requires you to move to a new location, learn about the new town or community. Start a community file. What information sources are there? Find out about the local library and newspapers, obtain a copy of the local community services directory, list the health and social services information help lines, and so forth. See if a community needs assessment study has been done. Write some preliminary notes below.

7. Learn your practicum setting's routines for obtaining files, using the telephone (long distance), advising the receptionist of your schedule, using government cars or keeping a record of mileage, keeping work/caseload statistics, using word processors, keeping documentation, taping and recording, getting office supplies such as forms. Don't forget to pay for your coffee!

8. Another important orientation activity is introducing yourself to various levels of agency staff. Check with your field instructor about how social work students are to introduce themselves. Read some typical client files or case records to become familiar with service delivery, documentation, and standards in your practicum setting. Read the policy manuals. Observe others: sit with the receptionist; attend an intake interview; attend a case conference or a court presentation; observe a home visit with a social worker.

9. Begin to develop a list of resources or agencies that may be of use to you or your prospective clients. Sources for your list include coworkers, your field instructor, other practicum students, and clients. All of these activities help in getting acquainted with the role of social workers in the practicum setting. List some resources that you feel will help your clients below.

10. Review relevant legislation that may affect social work practice within your practicum setting. List relevant legislation below.

11. Meet each staff member individually and get to know their roles and functions. Keep notes in your journal of your impressions of these contacts. List key staff members and their roles below.

12. Each of these activities will contribute to formulating specific learning opportunities in your setting. Use the orientation activities to begin developing a list of your goals and learning needs. Be as specific as possible. Record your developing list in the space provided below.

13. Plan some especially pleasurable and relaxing activity since this is going to be a tough week!

Exercise 3.3 may sound like a lot of work. In fact, it is work, but social workers are required to document and record any contact that has to do with clients, and you may as well form the habit early. There will also be forms to be completed and reports to be written. For example, some practicum settings will not require you to turn in a time sheet, but you may have to keep a detailed time sheet. Your time sheet may not be a simple matter of arrival at 8:15 AM, departure at 4:30 PM, with half an hour for lunch and an hour at the dentist. Instead, you may be asked what you did between 8:15 AM and 4:30 PM: how much of your time was spent in direct client contact, how much in working on the client's behalf, how much in administration, how much in supervisory conferences, and so forth. If you have not kept a daily record, much of your time sheet will be plain invention.

As the days go on, the entries you make in your journal will become more focused. For example, appointments, now more numerous, will be written in a separate appointment book. Anything to do with clients will be kept in the clients' files. You may need other files to separate out such things as treatment sessions observed with other workers, expense sheets, requisition forms, minutes of meetings, job-related legislation, community resources, and so forth. Your journal will now cease to be a general repository for every scrap of information and will become a record of your learning process.

The learning process will be discussed more fully later, but basically it will entail setting specific learning goals and objectives and doing specific activities that will achieve those objectives. For example, one of your learning goals might be to "develop group work skills in relation to rehabilitating cardiac patients." Your field instructor will want to know precisely what you have done to improve your group work skills, and it will help if you have devoted a couple of pages of your journal to this goal. For example, you might write down that on Monday you spent an hour with the group facilitator planning an agenda. On Tuesday, you reread a chapter from your group work textbook. On Wednesday evening, you spent two hours at a group meeting. On Thursday morning, you wrote up what happened during the group session and discussed it with the facilitator. By Friday, when you have your weekly supervisory conference with your field instructor, you will have forgotten all about Monday unless you have written it down. If you have written it down, you will be well prepared.

LEARNING THE RULES AND REGULATIONS

Most of the agency's rules, regulations, and routines will be explained to you during the first few days. If you have to take a public service oath or have a security check completed, you will be told about these procedures. The secrets of the many-buttoned telephone, the reluctant photocopying machine, and the finger-chewing paper shredder will be revealed to you in turn, along with the ways of obtaining stationery, booking interviewing rooms, borrowing dictaphones, receiving messages, and so forth. Although initially confusing, all of this is basically quite straightforward; however, there are subtleties.

For example, you might discover that it is a no-no for social workers, especially students, to use the photocopying machine without asking permission from Marj. It may be another no-no to copy your term paper for your practice methods class. Havoc may occur when you use Ms Tutty's coffee mug or remove Emmy's stapler. The remedy is to ask. Whenever you are in doubt as to the correct and accepted procedure, practice humility and *ask*.

FINDING OUT ABOUT YOUR AGENCY

During the first few weeks of your practicum, there probably will be times when nothing specific has been scheduled for you to do. Cherish such times—they may not occur again until you are drawing your Social Security checks—but also put them to productive use. For example, you can organize the information you have about your agency into a coherent system. In addition to the previous three exercises, Exercise 3.4 will help you understand the agency in which your practicum setting is housed.

EXERCISE 3.4
GETTING TO KNOW YOUR AGENCY SETTING AS A SOCIAL SYSTEM

To understand your social service delivery system (your agency) and how you fit in, you need to understand how your agency functions as a system. This is a complex task that requires a great deal of information and understanding of the dynamics of the organization. Read agency material and talk with your field instructor to help you complete this exercise. To learn more about the overall goals and objectives of your agency, you may wish to contact other professionals within the agency. Record your responses in the spaces provided. At your next supervisory conference, discuss your understanding of your practicum setting as a system with your field instructor.

1. Name of agency:

2. Name of practicum setting:

3. Agency's address and telephone number:

4. Practicum setting's address and telephone number:

5. Agency's goals and objectives:

6. Practicum setting's goals and objectives:

7. What does the agency generally set out to do; that is, what is its mission statement? What does it specifically set out to do; that is, what are its objectives?

8. What does the practicum setting generally set out to do; that is, what is its mission statement? What does it specifically set out to do; that is, what are its objectives?

9. Functions of agency:

10. Functions of practicum setting:

11. What services are provided to what types of clients in the agency?

12. What services are provided to what type of clients in the practicum setting?

13. Philosophy of agency:

14. Philosophy of practicum setting:

15. What value systems underlie the services to clients in the agency?

16. What value systems underlie the services to clients in the practicum setting?

17. History of agency and practicum setting: How did the agency get started? Through a voluntary association of people determined to right some wrong? By statute? As an off-shoot of another organization? Or perhaps by metamorphosis—an evolution from prevention of cruelty to animals, for example, to prevention of cruelty to children. Often, the present characteristics of an agency can best be understood in the context of its history. It may have a large volunteer component because it began as a volunteer organization. It may be perceived as a "child snatcher" by the community because it started as a Children's Aid Society. Record a brief history of your agency and your practicum setting below.

18. Geographical area served by the agency: Most agencies provide service only to people who live within a certain geographical area. If an agency is funded by the county government, for example, it may serve people who live within the county limits free of charge and accept others on a fee-for-service basis as space permits. An agency may serve only part of a city, as some child protection agencies do, or be responsible for a large rural area or operate inside an entire state. Describe the geographical area served by your agency below.

19. Funding base: Depending on whether your agency is a public or private organization, money may be obtained from one or more of the following sources: federal government, state government, grants from various government departments, private individuals or foundations, fees paid by clients, donations, investments, and fund-raising events.

    Since it is usually true that whoever pays the piper calls the tune, an analysis of your agency's funding sources will enable you to see where control of the agency's policies primarily lies. For example, you might find your agency described as a private, nonprofit organization administered by a voluntary board of directors. This means, in theory, that the people from the community who sit on the board are free to direct your agency's activities as they see fit. In practice, however, 90% of your agency's funding may come from government grants or contracts and the board will therefore be anxious to accommodate the government.

    There is nothing necessarily wrong with this, but it does mean that government policies, priorities, and regulations are very important even to private agencies. If you are to understand the system in which you work, and if you are to use it to benefit your client, you will need to know what regulations apply, what they really mean in terms of services to clients, and what the effects will be when they are changed. Your investigation of agency funding sources may lead you to a whole new investigation into government policies and legislation. Now describe your agency's funding base below.

20. Organizational structure and context: Organizational structure refers to the linkages between departments and the lines of authority within departments depicted in the organizational chart. Organizational context is concerned with whether your agency stands on its own or whether it is a part of, or affiliated with, some other agency. The board of directors, if there is one, will be at the head of the organizational chart. How many people are there on the board? Are they elected or appointed? Do they have decision-making power or do they serve in an advisory capacity? What activities do they engage in? What kinds of expertise do they have? The answers to these questions will tell you a good deal about how the agency runs. How specifically does your practicum setting fit into the overall structure of the agency (use your responses to the first 19 questions to guide your answer).

21. Staff and volunteers: The counting of staff and volunteer heads is only a beginning. In addition, you may want to know what kind of qualifications and experience are required of staff members. What roles and responsibilities must they fulfill in various positions? How much are they paid? What training programs are provided for them? Do they stay with the agency for life or is there a high rate of turnover?

    Similarly, you may want to find out what qualities are sought in volunteers. How are volunteers trained and supervised? What kind of work do they do? Are their services acknowledged through a volunteer day, a pin, an annual dinner, or merely a kind word? Does your agency in fact revolve around the work of volunteers or are they peripheral or not utilized at all?

    Some of this information may not be readily available. You do not want to beseige your field instructor with questions about the expertise of the board of directors; your agency manual may be sternly silent on the subject of high staff turnover. Nevertheless, if you make a beginning and you know what you are looking for, odd snippets of information will continue to come your way throughout the practicum. Provide answers to the above questions below.

Fit the new information from Exercises 3.3 and 3.4 into the pattern of the old and before long you will have built a coherent whole. You will then be closer to understanding how your agency functions and how you can use your practicum to help your future clients.

FINDING OUT ABOUT COMMUNITY RESOURCES

After you have explored your agency and practicum setting as a system, you may want to explore them as part of a larger system, that is, as part of the community in which they exist. Exercise 3.5 will assist you. For example, clients come from somewhere. Occasionally, they find the agency themselves through the telephone book or through a friend, but often they are referred by someone else. The someone else may be a doctor, schoolteacher, or relative, but usually it is another social service agency.

> **EXERCISE 3.5**
> **GETTING TO KNOW YOUR**
> **LOCAL COMMUNITY**

In addition to knowing your agency and practicum setting, you need to know the community in which they operate. This includes not only the other agencies and organizations that make up the network of social services in the area, but also the community at large. Record your responses to the 15 attributes below in the spaces provided. Then discuss your responses with other social workers in your practicum setting and your field instructor.

1. History and traditions of the community:

2. Size, territory, and boundaries of the community:

3. Major institutions, organizations, and characteristics of the community:

4. Demographic characteristics (e.g., age, gender, educational, ethnic, racial, religious groupings):

5. Mobility and residential characteristics:

6. Economic and social structure:

7. Occupational and income profile:

8. Other issues such as local politics, housing, and crime rates:

9. Value system of community:

10. Leadership structure (power):

11. Communication systems (e.g., newspapers, TV stations, radio stations, organizational newsletters):

12. Informal support systems (individuals, groups, or associations known for offering help, support, or material aid to others):

13. Services needed:

14. Feasibility of change in various areas of concern:

15. Other comments and observations:

Clients may also be referred to another agency after they have finished with you, or they may be receiving service from another agency at the same time they are coming to you. It is therefore important for you to know what is out there, not just in terms of social service agencies but in terms of the community as a whole.

For example, your community may seem to consist largely of small children. Probably this is an illusion, but it may be, in fact, a young community—or an elderly community, or a growing community, or a shrinking community. It may have a preponderance of mansions or apartments or cardboard boxes over heating vents. It may be conservative or revolutionary, violent or peaceful. It may have a strong religious or ethnic base.

All these factors and others will affect what services are most needed by the people in the community. You might want to note what information you can find under the headings in Exercise 3.5. Add additional headings so the information on your community reflects the unique person, problems, and environment in which you will function.

The reason for collecting all this information is to give you an idea of what major problems exist in your community. For example, there may be a large number of single-parent families who have problems related to housing and child care due to inadequate incomes. There may be youths with little education and no employment who are contributing to a rising crime rate. There may be a large percentage of the population with AIDS, and so forth.

The next step is to determine what is being done or can be done about the problems. Ideally, your practicum setting via the agency is part of the solution, and so are all the other agencies in the community's network of services. It is a good idea to list these agencies, making notes on what they do, whom they serve, and in what ways they interact with your agency. Critically analyze the community characteristics, then compare the services that are needed with those services that are provided. This can prove to be very revealing and most useful in understanding your local community. Exercises 3.5 and 3.6 will increase your understanding of how your agency functions within the community. This comparative information is not only valuable to you as a student but to your potential clients as well.

**EXERCISE 3.6
INCREASING YOUR UNDERSTANDING
OF YOUR COMMUNITY**

What steps can you take to increase your understanding of the local community in which your agency functions? Write your response in the space below.

Again, finding the information you want will probably be a matter of picking up bits and pieces here and there. Manuals, pamphlets, and resource books will be useful. Your field instructor will be the primary source for this information but you might ask other staff and fellow students and, if it seems appropriate, your clients. Some clients know far more about community resources than some social workers do. Many of them have learned "the system" the hard way. They know what is out there and, most importantly, what is not.

MASTERING YOUR IMPATIENCE

After spending a number of days filling your unscheduled time with the exploration of your practicum setting, exploration of the community, and countless cups of coffee, you might start to get impatient. It may seem that you will never meet with your first group, never interview your first client, never do anything more constructive than hover in the wake of very busy social workers. Use Exercise 3.7 below in your initial supervisory conference with your field instructor to address these emerging, or at least fleeting, concerns.

**EXERCISE 3.7
PREPARING FOR YOUR FIRST
SUPERVISORY CONFERENCE**

As you gain *credibility* in your practicum setting, you need to become more focused. This process begins in your supervisory conferences. Using your questions and comments from Exercises 3.1, 3.2, and 3.3, prepare for your first supervisory conference. Some possible questions and activities are listed below. Now you have an agenda for your first formal supervisory conference with your field instructor.

1. Discuss plans for your agency orientation, introduction, and beginning work within the agency. Share ideas from your list.
2. Review questions from your initial impressions. Verify your observations. This will help to validate your feelings and ideas of your agency as a system. The discussion may serve as a learning opportunity for your field instructor as well.
3. Review your student portfolio and the drafted list of possible learning interests and activities.
4. Establish supervisory conference times and practicum hours.
5. Discuss staff roles and responsibilities. How do you fit into your setting's organizational structure and social service delivery system? Are there service priorities of which you need to be aware?
6. Establish with your field instructor how much independence and consultation is required for your social work assignments.
7. Find out who is the back-up field instructor when your field instructor is unavailable.
8. Confirm your observations of your practicum setting's behavior codes for dress, breaks for coffee and lunch, making and cleaning up the coffee area, and socializing.
9. If necessary, arrange for a public service oath, a security check or photograph, and for any keys that may be required.
10. Summarize each supervisory conference in your journal.

From your field instructor's point of view, this is a time of assessment. If you are to observe another worker's counseling session, your field instructor has to be sure that the session and the worker chosen are appropriate to your learning objectives (to be discussed in a subsequent chapter). If you are to see a client right away, your field instructor will likely have several in mind, with goals that appear to be obtainable within the time frame of your practicum.

Some clients are good at training social workers because they have experience with "the system." They know what questions you ought to ask and obligingly answer them for you. They fill in awkward pauses, propose solutions to their own dilemmas, help you along when you falter in drawing a genogram, and generally guide you on your way.

While they are doing all this, of course, they are carefully failing to mention their real problem. You may hear harsh words from your field instructor later on the subject of allowing yourself to be controlled by your clients but, nevertheless, you will have learned. Your field instructor has to find a client for you whose problems will not overwhelm you, who will not be hurt by your inexperience, who can help you reach your learning goals and, in turn, can be helped by you. This is not easy and it takes some time. If you are patient, however, a range of clients will appear and the results will be more positive and challenging than you ever imagined.

SUMMARY

At the beginning of your practicum, you may find that there is both too much and too little to do. Small decisions you need to make may cause you unnecessary worry because you may be too anxious to make a good impression and do the right thing. If you use your common sense, compromise to some extent, and remember that as a social work student you are allowed to make a few mistakes, you will be able to put these worries into perspective.

At first, you will be overwhelmed with information and you may despair of ever being able to remember all the names, rules, and procedural details that everyone else takes for granted. The staff will help you if you ask them. The other social work students in your practicum setting also will help you once you have it clear among you that a practicum is a mutual learning experience and not a competition.

There are two useful techniques for coping with information overload. The first is to keep a journal in which you can write your questions, take note of things you are told, and express your confusions. The second is to organize your information. The journal will help you establish the habit of documentation and recording, which is very important for social workers. Organizing your information will help you to see your agency and practicum setting as a system.

Understanding the system is an essential part of social work, because it is only through the system that you will be able to help your clients. If you collect information about your practicum setting as you go through your practicum, the various parts and workings will gradually fall into place. Basically, it is a matter of seeing the connections between such entities as funding sources, value systems, legislation, goals, services provided, and so forth.

It is important, too, that you see your practicum as one link in a network of community services. You will need to know about other agencies because you will interact with them on behalf of your clients. If you write down the services each provides and integrate these services into an overall map, you will begin to see what problems within your local community are being addressed and where there are gaps.

If the services provided are to be useful, they should be based on community needs. These needs, in turn, relate to the unique nature of the community—its ethnic or religious base, its poverty or wealth, its disparities in education and employment, its political views, and so on.

Exploring your agency and practicum setting as a system in itself and as part of a larger community system will occupy many unscheduled hours at the beginning of your practicum. Nevertheless, after a while you might start to get impatient. It will be easier to contain your impatience if you remember that careful planning on the part of your field instructor is necessary to help you attain your learning goals. This planning takes time and, if you are prepared to wait, the results will be more satisfactory in the long run.

Soon you will need to write down your learning goals specifically in the form of a learning agreement. This will enable you, your field instructor, and your field liaison to see how well your goals are being met, in what areas you have progressed, and what remains to be covered. We will now turn to learning goals in conjunction with learning contracts, sometimes called learning agreements.

SELECTED REFERENCES

Campbell, R.P. (1989). Practice orientation of students in field instruction. In M. Raskin (Ed.), *Empirical studies in field instruction* (pp. 137–160). New York: Haworth.

Grossman, B., Levine-Jordano, N., & Shearer, P. (1991). Working with students; emotional reactions in the field: An educational framework. In D. Schneck, B. Grossman, & U. Glassman (Eds.), *Field education in social work: Contemporary issues and trends* (pp. 205–216). Dubuque, IA: Kendall/Hunt.

May, L.I., & Kilpatrick, A.C. (1989). Stress of self-awareness in clinical practice: Are students prepared? In M. Raskin (Ed.), *Empirical studies in field instruction* (pp. 303–320). New York: Haworth.

Schneck, D. (1991). Ideal and reality in field education. In D. Schneck, B. Grossman, & U. Glassman (Eds.), *Field education in social work: Contemporary issues and trends* (pp. 17–35). Dubuque, IA: Kendall/Hunt.

CHAPTER 4

The Learning Environment

CREATING A LEARNING ENVIRONMENT is like setting the stage for a play. The stage is the agency and the community is in the wings. In your roles as writer, director, and major actor, you are free to set up the props as you wish, guide the action, and establish the script. Remember, you are a beginning director. You will find that the other actors and directors have strong opinions, and the play itself will limit your options by its very nature.

THE LEARNING CONTRACT

The script sets out the story line. It tells the actors what is to happen, why it is to happen, and how the parts connect. The most important part—the theme of the play—is always the *why*. *Why* is the play being performed? What is it attempting to communicate to its audience? What did the writer have in mind when giving it birth?

Your learning contract and the field evaluation form (see Appendix A on pages 229–264) is the script for your practicum. Sometimes learning contracts are called learning agreements. The *why* parts—the various interrelated themes—are the goals you want to achieve while in your practicum. Reaching those goals is why you are here, why the play has been set in motion, and why the other actors are prepared to work to make it a success.

Writing Learning Goals

You define your learning goals when you write your learning contract. To some extent these goals will be defined for you, because your social work program will have certain minimum standards, via learning goals, that you are expected to reach in the practicum. Appendix A contains a generic student practicum evaluation form (mid-term and final). The evaluation form provided by your program will probably be laid out in a different way but essentially the areas covered in it will be much the same. The rest of this book uses the student generic practicum evaluation form in Appendix A. Your learning goals should always be linked to your mid-term and final evaluations. You can add as many learning goals as you and your field instructor feel would be suitable.

As you can see from Appendix A on pages 229–264, by the end of your practicum, you are expected to know how to *effectively function within a professional context* (first learning goal in the evaluation form on page 230). Since this goal can cover a multitude of competencies, objectives may be delineated to describe more precisely the ways in which you are supposed to function effectively within a professional context.

For example, Objective 1.4 for Learning Goal 1 on page 234 requires that you will have had to demonstrate your "ability to recognize the impact of [your] personal behaviors and values on others." Such an ability can be interpreted in various ways. At a very basic level, it means that you abide by a dress code and do not interrupt others at staff meetings. At a somewhat higher level, it means that you do not show disapproval of a client who has institutionalized her mother because you believe that children should care for their elderly parents.

Your field instructor will be asked to assess you on this particular ability and her assessment will probably depend on a number of secondary behaviors. The neatness of your dress will be taken into account; your ability to argue a point without implying that people who oppose you are mentally deficient; your recognition that removing the stapler drives Emmy into a frenzy; your ability to work with your clients from *their* value base, not *yours*; and so forth.

You will eventually have to look at yourself and see if you think you rate high in this particular area. If you think you do, and your field instructor agrees with you, very good. If you think you may have a problem, try to define it more precisely. For example, you may find that you can never present an opinion to a group without alienating at least half of the people present. If this is the case, it is probably your presentation, not your opinion, that is at fault; therefore your learning objectives may be to remedy the matter.

Phrase your learning objectives in educational terms. Your writing ability definitely counts as a behavior, and the impact of your words on others is one of the things you are expected to recognize. For example, you might write a learning objective as, "learn to participate in group discussions in a positive manner." Having written this objective, you have to take some action to prove to your field instructor that some learning is taking place. Pick an issue that is close to your heart, preferably controversial, and plan how you could present your case in a polite, professional, and reasoned manner. Plan how you will deal with your fellow student, Raymond, who is highly articulate, always opposed, stubborn as a donkey, and can grind you to dust with kind words. Practice.

Ask your field instructor to role-play Raymond so that you can learn to respond to opposition in the safety of her office. If you do not feel safe in your field instructor's office, ask someone else instead (and make a mental note that the relationship between you and your field instructor needs to be further explored).

You can go through all the other objectives in the same way. For example, Objective 1.2 on page 232 requires that you have to demonstrate "values consistent with those of the profession and an understanding of and commitment to ethical standards." This refers to the two *Codes of Ethics* (Figures 1.1 and 1.2 on pages

13-26). As stressed in Chapter 1, you should read these *Codes* carefully and make sure that there is nothing in them that creates a conflict with your own value system. If a conflict arises, discuss it with your field instructor as soon as possible. You may even want to review the exercises in Chapters 1 and 2 about values, ethics, and the profession.

Most probably, there will not be value conflicts and you will rate high on this objective, unless you commit some awful ethical blunder such as releasing a client report without authorization, or interrupting Raymond when he is counting his airline bonus points. If by chance there is a conflict, *discuss it with your field instructor*. Item 2 of Section H, Confidentiality and Privacy, of the American *Code* states:

> The social worker should inform clients fully about the limits of confidentiality in a given situation, the purposes for which information is obtained, and how it may be used (page 14 in this book).

You may believe that Mrs. Bank will not tell you that her husband is sexually abusing their daughter if she knows you will report the abuse to child protection services. Therefore, in an effort to protect their daughter, you may be tempted to get the information out of Mrs. Bank without mentioning "child protection services." Such devious manipulation of Mrs. Bank is unethical even though it is done with the best of intentions.

When conflicts like this arise, consult your field instructor at once. It is very easy to be drawn into a web of deceit where you cannot be honest with your client, you are afraid to tell your field instructor exactly what you did, and you are not very happy with yourself.

Interpreting Your Practicum Evaluation Form

There may be some learning objectives on the practicum evaluation form (see Appendix A) that are not completely clear to you. For example, Objective 1.1 on page 231 requires you to demonstrate "an understanding of the person-in-environment concept from a social work perspective." Since you will be evaluated on your field instructor's interpretation of this objective, you are entitled to ask for clarification if you feel you need it. One thing to keep in mind is that social work institutions approach words in the same way Norman's soldiers approach Saddam's minefields. In fact, to social work institutions, words *are* minefields.

Offended persons wait in hordes, ready to explode at ill-judged words. There must be nothing in written form that might conceivably prove to be offensive. There must be no hint, not even the remotest breath of a hint, that any group or person is less worthy, less virtuous, or less wholesome than any other group or person. No opportunity should be provided for allegations of discrimination or sexism or any other calamitous "ism." There are occasions when this necessary care impedes communication—no one is offended because no one understands what was said.

It is possible, therefore, that you will come across nebulous objectives that would tax the wisdom of philosophers, and you will need to ask for help. Never mind that the interpretation is arguable. For your purposes, the objective means only and precisely whatever your field instructor says.

Defining Your Learning Objectives

You will derive some of your learning objectives by carefully going through your program's practicum evaluation form to see where problems may arise. Other objectives will occur to you when you think about the problem areas. For example, Objective 1.5 on page 235 requires you to demonstrate "the ability to take initiative toward increasing knowledge and skills relevant to performance demands." This means that you do not blindly complete assignments and wait after each task to be told what to do next. Instead, you play an active role in your learning by suggesting to your field instructor that this or that activity on your part might help with such and such an objective.

You may find that you are quite incapable of suggesting anything to your field instructor; the very thought may reduce you to a shivering heap. When you consider your heaplike state—remember being ground down by Raymond—and realize that most of your clients manipulate you, the underlying problem will be clear—you are not able to assert yourself. Your learning objective, therefore, will be "to become more assertive."

After you have written this down, there is more to be said. How will you know when you have become more assertive? What behaviors on your part will tell both you and your field instructor that this objective is being achieved? Some behaviors will be evident since it was your lack of assertiveness that prompted the learning objective in the first place. Your objective now is "to make appropriate suggestions to your field instructor regarding your learning activities." Your other objective is "to participate in group discussions in a positive manner"; that is, not to allow yourself to be ground down by Raymond. Yet another objective is "to identify your clients' problems or concerns"; that is, not to allow Mrs. Bank to lead you off the topic.

Your field instructor will be able to assess these more precisely stated objectives. She can count your appropriate suggestions; she can note the number of polite and reasonable remarks you make to Raymond; she can tell from your process recordings (to be discussed) when you are zeroing in on Mrs. Bank's real problem. You have managed to work toward an overall learning objective—becoming more assertive—in a number of concrete activities.

Examples of Learning Contracts

Figures 4.1 through 4.4 present four distinctively different learning contracts for students in institutional, psychiatric, hospital, and community settings. These are only examples; every student's learning contract is a personal document developed by the student with help from the field instructor. Nevertheless, these examples may serve as a guide when it comes time for you to write your own contract. You may be ready now to draft a learning contract. If this is the case, see Exercise 4.1 on pages 119–121. Start by developing your headings as you read along with the text.

FIGURE 4.1

EXAMPLE OF A STUDENT LEARNING CONTRACT (INSTITUTIONAL SETTING)

Conceptual (Theory Development)

• To learn what being a resident means (e.g., possible loss of dignity, feelings of being controlled, fear of unknown) • To examine institutional values versus individual personal values and if or how they are reconciled • To understand defense mechanisms that arise when people feel threatened • To gain an understanding of the theory behind group dynamics and individual counseling • To understand the social concept of "deviance" and to examine it in relation to substance abuse and prevention programs • To become aware of the roles of the various voluntary agencies (e.g., AA, Salvation Army) and how they relate to the institution and substance abusers • To understand the role and purpose of the bureaucracy and hierarchy of the institution and look at what effect this can have on staff relations, service delivery, and clients

Technical (Skill Development)

• To develop skills in working with a patient group (where focus may be both educational as well as therapeutic) • To acquire skills for individual counseling • To develop assessment and diagnostic skills (in particular, assessment when intensive intervention is indicated) • To develop skills in staff groups such as (1) presenting group dynamics and process and individual case studies, (2) chairing a meeting, (3) giving feedback to other staff, and (4) presenting relevant information to staff • To examine personal and professional roles—can they be combined or must they be separate? • To participate in therapeutic discussions with colleagues, offering a social work perspective and gaining from their expertise • To become skillful in the role of a group worker

Community and Project Work

• To become involved in relevant projects and community work where time allows

Strategy

• Formal, regular supervisory sessions for receiving feedback • Tape recordings of client interviews • Summary recordings on charts • Report writing (identify specific reports) • Tape recordings of supervisory sessions

FIGURE 4.2
EXAMPLE OF A STUDENT LEARNING CONTRACT (PSYCHIATRIC SETTING)

Aim

• To work as a member of a professional team in the role of a psychiatric social worker • To gain an understanding of what it means to be a social worker in this agency • To understand why a social worker acts/reacts/interacts to situations as they arise • To develop a basic theoretical framework to which further thoughts and actions can be related • To establish how this agency fits into the community, and then, from the agency's viewpoint, where the profession of social work fits in

Conceptual (Gain an Awareness of the Teamwork Model)

• To look at models of community interaction and how they apply to this agency • To gain knowledge of community functioning, that is, how the agency works for various sectors of the community, appreciation of associated agencies, knowledge of resources available • To look at how different people cope or do not cope with their situations; to establish models of coping, develop a style of assistance that suits myself • To become proficient in understanding of psychotropic medication

Operational (Develop Skills)

• Relating to people • Constructive interviewing (i.e., relating as a helping person to a client on a professional level) • Relating as a professional to other professionals in the team (look at networks) • Working as a member of an interdisciplinary team for the sake of the client • Report writing, fulfilling the accreditation standards of the agency • Developing assessment and diagnostic skills

Personal

• Aiming to feel confident in dealing with people in general • Being able to deal with various people with differing problems and different degrees of problems, with confidence • Facilitating personal growth, self-development • Gaining an understanding as to why one thinks a certain way—becoming aware of own actions and the effect that background and upbringing have on these actions

Strategy

• Weekly supervision sessions • Weekly review of cases to see if they are being dealt with in the most beneficial way for the client • Diary for planning weekly activities, as well as a record of tasks completed • Agency visits • Taping interviews

FIGURE 4.3

EXAMPLE OF A STUDENT LEARNING CONTRACT
(HOSPITAL SETTING)

S = Student; FI = Field Instructor

Aims

• S aims to increase knowledge of available and relevant community resources and to develop skills to understand appropriate use of the referral process to these resources • S aims to gain an appreciation and understanding of the roles played by other professionals (e.g., occupational therapists) in the delivery of health care services within the hospital • S aims to enhance understanding of the policies and practices of the social work department by undertaking relevant reading and by discussions with departmental staff • S aims to enhance skills in identifying client problems and in building and utilizing repertoire of interventive techniques • S will aim to increase the knowledge of disease processes through reading and discussions with medical staff

Strategy

• S will arrange to record two or three interviews with clients and/or their families. These clients and families will be informed of the reasons for the recordings, asked if they will participate, asked if they wish later to listen to the recordings and/or to be present when they are erased. S and FI will subsequently analyze content and process of such interviews for the purpose of increasing S's professional social work knowledge and skills • S will ask FI to be present during two or three interviews, either in the hospital or during a home visit. Both S and FI will subsequently analyze the interview with respect to its content and process thereby increasing S's professional knowledge and skills • S and FI will regularly undertake process recording; that is, S will record the interviews and inform FI of the content, and together they will examine the processes operating during the interviews • S and FI will spend one hour per week in supervisory conferences, S taking responsibility for selecting topics for discussion for each session • S and FI will review this contract every three weeks

FIGURE 4.4

EXAMPLE OF A STUDENT LEARNING CONTRACT (COMMUNITY CENTER SETTING)

Conceptual

• To test the center's ideas in the development of an individual perspective and conceptual framework for community work practice • To examine various models of community development work and assess their applicability to the center • To understand the unique structure of this community and relate this understanding to various concepts of community work and changes occurring in communities • To understand the basis of community involvement in the center's management and the relationship of the worker to the management committee

Operational

• To develop communication skills in working with community members, as participants at the center, as members of management committee, and as leaders in the community; in working with other staff at the center and workers in other agencies; in report writing and submission preparation; in contacts with the media and the public presentation of the center; and in negotiating with external agencies • To develop skills in recording and evaluating one's activities and the work of others in the community setting • To identify formal and informal networks and utilize them for the benefit of the center • To develop an initial familiarity with the basic processes of some of the different approaches to community work

Personal

• To identify and explore own beliefs and views about community work as a strategy for change • To arrive at a perspective on own role as a community worker in the center, in the surrounding community, and in society at large • To learn to work with people and tasks with which I am not personally comfortable • To experiment with different behaviors in different situations, leading to the development of a personal style as a community worker and to become comfortable with that style

Strategy

• To read as widely as time will permit; prepare at least three book reviews for discussion with my supervisor • To maintain a daily diary and prepare process recordings on activities undertaken • To plan a program of discussions with center workers and selected members of the community • To prepare a proposal of planned work, together with a justification of the activities planned, for each supervisory conference; do an analytical review of the previous week's work

**EXERCISE 4.1
YOUR LEARNING CONTRACT**

The field educational learning contract is designed to

1. specify the responsibilities of you and your field instructor;
2. assist in the formulation of an individual educational practicum plan; and
3. ensure that you have the appropriate opportunities to learn and demonstrate competence on each of the evaluation criteria identified on your program's practicum evaluation form (see Appendix A as an example).

The primary task of formulating the learning contract rests with you; however, responsibility for completing the contract is shared by you, your field instructor, and your field liaison. After completing your learning contract, it should be negotiated, documented, and signed by all parties prior to the end of the first three weeks of your practicum. The contract should be reviewed during your mid-term and final evaluations and may be revised as need arises. Copies of the learning contract and any revisions should be kept by you, your field instructor, and your field liaison. Complete your learning contract on the following pages using Figures 4.1 through 4.4 as guides.

Your name:

Your agency:

Your practicum setting:

Today's date:

Your field instructor's name:

Your field liaison's name:

Your practice methods instructor's name:

Learning Contract (continued)

Learning Contract (continued)

Field Instructor's　　　　　Student's　　　　　Field Liaison's
Signature　　　　　　　　Signature　　　　　　Signature

_____　　_____　　_____

Preliminary Assessment

After completion of the learning contract, the preliminary assessment of the beginning phase of the practicum experience takes place. The purpose of the preliminary assessment is to provide you with feedback related to strengths that are beginning to emerge and to alert you to areas that need immediate attention. This assessment will help you begin to practice with the confidence that you are on the right track. Even though each supervisory conference with your field instructor provides feedback, preliminary assessment constitutes your first formalized (written) feedback.

Organizing Your Learning Contract

As you can see from Figures 4.1 through 4.4, learning contracts, or learning agreements, are not organized in the same way as your program's practicum evaluation form. This is because the evaluation form is a generic one and the learning contracts were extracted from programs that did not use the same evaluation form that is contained in Appendix A. The examples of learning contracts have been deliberately taken from different places to reinforce the point that student contracts are *individual*. The practicum evaluation forms will be different for each program and the learning contracts will be different for each student. You are free to organize your contract in any way that appears reasonable, unless your program has a specific format it requires you to follow.

Probably, the most sensible way to start organizing your learning contract is to follow the headings on your program's evaluation form. This form could have four learning goals and four headings, such as those presented in Appendix A on page 230:

1. Functions effectively within a professional context
2. Functions effectively within an organizational context
3. Functions effectively utilizing knowledge-directed practice skills
4. Functions effectively within an evaluative context

Perhaps under one heading you will not have the identical objectives as others because you feel you have already reached the required standards in the area. If you have a number of learning objectives under one goal, you may find that some of them have to do with using theoretical knowledge and some of them have to do with acquiring practice skills. For example in Appendix A, Learning Goal 3 on page 244 lists 16 objectives required to function effectively utilizing knowledge-directed practice. Objective 3.1 on page 244 requires that you will have "demonstrated the ability to engage others and identify problems or concerns." You may have formulated an additional learning objective around Learning Goal 3, for example, "to learn to identify clients' problems or concerns." This then could be added as Learning Objective 3.3 on page 246.

Achieving the learning objective you added is obviously a very practical matter. You have to interview Mrs. Bank, form a relationship with her, and persuade her to divulge the real reason she came to the agency. In contrast, Objective 3.5 on page 248 requires that you will have "demonstrated the ability to articulate a comprehensive assessment." Part of this is practical—you have to complete an assessment on Mrs. Bank—but part is theoretical. You have to know, from theory, what information about Mrs. Bank and her family should be included in an assessment. Your learning objective here might be "to learn how to formulate a comprehensive assessment."

Under one heading, or goal, you may end up with a number of practice-oriented learning objectives and a number of objectives that are more concerned with theory. It may seem worthwhile then to group them under the subheadings *theoretical and practical*, or *conceptual and technical*, or *skill development*, or whatever words appeal to you.

Do not forget that your individual learning objectives should be related to the nature of your practicum setting as well as to the standards set by your social work program. For example, the information contained in a comprehensive assessment of Mrs. Bank will depend on why you are assessing her situation. If you are working in a nursing home and Mrs. Bank is applying to become a resident, you may need information about her financial status, her medical history, her likes and dislikes, local community programs, and so forth.

If Mrs. Bank is to enter a drug rehabilitation program or a therapy group for sexual abuse survivors or a foster parent training program, the required information will be different. You may want to write your learning objective about assessments more specifically in order to reflect this. For example, your objective might be "to learn to formulate a complete assessment of prospective foster parents."

Some of your learning objectives will not be concerned with either practical or theoretical learning. Instead, they will refer to personal development, and you may wish to put them under a separate heading as illustrated in Figures 4.1 through 4.4. For example, you might list your objectives about becoming more assertive under the *Personal* heading. Keep in mind, however, that personal objectives need to be related to your professional development as a social worker.

A learning contract should also include the following administrative information: the number of days per week you spend at the practicum setting and the number of hours per day; the frequency and length of supervisory conferences; supervision method (e.g., individual supervision or group supervision); the number and type of case or project assignments you are to be involved with over a specific period of time; documentation and recording procedures expected by the practicum setting; and any special arrangements you have made with the agency.

All this could well go under another heading, *Strategy*, for example. After all, the strategies or methods you use to help you achieve your objectives include such things as regular supervisory conferences, videotaping your interviews, process recordings, and so forth—and if you were not regularly present at your practicum setting, you could not do any of those things.

When you look at your finished list of objectives, it may seem that there are more headings and subheadings than there are objectives. If this is the case, reorganize it so that it looks better. If possible, use the headings on your student practicum evaluation form (see Appendix A) to ensure that your learning goals and objectives will enable you to meet your program's minimum standards. But it is the learning objectives tied to the goals, not the headings, that are important. If only a few headings make your list look more coherent and sensible, just use those headings.

Negotiating Your Learning Contract

When you have defined and organized your learning goals and objectives, you will have to submit them to your field instructor and your field liaison for final approval. It is more practical to discuss them with these two people as you go along; use their feedback to revise them and make additions. Occasions do arise, however, when the field instructor and the field liaison believe the student's objectives are unrealistic and the student, of course, believes that the field instructor's and liaison's expectations are too low. If this should happen in your case, remember that learning contracts are not written in stone. They can be revised at any time during your practicum if the learning experience does not proceed precisely as expected, or if new opportunities and needs arise. We suggest, therefore, that you accept their advice at the beginning. If it turns out that you have set your sights too low or in a direction that is slightly wrong, you can rectify the error later.

THE ACTORS

Once you have set the theme for your practicum play, that is, decided on your learning goals and objectives, your next consideration will be the actors. The most important actor, apart from yourself, probably is your field instructor. The relationship you establish with her will improve or inhibit your learning experience. There are a number of factors that may affect this relationship.

Your Field Instructor

A key factor in establishing a relationship with your field instructor involves differences in expectations and attitudes due to different ethnic or religious backgrounds. Another factor is concerned with age and gender differences; another is concerned with stresses due to physical handicap. Still other issues of significance are how each party learns, personality meshes or clashes, and how each one deals with authority. A further factor is the matter of organizing and managing supervisory conferences. All these will be discussed when our focus is on practicum management discussed in Chapter 5.

An important aspect in establishing a relationship is your understanding of your field instructor's responsibilities. Most likely she is a supervisor. She has staff to supervise, other administrative matters to attend to, and probably a client caseload as well. There will be times when she is not available to help you, perhaps even times when she is impatient and irritable because she has other things on her mind. Make allowances for these times. Do not pounce on her when you know she is on her way to an important meeting.

Do not expect her to extend your supervisory conference time without notice because you are suddenly facing a crisis. If it is a real crisis, of course she will put other things aside. But the definition of a "real crisis" depends on the person doing the defining. Try to see your own crisis as one of a hundred looming disasters, all about to rain on your field instructor's head.

A relationship depends to some degree on knowledge. If you learn about the particular problems your field instructor may be facing at your practicum setting, you will not only add to your own experience but you will be able to be appropriately sympathetic when the occasion arises. Occasions may also arise for an exchange of more personal information about families, hobbies, mutual acquaintances, past experiences, and so forth. A student and a field instructor who both belong to a specific social action group can easily form a deep and satisfying bond.

Your Field Liaison

You may see your field liaison rarely or on a regular basis depending on whether or not your integrative seminar is taught by her. She is the person to talk to if you have a problem you cannot resolve with your field instructor. Even if you do not have a problem, it is a good idea to keep her informed of your progress, because she will be involved (to various degrees) in your mid-term and final evaluations (Chapters 7 and 9). She may even have a major say in the assignment of your grade.

Since it is difficult to telephone someone you do not know well in order to say nothing in particular, you might prefer to maintain contact subtly. If you take a class with her, the opportunity will arise in class. If she is not one of your instructors, a word in the hallway might suffice, or a moment in her office when the door is open. You just want to ensure that there has been some positive contact between the two of you before the time arrives for your mid-term evaluation.

You, The Student

The most important actor in your practicum experience is undoubtedly you. You differ from other students in skills, personality, background, value systems, and learning style. A learning style does not refer to what you have learned already. It refers to *how* you learn—to the way in which new material ought to be presented so that you can absorb it most effectively. For example, if you want to acquire more interviewing skills, you might read about interviewing, listen to someone tell you about it, watch a videotape, practice a role-play, or participate in group discussion. Probably, you will do all of these things, but one or two of them are more likely than the others to be more effective for you.

It is important to understand how you learn best so you can maximize available learning situations for yourself during your practicum. Of course, you will learn in many different ways. The fact that you learn best in one way does not mean that you cannot learn in all the other ways. Nevertheless, if you know you learn well by reflective observation (watching), for example, you should find as many opportunities as you can to watch other people doing things. If you learn better by abstract conceptualization (thinking), you should spend more time reading and trying to fit the information you acquire into a theoretical framework.

Your field instructor should understand your learning style as well. After all, she is going to be deciding on your learning assignments, particularly in the first few weeks when you are not yet ready to create your own learning opportunities. If she knows how you learn best, she will be more able to find assignments that will suit you. She will also be able to deliberately find assignments that do not suit you in order to encourage you to learn in other ways.

It might be interesting to find out what her learning style is. People who learn best in one particular way and have always done so have a tendency to assume that other people learn the same way they do. Therefore, they teach that way and may not have considered that there are other ways to teach.

Other Actors

Other actors in your practicum play are other professionals, other students, and all the agencies in the community that interact with your agency. You may be supervised by one or more professionals in relation to some particular project. These professionals will then consult with your field instructor about your "overall" progress. There should be no difficulty here so long as you are honest with both. Problems with another professional should be resolved directly with that individual if at all possible. You do not want to put anyone in a position where he or she is expected to take sides.

Your relationships with other students can become some of the most positive experiences of your practicum, if you remember that learning is a cooperative and not a competitive effort. With regard to other agencies, remember that relationships between agencies are not always as good as might be hoped. If you sense that there is conflict between your own and another agency, *do not offer your opinions on the subject of the conflict*. The conflict is their problem, not yours, and you will do much better if you do not become involved.

HOW TO LEARN BEST IN YOUR PRACTICUM

In general, there are five principles of effective learning that can be applied to your practicum experience.

Highly Motivated Student

Students learn best when they are highly motivated. This principle covers two possible situations: first, you think you already know all there is to know about a certain subject area and so have nothing to learn; second, you see no reason why you should have to know whatever it is you are being taught. Unless you are particularly arrogant, the first situation is unlikely to arise.

The second arises quite often. Students do not see, for example, why they need to know anything about the theory of organizations. They intend to spend their lives talking to Mrs. Bank about the wisdom of institutionalizing her mother and they do not see how organizational theory will assist in this endeavor. If it is not clear to you why you are being taught something or why you are being instructed to do something, *ask*. Ask politely, without implying that the field instructor's pet topic is irrelevant nonsense, but ask.

Energy Devoted to Learning

Students learn best when they devote their energy to learning. This principle concerns distractions. If your dog has died, your best friend has left the country, and your father has become ill, you will probably not learn very much. Perhaps your love life, social life, home life, and other classes take up so much of your time that you have little energy left to devote to practicum learning. This is definitely a moment for compromise. You need to take time to get some pleasure out of life and give yourself some rewards. On the other hand, maybe *one* of your leisure time activities could go, or you might consider dropping that extra class on statistics you thought you could handle.

Students learn best if they are involved in the learning process. So, as we said earlier, you will learn more if you create your own learning opportunities rather than waiting to be told what to do.

Positive Satisfaction

Students learn best when learning is followed by positive satisfaction. Consider these three possibilities: your field instructor has overestimated your capabilities so that the tasks you are assigned are too difficult; you are never praised when you have done something well; or you are always praised even though you regularly make mistakes. If you find that you are unable to cope with assignments, you should say so. Social workers are taught to start where the client is; educators are taught to start where the student is; but your field instructor may not know where you are. She may be basing your assignments on false assumptions about your knowledge level and skills, not realizing that the social work student she had before was on his second practicum, while you are on your first.

If you are to learn anything at all in this situation, you will have to practice humility. Be candid about what you do not know and cannot do. Suggest that you work up to your impossible assignment by way of a number of easier assignments. Ask your field instructor for help.

If you are never praised when you have done something well, there is always the possibility that you have not done as well as you thought. Perhaps your field instructor does not want to give you negative feedback and is avoiding the issue by giving you no feedback at all. Again, the thing to do is ask. Select some part of an assignment that you think you did particularly well and ask if you did it correctly. In what ways did you not do it correctly? How could it have been improved?

This approach might elicit a number of gentle criticisms that may surprise and dismay you. When you have recovered from the blow, you will have to consider not just that particular assignment but the whole relationship between you and your field instructor. Perhaps you do not respond well to negative feedback and have been sending nonverbal signals to that effect. Maybe she is sacrificing your learning for fear of injuring your self-esteem. This is a matter which definitely needs to be discussed. If she does not initiate the discussion, then you will have to, perhaps by asking politely why she did not mention these negative aspects before. It is always possible, of course, that your accomplishments have been brilliant in every respect but your field instructor considers praise bad for the character.

If you are praised continually, even in situations where you have doubts about your performance, you will eventually lose faith in your field instructor's judgment. You might mention delicately that you did this or that badly and you would feel more comfortable if you believed her praise was earned. If you are then praised for your courage in admitting to your faults, at least you will know that she, too, thought they were faults.

Content Presented Meaningfully

Students learn best if the content is presented meaningfully. First, the content has to be meaningful in the student's perception, as stated previously. Second, it has to be presented in a way that makes sense. Sensible methods of presentation involve a number of factors. Difficult material should be presented more slowly and repeated more often than easier material. Not too much should be presented all at once. Repetition should include different ways of teaching the same thing to make use of different learning styles. Material should be presented in stages, building from the simple to the complex, each stage related to the stage that went before it. Periodically, everything presented to date should be summarized.

There is nothing difficult about this except actually doing it. For example, your field instructor may be quite prepared to present difficult material more slowly if she knows what you find difficult. She will accommodate your learning style if she knows what it is. She will repeat what needs to be repeated and summarize what needs to be summarized, but she will not be able to do any of this without your active participation.

Uniqueness Taken into Consideration

Students learn best if their uniqueness is taken into consideration. Uniqueness of a learner involves three considerations. What do you *want* to learn; that is, what are your learning goals? What *can* you learn, based on what you already know? *How* will you learn best; that is, what are your learning styles? Again, your field instructor will not know what you want to learn, what you have already learned, and how you learn best unless you give her this information.

PRELIMINARY PRACTICUM EVALUATION

You are learning a great deal at this point. One thing is certain: you are also starting to feel more comfortable and are becoming a part of your practicum setting.

Now that your learning contract is done, it is an ideal time to evaluate how well you are doing to date. A preliminary practicum evaluation of your learning can be used as a way to provide you with an early evaluation of your beginning during this phase of the field education process. This can be done by the third week.

Generic preliminary practicum evaluation forms are contained in Exercises 4.2 (page 129), 4.3 (page 130), and 4.4 (page 131). Early and formal feedback tends to keep both you and your field instructor clearly focused on your emerging strengths and areas requiring attention. It is also a time for you and your field instructor to correct the learning contract and make adjustments, rather than waiting until the mid-term evaluation. Exercise 4.5 (page 132) will assist you in identifying the measures necessary for correcting or maintaining initial efforts. You are doing a good job, so keep going.

**EXERCISE 4.2
YOUR PRELIMINARY
PRACTICUM EVALUATION**

Complete this preliminary practicum evaluation. Comment on your initial adjustment to your practicum setting and initial work with various client systems. Add any other comments about the beginning phase of your practice in the practicum setting. This form should be completed around the third week of your practicum.

1. The orientation process:

2. Beginning work with client systems:

3. Other comments:

**EXERCISE 4.3
YOUR FIELD INSTRUCTOR'S
PRELIMINARY EVALUATION OF YOU**

Ask your field instructor to also record a preliminary impression of your adjustment to your practicum setting and of your activities related to your objectives. Make sure that all comments related to your strengths and limitations which emerged in the beginning phase of practice are recorded in the space provided below.

1. Adjustment to the setting and learning related activities:

2. Emerging strengths:

3. Emerging concerns:

4. Other comments:

EXERCISE 4.4
YOUR DEVELOPING ABILITIES

Using Exercises 4.2 and 4.3, discuss with your field instructor beginning perceptions of your developing practice abilities. Such discussion provides an opportunity for both you and your field instructor to comment on the initial stages of working together. Identify any differences in perceptions here.

**EXERCISE 4.5
RESPONDING TO FEEDBACK**

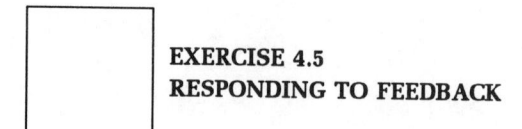

What steps can you take to respond to the feedback you received in your field instructor's preliminary practicum evaluation (Exercise 4.3)? Write your comments in the space provided below.

SUMMARY

Creating a learning environment involves paying attention to the goals and objectives of your practicum and to the actors who will make your dreams a reality.

You define your goals and objectives when you write your learning contract, sometimes called a learning agreement. They must be related to your practicum and to the achievement standards required by your program, which may be similar to those set out in Appendix A. To ensure that all your objectives will be met, examine your social work program's practicum evaluation forms at the beginning of your practicum. You can then identify potential areas of weakness and formulate your learning goals and objectives to improve these areas.

With regard to yourself, creating a learning environment demands attention to the way you learn. Once you have evaluated your learning style, you can create opportunities that will enable you to learn most effectively. Misunderstandings with your field instructor regarding assignments and learning in general may be avoided if you are both aware of the principles of learning and your respective learning styles.

We will now turn to the factors that affect the management of your practicum.

SELECTED REFERENCES

Amacher, K.A. (1976). Exploration into the dynamics of learning in field work. *Smith College Studies in Social Work, 46*, 163–217.

Barnat, M.R. (1973). Student reactions to the first supervisory year: Relationship and resolutions. *Journal of Education for Social Work, 9*, 3–8.

Berengarten, S. (1961). Educational issues in field instruction in social work. *Social Service Review, 35*, 246–257.

Blake, R., & Peterman, P. (1985). *Social work field instruction: The undergraduate experience.* New York: University Press of America.

Brennen, E.C. (1982). Evaluation of field teaching and learning. In B. W. Sheafor & L. E. Jenkins (Eds.), *Quality field instruction in social work* (pp. 76–97). White Plains, NY: Longman.

Brownstein, C., Smith, H.Y., & Faria, G. (1991). The liaison role: A three phase study of the schools, the field, the faculty. In D. Schneck, B. Grossman, & U. Glassman (Eds.), *Field education in social work: Contemporary issues and trends* (pp. 237–248). Dubuque, IA: Kendall/Hunt.

Dea, K. (1972). The collaborative process in undergraduate field instruction. In K. Wenzel (Ed.), *Undergraduate field instruction programs: Current issues and predictions* (pp. 50–62). New York: Council on Social Work Education.

Dwyer, M., & Urbanowski, M. (1981). Field practice criteria: A valuable teaching/learning tool in undergraduate social work education. *Journal of Education for Social Work, 17*, 5–11.

Fishbein, H., & Glassman, U. (1991). The advanced seminar for field instructors: Content and process. In D. Schneck, B. Grossman, & U. Glassman (Eds.), *Field education in social work: Contemporary issues and trends* (pp. 226–232). Dubuque, IA: Kendall/Hunt.

Green, S.H. (1972). Educational assessments of student learning through practice in field instruction. *Social Work Education Reporter, 20*, 48–54.

Hartung Hagen, B. J. (1989). The practicum instructor: A study of role expectations. In M. Raskin (Ed.), *Empirical studies in field instruction* (pp. 219–236). New York: Haworth.

Johnston, N., Rooney, R., & Reitmeir, M.A. (1991). Sharing power: Student feedback to field supervisors. In D. Schneck, B. Grossman, & U. Glassman (Eds.), *Field education in social work: Contemporary issues and trends* (pp. 198–204). Dubuque, IA: Kendall/Hunt.

Kettner, P.M. (1979). A conceptual framework for developing learning modules for field education. *Journal of Education for Social Work, 15,* 52–58.

Larsen, J., & Hepworth, D. (1980). Enhancing the effectiveness of practicum instruction: An empirical study. *Journal of Education for Social Work, 18,* 50–58.

Lemberger, J., & Marshack, E.F. (1991). Educational assessment in the field: An opportunity for teacher-learner mutuality. In D. Schneck, B. Grossman, & U. Glassman (Eds.), *Field education in social work: Contemporary issues and trends* (pp. 187–197). Dubuque, IA: Kendall/Hunt.

Raskin, M. (1989). Factors associated with student satisfaction in undergraduate social work field placements. In M. Raskin (Ed.), *Empirical studies in field instruction* (pp. 321–336). New York: Haworth.

Schneck, D. (1991). Integration of learning in field education: Elusive goal and educational imperative. In D. Schneck, B. Grossman, & U. Glassman (Eds.), *Field education in social work: Contemporary issues and trends* (pp. 67–77). Dubuque, IA: Kendall/Hunt.

Tsang, N. (1989). Factors associated with fieldwork performance in a social work course in Hong Kong. In M. Raskin (Ed.), *Empirical studies in field instruction* (pp. 337–358). New York: Haworth.

Walden, T., & Brown, L. (1985). The integration seminar: A vehicle for joining theory and practice. *Journal of Education for Social Work, 21,* 13–19.

Waldfogel, D. (1983). Supervision of students and practitioners. In A. Rosenblatt & D. Waldfogel (Eds.), *Handbook of clinical social work* (pp. 319–344). San Francisco: Jossey-Bass.

CHAPTER 5

Management

MANAGEMENT CAN BE DEFINED as the planning, organizing, coordinating, directing, controlling, and supervising of any activity with responsibility for results. If you are engaged in at least some of the planning, organizing, or coordinating functions, it may be said with fairness that you are managing your practicum.

You are certainly responsible for the results of your practicum, that is, achieving your learning goals and objectives, as discussed in the previous chapter. You are also responsible for planning, that is, defining your goals and objectives and suggesting specific assignments (opportunities) that will help you to achieve them. You are responsible for organizing your learning assignments to accommodate the schedules of all those involved; and you are responsible for coordinating these assignments so that they form a coherent pattern of your overall learning goals. Therefore, a central function apparent in both daily and overall practicum activities requires management tasks on your part.

For example, one of your learning goals may be *to acquire interviewing skills* and one of your specific learning objectives related to that goal may be "to learn to define the client's problem in a generalist family service setting." With this objective in mind, you can coordinate a number of activities: reading whatever you can find about defining client problems; observing other social workers define problems with their clients; watching relevant videos; recording and discussing with your field instructor your own attempts to define problems with your own clients; having your field instructor role-play a client who is absolutely determined not to tell you why she came to the agency; and exploring in theory the many reasons people have for nurturing and clinging to a problem as though it were a baby.

The directing, controlling, and supervising parts of your management role are less clear since you are the one being supervised. But there are ways that you can and should direct your practicum supervision.

SUPERVISORY CONFERENCES

Your supervisory conferences with your field instructor are not social occasions. Each session has its own purpose: to determine the degree to which you are achieving one or more of your learning objectives. Therefore, you need to plan these sessions in the same way as you plan for your practicum. What will be the particular focus of this session? What do you hope to achieve in it? What do you need to have prepared to realize your expectations? What similar or different expectations might your field instructor have? What other factors might affect the session? Basically, there are two types of factors that affect your practicum supervision: practical factors and relationship factors.

Practical Factors

Practical factors related to your supervisory conferences are largely concerned with what, when, and how: *what* are you going to talk about, *when* are you going to talk about it, and *how* can you facilitate the discussion. In all probability, the *when* will arise on a regular basis—from 2:00 to 3:00 on a Friday afternoon, for example. Occasionally, the Friday session may become a Wednesday session or you may skip a week or schedule an extra session to meet a particular need. *When* is not at all important so long as both you and your field instructor *know* when, because both of you need to be prepared.

What is a different matter. Of course, you will know in advance of the session that you want to discuss Mrs. Taylor's refusal to tell you her *real* problem. You will probably have to let your field instructor have Mrs. Taylor's file and a videotape or a process recording of your last interview with her. You will have to formulate some tentative hunches about where you think the *real* problem lies and why you think she is avoiding the *real* issue. You will have to be prepared to discuss which interviewing techniques learned in your interviewing skills course you used to elicit the information and why you feel they were unsuccessful. You will have to be ready with suggestions as to what you will say to Mrs. Taylor next time and why you think this different approach might prove to be more effective than the previous ones.

All this will be in vain if your field instructor wants to discuss your weekly time sheet instead. Accordingly, you must come to an agreement with her about the focus of the supervisory conference well *before* the session starts. If you cannot plan for next week at the end of last week's session, you should schedule five minutes during the week to decide whether the agenda will be Mrs. Taylor or time sheets. A brief written agenda will keep both of you focused. If it is to be Mrs. Taylor, your field instructor will then have the opportunity to reread her file. If it is to be time sheets, you will have a chance to reflect over where you may have gone wrong.

You might also find that *when* is intimately connected with *what*. Your disappointment over the time sheets might occupy a brief five minutes; Mrs. Taylor, on the other hand, might take ten times as long. You should therefore ensure that you and your field instructor have enough time available for the topics you have to discuss. If there is not enough time, ask for extra time in advance of the session, or divide the material into two sessions, or select just the most important points.

How may also affect *when* and is definitely connected to *what*. For example, the resolution of Mrs. Taylor's distressing obstinacy may involve letting your field instructor watch your videotaped interview with her. To do this, you have to have a video machine. The video machine may only be available for a certain time and in a certain place. You will have to negotiate for the machine with all of the other social workers and students who are waiting in line and with your field instructor about when and where you are to view your tape.

In addition remember that a half-hour tape will take about ten times as long to view and discuss, so either you will need extra time or you will have to choose the vital parts in advance. By the time you have done all this, you will have acquired considerable expertise in the negotiating, organizing, and coordinating aspects of practicum management.

Relationship Factors

We have already mentioned that successful practicum supervision has a great deal to do with the relationship between you and your field instructor. This relationship can be affected by a number of factors: differences in expectations and attitudes due to differences in ethnic, cultural, or religious backgrounds, differences in age, differences in gender, and difficulties due to physical handicap.

Differences in Ethnic, Cultural, or Religious Backgrounds. If you are a majority white North American and your field instructor is a minority, you may be tempted to ignore her "minorityness" either because you feel it is rude to notice or because you are determined not to let it make a difference. Such a determination is doomed to failure; not only is it doomed, it is absurd and insulting. Your field instructor knows she is a minority in a majority culture. She is proud to be who she is.

Because she has become a social worker, she knows what the differences are between her own culture and yours. She knows how to use those differences to benefit her clients and improve the lot of minority groups, particularly her own. She knows that being of equal worth does not mean being all the same. If you have an instructor from a minority group who can teach you all this, you are fortunate indeed. If not, you must try to learn it anyway before you interact with a client whose skin color you have failed to notice.

People from different cultures react differently to such things as authority figures, the age or gender of the worker, and the very notion of receiving professional help. You may find with some clients that the process of engagement takes a long time because the client does not really believe that help ought to be given by strangers. This kind of help, in the client's culture, may be a private matter reserved for family and friends. In contrast, you may find that the client perceives you as a godlike being, because you represent a form of authority. There will be no mutual problem solving, no sharing of ideas, no corrections to your wrong assumptions, because the client feels one should not correct a god. There may be no eye contact if the client believes eye contact is rude, no filling of conversational gaps if the client is politely maintaining silence.

If you are older than the client, you may be deferred to because of your age; if younger, you may be rejected as a helper. If you are a woman with a male client, you may realize gradually that from his perspective you have no status.

All such barriers to the client-worker relationship may also impede the student-field instructor relationship. Essentially, there are five possibilities, the last of which has already been discussed: you and your field instructor both belong to the same majority group, you belong to the same minority group, you belong to different minority groups, you are minority while she is majority, and vice versa. In any case, your field instructor can assist your development toward being culturally sensitive, responsive, and more competent.

Same Majority Group Student and Field Instructor. The majority group in North America is not a homogeneous mass as everyone incorrectly believes; it is composed of vast numbers of subgroups and sub-subgroups, each with its own individual conventions, quirks, standards, and resentments—all with uneasy doubts about the rest. Nevertheless, the range of commonly accepted beliefs and behaviors is usually wide enough to avoid misunderstandings based on culture. You may not agree with your field instructor when she suggests that you should have put your arm around the tearful Mrs. Taylor, but your discussion on the subject will be based on similar beliefs about touching.

Same Minority Group Student and Field Instructor. If you come from the same minority group as your field instructor, your common heritage may be the basis of an instant bond. You may be more comfortable sharing value conflicts; your instructor may anticipate these conflicts because she has had to deal with them herself. She may mediate for you with the majority group or teach you how to cope with majority colleagues more effectively.

She may also make special allowances for you, which could endanger your learning. On the other hand, she may not accept substandard performance based on supposed language or cultural difficulties because she knows the difference between a problem and an excuse. She may even expect a great deal more from you than she would from a majority student. Expectations that are too low or too high can be equally disastrous. It is up to you to point out that you are capable of more if you feel you are being coddled, or that you need to go slower if you are feeling overwhelmed.

On a few occasions membership in the same ethnic group may lead not to a bond but to a feeling of instant loathing. Some conflicts between subgroups of the same ethnicity can be more deep-rooted and violent than any conflict between members of different groups. If you have been taught from infancy that the subgroup to which your field instructor belongs is the spawn of the devil, your practicum is not the time to try to alter this belief.

By now you should have reached the stage where the devil's spawn seems less devilish than you have been led to expect. If this is the case, you might try to get along, watching yourself carefully for irrational reactions, prepared to admit that you are not fighting your prejudice as successfully as you had hoped.

If you are still an unfortunate disciple in the matter of devils, it is far better for you to say so. You might find it difficult to admit your prejudice to your field instructor, and she might wish that you had taken it into account before you accepted the practicum setting. Nevertheless, it is quite reasonable to have a prejudice, acknowledge that you have it, attempt to overcome it, fail, and ask for a transfer to another practicum setting. Transfers tend to be rare but they can be achieved if there are *valid* reasons. You will then be free to do long-term battle with your prejudice at a time when it will not interfere with your practicum learning.

Different Minority Group Student and Field Instructor. Many of the same considerations apply to students and instructors who come from different minority groups. The very fact of belonging to an ethnic minority can create a bond, with all its accompanying advantages and hazards. The difference, of course, is that your field instructor will be less well equipped to know when you have a problem and when you are making excuses. You may be tempted to inappropriately take advantage of this. The result will be that you will acquire fewer skills than you would have otherwise and your clients will eventually suffer as a result.

Minority Group Student and Majority Group Field Instructor. Minority group students sometimes have real difficulties when they work within the majority culture. To begin with, there are the discriminatory slights and rejections which minority peoples still suffer. Such discriminatory acts make it difficult for a minority student to play a full part in the professional community, in addition to the planning, organizing, cooperating, and negotiating as the practicum task demands. There is also the possibility of rejection by majority clients, a possibility that adds to the inevitable tension of conducting the first interview with a new client, probably while being observed.

Then, there is the matter of differing value systems. For example, one of the aims of this book is to get social work students to be proactive rather than reactive; that is, we believe you are supposed to take a primary role in setting your learning goals and objectives, suggesting assignments, organizing activities, and resolving conflicts. These responsibilities, in turn, necessarily involve a certain attitude toward authority. If you have been taught that persons in authority should rarely be questioned and never be challenged, you may have difficulty in disagreeing with your field instructor. On the other hand, if you have been taught that admitting to a problem will cause you to lose face, you will be more likely to pretend that the world is a bed of roses.

It is quite essential that you are aware of these conflicts between your own values and the values of the majority, but such awareness may not help you much. You may *know* that frankness in expressing your problems is held to be a virtue; however, you may not really *feel* that it is a virtue or even that it ought to be considered as such. Should you then try to change your beliefs to fit the majority values? If your effort is successful, to what degree have you betrayed your own culture? To what degree have you abandoned what may be still the *truth*?

Such questions can only be answered on a personal level by the individual concerned. Ideally, your field instructor will understand that your problems are culture based, will be sensitive to them, and will be ready to explore them with you when you are ready and able to explore them. However, the solutions, as always, can only come from within.

If you are a member of a minority group working with clients from your own culture, you may understand your clients better than your field instructor does. This can be threatening to an instructor who as a result not only perceives herself to be without a teaching role but finds that her own helping interventions may be ineffective. In fact, she has a dual role: to learn the ways of your community and culture and to teach you to analyze your helping techniques and develop new ones. If you can interchange your own respective roles as teacher and learner, the two of you together can make a real contribution to the ethnic community and the social work profession.

Differences in Age. Students, by tradition, are thought of as young. They are generally thought to be younger than the people who teach them. If you are a mature student, you are not alone; older social work students are becoming more common. Nevertheless, age has its problems and it is absurd to pretend that it does not.

To begin with, if you are a mature student you are trying to form peer relationships with other students who, in some cases, may be younger than your children. This situation is even more difficult than it sounds since they can easily socialize at parties while you may feel more comfortable being at home. The relationships you form may be cordial and supportive, but the quality of the support is rarely the same as it would have been with same-age peers.

It may have been a long time since you were last in school. You may wonder if your brain cells are still intact, if the other students will laugh at your efforts, if your professors will laugh, or—worse yet—if they will all treat you with the patient, patronizing kindness which is only inappropriately afforded to the very old. A particular nemesis is often the computer. Younger social work students may have little affection for computers but at least they have met them before, if only through video games. Older students who did not have the opportunity to take typing classes in high school have more of a tendency to regard the computer as a dangerous and alien beast. The very fact that you are back in school means you are ready to *learn* new things. It is only a matter of combining this positive attitude with a willingness to ask for help when you find you do not understand.

Sometimes, asking for help is difficult for older students. Gray hairs, although they have nothing to do with wisdom, are certainly supposed to indicate experience. Clients and other professionals may show surprise when you introduce yourself as a social work student. You may even read on Mr. Rothery's face that if you are *still* a social work student at your age, he has little hope in solving the authority conflict he is having with his immediate boss.

All this can be especially difficult if you have recently changed careers. You were probably competent in the job you had before, but in this new field you may believe you have lost your accustomed sense of usefulness and worth. Not only may you *feel* useless, you are obliged to submit your perceived "uselessness" to the scrutiny of your field instructor. It is up to your field instructor to point out to you that your experience *does* count. If your prior experience was in a related field, you should be able to use parts of it to shed light on some aspects of your new work, perhaps on the social problems faced by the agency or its system of organization or recording. If your experience is unrelated, it is still experience. Your previous experience has likely taught you how to interact with people, has given you emotional maturity, and has provided you with a long-term perspective on the purposes of learning.

Some difficulties may arise if your experience has been in an area where self-determination is less important than control. For example, nurses usually do not discuss with patients the advisability of taking medication. Teachers do not debate with students the wisdom of attending school. If you have been accustomed to making decisions *for* people, it might be hard for you to let your clients make them on their own, particularly if you disagree with the decisions they make. Discuss your dilemmas with your field instructor.

An instructor-student relationship may be difficult if the student is older than the instructor. The instructor may feel uncomfortable acting as teacher to your older age, and you may feel just as uncomfortable in the role of a social work student.

Probably, the instructor will take the initiative in discussing the age matter with you as a preliminary to exploring your other feelings about your new student role. If she does not, it is up to you to make it clear that in this particular setting *you* are the social work student and *she* is the field instructor. You accept that; you expect that on the basis of this understanding she will share with you her greater knowledge of social work and you will share with her your wider experience of life in other fields.

If you have worked in a social work setting before, you may present your field instructor with an even greater challenge. You may feel that you are as competent as she is and resent her instruction. On the other hand, you may play down your experience because you would like to be just another social work student, the same as everybody else. Either of these attitudes will lead you to disaster. A student may have worked, yet not put the knowledge later learned in the classroom into action. Without realizing it, many people continue to do the wrong thing for years.

Work experience, even in social work or a related field, does not necessarily put a student ahead of one without that experience. The most sensible thing to do is to ask the instructor's help in deciding what you know, what you do not know, and how you can best fill in the gaps. You may begin at a higher level than the other students but the process of setting learning goals and objectives, doing activities to meet the objectives, and analyzing failures will remain the same. For you, challenging yourself is surely one of your personal learning goals.

Differences in Gender. North America is a society in which male and female roles are in a state of tumultuous transition. Men who open doors for women are not sure whether they are being patronizing or considerate; women who fetch coffee for men are not sure whether they are being helpful or betraying the sisterhood. Most of these dilemmas can be resolved by using common sense. The person who reaches the door first opens it; the person who is least busy fetches the coffee; the person who has the greatest amount of knowledge in any situation assumes the lead.

Nevertheless, people are men or women. Hormones continue to flow despite all efforts to subject them to equality. Sparks leap, jealousies fester, looks pass. A relationship between two individuals—even the most formal and professional of relationships—will contain currents that need to be acknowledged. It goes without saying that these currents have to be examined. Any kind of sexual contact with clients by social work students is expressly forbidden. The same applies to social workers and field instructors. Unwanted sexual touching and suggestions from those persons who are in positions of power or authority are recognized as sexual harassment. Such situations require you as a student to report the information and adhere to ethical obligations and responsibilities.

Sexual contact with other staff members is not forbidden; romance will flourish in even the strictest of circles. Emotional entanglement for students, however, is an extremely dangerous game. It is even more dangerous if it occurs between student and field instructor. Yearnings are all very well, but subsequent behaviors will undermine the student's ability to learn and the field instructor's ability to teach.

Attitudes that are gender related may also be problematic. For example, a male instructor may expect less from a female student than he would from a male student. He may expect her to be good with children even though she has no experience with children. He may defend and protect her when she needs to learn to defend and protect herself. In the same way, a female field instructor with a male student may feel uncertain about her authority. She may adopt an overly authoritarian or passive attitude, either of which will interfere with the student-instructor exchange. A seasoned instructor will be aware of these potential traps, will be able to avoid them, and will help you to avoid them. Nevertheless, awareness on your part is essential if you are to establish and maintain a positive learning relationship.

Another area of increasing concern is that of sexual harassment. It is still a reality that some people may be subject to such unwanted attentions as discriminatory remarks, snide leers, and improper suggestions. Laws have been passed, education is proceeding, and committees are locked in debate. Nevertheless, while the law, the schools, and the committees pursue their cumbersome paths, we have to cope with reality.

No number of laws or committees will protect the ordinary woman in the ordinary workplace until attitudes have undergone a fundamental change. Attitudes change slowly while harassment, for many women, is an ongoing reality. If you are a female student, try to develop your own coping mechanisms so that comments, looks, or touches will lose their power to annihilate you.

Appealing to a higher authority may be necessary if you cannot cope; most universities nowadays provide some formal avenue through which complaints can be lodged. You cannot, however, spend your life lodging one complaint after another and, eventually, you will have to learn to fend for yourself. It may not seem fair that you are expected to deal with a situation which, by every law and every social work value, ought not to be allowed to occur. It is *not* fair. There will be other things in your practicum—and in your life—that are not fair either. Unfairness is one of those things with which you must learn to cope. If you cannot cope with unfairness, and you have a tendency to lead "trendy" crusades, you do not belong in social work.

Differences Due to Physical Handicap. A physically handicapped student can present a special situation for both your practicum setting and your social work program. The most common physical problems include motor disabilities, which may necessitate a wheelchair, and hearing or vision defects ranging from moderate impairment to profound deafness or blindness. Most universities are now making arrangements to allow physically handicapped students to move around the campus and have access to most classrooms. Special assistance in the form of readers, attendants, interpreters, Braille texts, and special electronic equipment has made it possible for students to keep up with classroom work.

A practicum, however, is a different matter. Handicapped students face the community daily and are well aware of what they need to function, but facing the community as a private individual and facing it as a beginning social work student are very different things. To begin with, there is the matter of access. Public buildings are increasingly being made accessible to the handicapped, but there are still smaller agencies with offices that can only be reached by circumventing obstacles in the hallway and climbing up three flights of stairs. If you are a handicapped student, you will probably be more limited than other students in making initial practicum choices.

One answer to this, of course, is a practicum setting in a rehabilitation agency. Facilities will be on hand since you will be working with handicapped clients. You will have the opportunity to begin your professional life with colleagues and members of the public who are accustomed to interacting with handicapped people. You may be more comfortable, your colleagues may be more comfortable, and your personal experience may be invaluable to your clients.

Some social work educators and handicapped students feel strongly that a practicum in a rehabilitation setting is not an answer at all. Instead, they feel it is a statement that handicapped people should only work with other handicapped people because they cannot function anywhere else. This is a value question that you must decide for yourself. Given the limitations of stairs and cluttered hallways, you have the same opportunity as any other student to decide what you want from your practicum and what you do not want.

Next is the question of acceptance. Acceptance by agency staff and other professionals is vital to all social work students but, for the handicapped student, it is critical. There are still many people, including a few social workers, who are unable to see past the handicap to the person. They have a vague notion that because the legs no longer function, the brain must be affected too. In most cases, such fears can be avoided by a frank discussion with agency staff about the nature of the handicap, the limitations imposed by the handicap, and the large number of things you are able to do despite the handicap. Normally this discussion will take place before you arrive at the practicum setting and, for it to be useful, your field liaison should have your permission to discuss your handicap with your field instructor and other agency staff.

When you arrive, you may find that other people are uncomfortable in your presence. You will know by now that initial embarrassment fades quickly with familiarity, but your field instructor may still be reluctant to assign you clients. There is reason in this. Clients may be reluctant to share problems with someone whose life situation seems much worse than their own. Their embarrassment may add to their existing stress. If you need to have an attendant or an interpreter with you during the interview, the presence of this other person may distress the client and lead to problems about confidentiality.

None of these problems are insurmountable. Indeed, when the initial barriers have been overcome, you may find that your handicap enables you to interact with your clients more readily. Handicapped people are less likely than others to be perceived as threatening. Your coping and problem-solving skills are probably well developed, and you may be able to engender a hopefulness in your clients along the lines of, "I can cope with this if you can cope with that." Nevertheless, you should still be aware that finding the right client for any beginning social work student is a time-consuming and careful process. In your case, it may take longer and you may have to be more patient.

It is possible that your field instructor and other colleagues will make allowances for you in ways that may endanger your learning. For example, lateness in completing an assignment may be tolerated on the grounds that you cannot walk. Sometimes, this is reasonable. You may indeed be late because it took you longer to get from one place to another. At other times, however, the task from which you are being excused may bear no relation to your disability.

Such situations should not occur if you have discussed with your field instructor the precise nature of your disability and have agreed with her about the accommodations that may have to be made. The learning requirements of your social work program and the expectations of your practicum setting must be met whether you are handicapped or not. It is up to you and your field instructor together to see that they are met by setting realistic learning goals and objectives and ensuring that any allowances made are specific only to your disability. If your instructor has underestimated your coping skills, you should point out your capabilities, emphasizing that your handicap is one factor in your life and not the whole of it.

Exercises 5.1 on page 145 and 5.2 on page 146 are to help you prepare for your supervisory conferences.

GROUP SUPERVISORY CONFERENCES

So far, the practical and relationship factors affecting your practicum supervision have been discussed as though the individual supervisory conference is the only form of supervision that exists. Group supervisory conferences are also an important part of your practicum experience, however.

If you are placed separately from your fellow social work students, particularly if you are located in a different department, group supervisory conferences may be one of the few opportunities you have to meet with them and find out what they are doing. Group supervisory conferences enable you to see their individual problem-solving approaches and, inevitably, you will be able to compare their experiences with your own. You can learn a lot so long as you remember that you are not in competition with one another. Their approaches may be different from yours but "different" does not mean better or worse.

Group supervisory conferences allow a wider selection of learning experiences to be undertaken. For example, a film is far more useful if you watch it and discuss it afterwards with someone else. Lectures and presentations are normally only provided to groups; even role-plays can be more effective if there are a number of participants, each watching and trying to improve on the performance of the others. Some students need group supervisory conferences to develop a sense of professional identity. Some students learn better in group settings. Some are not able to challenge the field instructor without the feeling of moral support and safety provided by other students. If at all possible, individual supervisory conferences should be balanced with group supervisory conferences.

**EXERCISE 5.1
PLANNING FOR
SUPERVISORY CONFERENCES**

Planning on the part of both the student and field instructor is important in supervisory conferences. As a student, you need to take an active part in planning, organizing, and directing your learning during supervisory sessions. Such activities will help you maximize the time directed toward practicum supervision.

In preparation for each supervisory conference, the following outline can help you plan for your sessions. Fill in the spaces provided before you attend your supervisory session. Then take the form with you to your meeting.

Supervisory conference meeting date: _____

These are the results I expect today:

These are the tasks I want to prepare for my next supervisory conference:

**EXERCISE 5.2
QUALITIES OF EFFECTIVE
SUPERVISORY CONFERENCES**

Everyone learns in different ways. Knowing how you learn best is something that will develop over a period of time. At this time you can begin to think about ways that help you learn most effectively. Identify the qualities in supervisory conferences that you feel will help maximize your learning. Consider the qualities, activities, and the process that must be present on the part of both you and your field instructor. Write your responses in the space provided.

1. What do you believe are the qualities of an effective supervisory conference?

2. In your opinion what can your field instructor and you do to stimulate a positive learning environment during supervisory conferences? List the responsibilities for both.

Field Instructor Contributions   *Your Contributions*

3. Reflect back on your last supervisory conference session. In what ways might you take more responsibility for the outcome of the next session?

**EXERCISE 5.3
EVALUATING YOUR
SUPERVISORY CONFERENCES**

Consult your journal to review your last supervisory conference session. Analyze the session using the eight questions presented here. Write your responses in the spaces provided.

Supervisory conference session date: _____

Time spent: _____

Theme of session: _____

1. Was there enough time for you to prepare for the supervisory conference? If not, why not?

2. Was the focus of the session clearly established by you *prior* to your meeting time? Explain in detail.

3. In your opinion, did the teaching style of your field instructor encourage you to be active and to participate in the supervisory conference in a useful manner? Explain in detail.

148 Part Two / The Practicum

4. In your opinion, did you present yourself in a manner that is active and open to learning during supervision? Explain in detail.

5. Did you and your field instructor keep focused on the topic or theme in order to accomplish your purpose? How? If your answer was no, explain why you are unable to remain focused.

6. Did the session achieve the mutually stated purpose for both you and your field instructor? If not, where did it fall short?

7. Were you able to present your ideas and feelings on the topics easily? Explain in detail.

8. Did the session provide effective support? If no, why not?

**EXERCISE 5.4
STEPS TO INCREASE THE EFFECTIVENESS
OF SUPERVISORY CONFERENCES**

Have your field instructor complete Exercise 5.3 on pages 147–148. Together discuss the results of the analysis. What steps might you take to increase the effectiveness of future supervisory conferences? Write your responses in the space provided below.

**EXERCISE 5.5
USING FEEDBACK FROM
SUPERVISORY CONFERENCES**

One of the functions of the supervisory conferences during your field placement is to provide you with feedback about your developing skills and abilities as a professional social worker. Because you are receiving regular feedback from your field instructor, there will be no surprises about your abilities when it's time for your mid-term evaluation (Chapter 7).

Feedback can be positive and/or negative. Learning to deal with negative feedback is difficult. So, how are you doing? What is your reaction or feelings to criticism? How sensitive are you? Write your response in the space provided.

What steps might you take to react in a way that is more productive to your future learning? Write your responses in the space provided.

**EXERCISE 5.6
KNOWING YOUR STRENGTHS**

In your opinion, what new strengths and abilities are you developing at this point in your practicum learning? List them in the space provided below.

OTHER ASPECTS OF PRACTICUM MANAGEMENT

Supervision is only one aspect of practicum management. Other aspects include selecting activities to achieve your learning objectives, and then organizing, planning, and carrying out these activities, and recording the results. One activity that requires careful planning is interviewing clients, particularly the first client.

Preparing for Your First Interview with a Client

When you are ready see your first client, you may feel heightened anxiety. You can offset anxiety to some degree by providing yourself with as much information as possible. Read your client's file if one is available. Read whatever you can find about the client's problem area if you know it in advance. Ask yourself how you might use this theoretical data to assist the client. Ask yourself, too, if you have any values or biases that might affect your performance in this particular area with this particular client.

With the client in mind, you might then reread some of the principles and techniques in your interviewing textbook. How do you engage a client? What particular techniques might be useful in engaging this client? How do you set a goal for an interview? What goals might be set for this interview?

Once you have some ideas, discuss them with your field instructor. She may be willing to role-play the client for you so that you can resolve such difficulties as where to meet the client, what to say first, how to make the seating arrangements, and whether to offer coffee. She may take the role-play further into engagement and goal setting. But even if she does not, you will have gained an initial feeling for your role as a worker with a client.

At the beginning of the interview, introduce yourself as a social work student; give your name and an explanation of what the agency does, if the client has not been there before. You can then begin to gather information. Encourage the client to participate in such practice activities as drawing a genogram (family map) or an eco-map (diagram of social contacts).

If you remember the basic core interpersonal helping skills—empathy, respect, and authenticity—and you are not afraid to ask for clarification when you do not understand, the first interview will not be as traumatic as you may have feared. The second will be easier; the third will be easier yet. The fourth may be more difficult because you will be much more critical of your own performance, but this kind of difficulty should be welcomed as a positive sign of learning. As we stated in the preface for instructors, interviewing skills are not covered in this book, as they are covered in-depth in other books and we suggest you read them carefully *before* you see your first client. We have only identified basic elements of practicum management that you should be alerted to when it comes to interviewing clients.

Documenting Your Activities

Keeping careful documentation is not only important to the IRS, it is also an important part of practicum management. A major reason for keeping records is to enable you to determine the best plans for your clients. You also need to document your activities thoroughly not only as a learning experience but to fulfill agency requirements and prepare yourself for your mid-term evaluation (if there is one).

SUMMARY

Managing your practicum means that you accept responsibility for defining and achieving your goals and objectives; suggesting, organizing, and documenting your activities; and participating actively in the field instruction process. Effective field instruction depends on both practical and relationship factors. The practical factors involve arranging a time and place for the conference, agreeing on the session topic in advance, gathering all available information about it, and ensuring that adequate time is allowed to discuss it. Relationship factors may be affected by differences in expectations and attitudes due to different ethnic or religious backgrounds, differences in age, differences in gender, and difficulties due to physical handicap.

Often, field instructors and students both belong to the same majority cultural group and share a common value system. There may be disagreements but there will be few misunderstandings based on cultural differences. Sometimes, however, a minority group student is placed with a majority group instructor, or vice versa. Misunderstandings can occur in these cases, often based on differing attitudes toward authority figures or different values about the expression of client problems. When student and instructor belong to the same ethnic minority, strong bonds may be formed which sometimes result in too much or too little being expected of the student. Awareness of cultural differences on the part of both field instructor and student can smooth the path, promote learning, and make a real contribution to the ethnic community.

Mature students, or very young students, present a special challenge to field instructors. Initial discomfort may be overcome if students and instructors are frank about the issues. For both the very experienced student and the inexperienced student, the process of setting learning goals and delineating objectives will still be just about the same.

Gender differences between the student and field instructor may lead to reduced or heightened expectations about student performance. In rare cases, they may lead to the dangerous arena of sexual entanglement. Laws prohibiting harassment are often ineffective in affording real protection for women in the daily interactions of the workplace. Students, male or female, for whom sexual harassment is a problem should therefore consider developing their own coping mechanisms. If these strategies fail and the problem continues, there is always the alternative of lodging a formal complaint.

Physically handicapped students may face some difficulty in obtaining a practicum where facilities are adequate and suitable learning opportunities are provided. Such students may also have to cope with discriminatory attitudes on the part of colleagues and clients. Once the initial barriers have been overcome, a physical disability may even prove to be an advantage in relationships with clients. Provided that expectations are tailored to the student's abilities and needs, the practicum should be as positive an experience for the handicapped student as it is for any other student.

Although the individual supervisory conference is still considered primary, group conferences can enrich the practicum experience in a variety of ways. They allow a wider range of learning activities to be undertaken, provide experience in group interaction, give the student a sense of professional identity, and provide a sense of support which may be necessary if the student is to learn by challenging the field instructor.

Other aspects of practicum management include planning and documenting activities. Planning for the first client interview is particularly important and can alleviate much of the stress that all beginning social work students feel.

We will now turn to documentation in the context of preparing for your midterm evaluation.

SELECTED REFERENCES

Barnat, M.R. (1973). Student reactions to the first supervisory year: Relationship and resolutions. *Journal of Education for Social Work, 9,* 3-8.

Barth, R., & Gambrill, E. (1984). Learning to interview: The quality of training opportunities. *Clinical Supervisor, 2,* 3-14.

Behling, J.C., Curtis, C., & Foster, S.A. (1989). Impact of sex-role combinations on student performance in field instruction. In M. Raskin (Ed.), *Empirical studies in field instruction* (pp. 161-168). New York: Haworth.

Benavides III, E., Lynch, M.M., & Velasquez, J.S. (1980). Toward a culturally relevant field work model: The community learning center project. *Journal of Education for Social Work, 16,* 55-62.

Berkun, C. (1984). Women and the field experience: Toward a model of nonsexist field-based learning conditions. *Journal of Education for Social Work, 20,* 5-12.

Bogo, M., & Vayda, E. (1991). Developing a process model for field instruction. In D. Schneck, B. Grossman, & U. Glassman (Eds.), *Field education in social work: Contemporary issues and trends* (pp. 59-66). Dubuque, IA: Kendall/Hunt.

Cournoyer, B. (1991). *The social work skills workbook.* Belmont, CA: Wadsworth.

Dwyer, M., & Urbanowski, M. (1981). Field practice criteria: A valuable teaching/learning tool in undergraduate social work education. *Journal of Education for Social Work, 17,* 5-11.

Grossman, B., Levine-Jordano, N., & Shearer, P. (1991). Working with students—emotional reactions in the field: An educational framework. In D. Schneck, B. Grossman, & U. Glassman (Eds.), *Field education in social work: Contemporary issues and trends* (pp. 205-216). Dubuque, IA: Kendall/Hunt.

Kaplan, T. (1991). A model for group supervision for social work: Implications for the profession. In D. Schneck, B. Grossman, & U. Glassman (Eds.), *Field education in social work: Contemporary issues and trends* (pp. 141-148). Dubuque, IA: Kendall/Hunt.

Lemberger, J., & Marshack, E.F. (1991). Educational assessment in the field: An opportunity for teacher-learner mutuality. In D. Schneck, B. Grossman, & U. Glassman (Eds.), *Field education in social work: Contemporary issues and trends* (pp. 187-197). Dubuque, IA: Kendall/Hunt.

Marshack, E.F. (1991). The older student: Social work's new majority. In D. Schneck, B. Grossman, & U. Glassman (Eds.), *Field education in social work: Contemporary issues and trends* (pp. 295-300). Dubuque, IA: Kendall/Hunt.

Mayers, F. (1970). Differential use of group teaching in first year field work. *Social Service Review, 44,* 63-70.

Raphael, F.B., & Rosenblum, A. (1991). The open expression of differences in the field practicum: Report of a pilot study. In D. Schneck, B. Grossman, & U. Glassman (Eds.), *Field education in social work: Contemporary issues and trends* (pp. 301-309). Dubuque, IA: Kendall/Hunt.

Schneck, D. (1991). Integration of learning in field education: Elusive goal and educational imperative. In D. Schneck, B. Grossman, & U. Glassman (Eds.), *Field education in social work: Contemporary issues and trends* (pp. 67-77). Dubuque, IA: Kendall/Hunt.

Thyer, B., Sowers-Hong, K., & Love, J.P. (1989). The influence of field instructor-student gender combinations on student perceptions of field instruction quality. In M. Raskin (Ed.), *Empirical studies in field instruction* (pp. 169-179). New York: Haworth.

CHAPTER 6

Documentation

EACH PHASE OF YOUR practicum experience has been preparing you for your mid-term and final evaluations, first by formulating your learning contract's goals and objectives and then by documenting and recording all the activities necessary to reach your learning objectives.

Documentation and recording are not synonymous terms. Documentation occurs when you simply put the client's name, the date of application, and the type of service requested in the client's file. Recording is a special kind of documentation. Recording tells the recorder what went on during the provision of service. Description of an individual treatment session is an example of recording. Documentation and recording are important both as learning tools and as evidence of what you have accomplished. After all, despite your struggles and failures, you have had your moments of glory, and you would like these to be branded on your field instructor's memory as she starts to prepare your mid-term evaluation.

By now you should have accumulated various files on different subject matters, all filled with collected information. Attempts have been made to collate the information into some coherent pattern—contacts made, tasks accomplished, tasks still to be accomplished, and so forth. Among this vast array, certain records might be particularly important in terms of your mid-term evaluation. These include your journal, notes in your clients' files, notes on supervisory conferences with your field instructor, notes from meetings and consultations, and process recordings you have made of interviews with clients. Videotapes and audiotapes also represent an important form of recording.

YOUR JOURNAL

Your journal should be a record of your learning during your practicum experience. Learning has two initial stages: collecting information and making sense of the information in relation to previous knowledge, experience, and identified goals.

Your journal therefore should contain two separate sections for each recorded item: a summary of the information acquired and your interpretation of the meaning of that information.

For example, you may have observed an interview with a client conducted by another staff member. Under the *Summary of Information* heading you can describe what you saw. When and where did the interview take place? Who was present? What use was made of video or audio equipment? What questions were asked? What body language was used? How did the client respond to the questions and the body language? Did the interviewer take notes? Were any measuring instruments employed, such as a written questionnaire? Were specific tasks set for the interviewer or client to complete before the next session? What tasks? What arrangements were made regarding the next session? You may want to write all this down in a column on the left side of the page under the *Summary of Information* heading.

The right side of the page can then be devoted to your interpretation of each event under the *Interpretation* heading. For example, your observation of an interview between a worker and a couple may have been that the husband was present at the interview. You would then record this under the *Summary of Information* heading. Under your *Interpretation* heading you might remark that this was the first time the husband had attended with his wife. The husband's presence was significant because (1) this interview marked the beginning of couple counseling as opposed to individual counseling, or (2) the husband was becoming more supportive of his wife, or (3) the husband had accomplished the first major step of acknowledging the existence of a problem and deciding to ask for help, or (4) another person, such as a child protective services worker, had indicated to the husband that if he did not attend counseling sessions worse things might befall him.

If you are not sure which of many possibilities is the correct interpretation, you might make a note to ask the interviewer or your field instructor later on. Alternately, all might become clear when the husband remarks that his wife is nuts, the interviewer is a useless do-gooder, and child protection services has no right to interfere in his business.

In a similar way, you might observe that no video or audio equipment was being used. This was because (1) the equipment was unavailable, (2) this particular interviewer rarely uses such equipment, or (3) the husband voiced a vociferous protest and refused to sign the consent form. In this connection, you might note later that the interviewer took copious notes because she needed a complete record to analyze a difficult interview and because the information was required by another social service agency.

You may think that the interviewer performed well under difficult conditions. If so, you can write down in what ways you believe she performed well and share this with her later. If you have questions, your specifically directed praise may mean that she may answer your questions more readily.

You may also feel that she may have made some errors and, had you been the interviewer, you may have taken a different approach. If you have recorded the errors you believe she may have made, why you feel they were errors, and what you would have done instead, she may be prepared to discuss this with you. Such discussions are always delicate. She may perceive your comments not as an attempt to acquire wisdom but as a direct criticism of her abilities. She may be concerned that you will communicate your criticisms to your field instructor who also may be her direct supervisor. She may be afraid that you will discuss the negative aspects of the interview openly with other staff members or even with staff from another agency.

Usually, none of this will occur because your field instructor will have selected the staff members you are to observe as carefully as she has selected the clients you are to see. Such workers are normally open to challenge and are ready to consider suggestions, admit to errors, and point out why the errors you noted were not errors at all. Nevertheless, care and sensitivity on your part are also needed.

Be sufficiently aware of which social workers are particularly vulnerable and when some innocent action on your part might aggravate tension or lead to conflict. You should not discuss one worker's performance with another worker, and you should not discuss your agency at all with members of a different agency.

Occasionally, despite all your care, you might become embroiled in a dispute. For example, it might be said that you have unethically shared confidential information with someone else, or you have carried tales, or you have failed to cooperate with some social worker on a particular project. If you have been in the habit of taking notes on what occurred, under what circumstances it occurred, and why you believe it occurred, you will be able to use these notes to defuse the conflict or, in the worst case, to defend your position. Thus it is important for many reasons that your notes be accurate, coherent, and complete.

If you try to take accurate, complete, and coherent notes on everything that occurs in the course of a day, you will do little else. Your journal should not be a record of every event but only a record of significant events. For example, you may want to leave out the fact that you had lunch with Pam if all you did was eat and talk about life. On the other hand, if lunch with Pam marked a change in your relationship or if you discussed some vital aspect of a group you both facilitate, this is worthy of note. The difficulty, of course, is deciding what counts as a significant event. Inevitably, you will fail to record a momentous something which did not appear in the least momentous at the time you ignored it.

All you can do is try your best to identify significant events in relation to other events. For example, every learning experience is significant because it relates directly to achieving your learning objectives. Events around relationships are significant because relationships—your own and other people's—affect both your learning and your personal satisfaction in your practicum setting. Supervisory conferences with your field instructor are definitely important. So are events around contentious issues, because they might be important in the future even if they do not seem so at the time.

Another significant area is your reaction to the event you have recorded. Did you feel satisfied after your lunch-time talk with Pam or were you left with a vague feeling that something was wrong? If you took part in a group discussion, did you feel comfortable with the group or did you feel that your suggestions and comments were largely ignored? Did you feel bad about a canceled appointment or an unreturned telephone call? Did you feel good when Mr. Gutman eventually told you his *real* problem?

At the end of the week, when you have written down what events occurred, what they meant, and how you felt about them, you need to write a summary. In other words, you need to pick out the most significant events from your list of significant events to see if they form a pattern. The questions in Exercise 6.1 on the following three pages may serve as a guide.

**EXERCISE 6.1
QUESTIONS TO PONDER**

1. What was the most significant thing you learned at your practicum this week? Why?

2. Were you able to actively participate in any staff meetings this week? What did you learn there?

3. What was the high point of the week? Why?

4. Whom did you get to know better this week? Why?

5. What new skill from your practice skills book did you try to use this week? Did it work? If not, why do you think it did not?

6. Did you use your time effectively this week? If you did not, was there a particular reason?

7. What learning goal have you made progress with this week? What goal do you need to work on most? How will you work on it next week?

Do not forget that your field instructor and field liaison may need to read some or all of your journal. The journal should be reasonably tidy so that it will not embarrass you, and it should be written in a language that will not embarrass you either. For example, you may be tempted to express your feelings about some incident or your opinion of a social worker's behavior in the strongest of terms. This is unwise. Instead, if you make an attempt to write objectively, taking into account the worker's possible point of view, you might even discover some point of empathy. If this does not occur, a reasoned account of what took place is still more impressive than an outburst of emotion. If you are referring to clients in your journal, it is better to use initials. Your journal will not be stored with the same careful security as your clients' files and you do not want to risk any accidental breach of confidentiality.

NOTES IN CLIENTS' FILES

Much of your material about clients is recorded in the clients' files. Files tend to be read by people other than the writer, and the information contained in them is not only shared with other social workers but may affect decisions regarding your client. Take care therefore to write as accurately as possible. If you can justify giving the client the benefit of the doubt, do so. If your comments must be negative, make sure that you have evidence to support your position. Where your comments are not backed up by facts, say they are your impressions or the impressions of others. Do not record impressions as facts. References to other workers must also be made with circumspection since they and others will read what you say.

You might take your material either from a tape of the interview or from notes you made while it was going on. Such note taking is always a delicate balance between writing every word verbatim and making a few cryptic scrawls which you hope you can interpret later on. There are also the feelings of the client to be considered. If you write extensively, for example, Mr. Gutman may wonder how many more dreadful things you can possibly find to say. If you write very little, he may think he is not saying anything that is worth writing down.

As always, it is a question of compromise. Write facts, for example, Mr. Gutman's negative relationship with his boss and his gloomy outlook on life if you are discussing that. Write memory joggers: he mentioned he was having a great deal of difficulty at work. Write impressions: he is not afraid to go to the union. Particularly, note tasks that you have promised or he has promised to accomplish, arrangements for the next contact, and any special considerations.

Tell your clients at the beginning of the interviews that you are just going to take a few notes to remember something important. If your clients seem uneasy, tell them as you go along what you are writing down. As soon as you can, after the interview, amplify your notes and write them in coherent form. The longer you wait, the more likely it is that you will forget or distort something, particularly if you have seen another client in the meantime.

NOTES ON SUPERVISORY CONFERENCES

You may have a separate file that you use to prepare for your supervisory conferences. If so, you should write down the focus of the session, when and where it is to take place, what materials you need to take, what questions you want to ask, and what you hope to have achieved when it is over. In this same file are your notes taken from previous sessions. Record your field instructor's analyses and suggestions and write down any tasks that you or she has agreed to perform.

Probably your instructor will also be taking notes, and these notes will guide her when she comes to prepare your mid-term evaluation. It may be stressful for you to watch her writing if you are not quite sure what she is putting down. Usually, she will be writing what has been said, recording her impressions of the material you have provided, and noting your progress, areas to be worked on, tasks to be accomplished, and so forth. All she is doing is putting her audible feedback into written form so that she will not forget about it later. Ideally, nothing should be written down that she has not told you.

If you are still uneasy, you might remember that her supervisory notes are usually open to inspection by your field liaison. These notes, along with other records, form the basis for your grade (whether pass/fail or letter grade), and your field instructor needs documentation to support her opinion of you in the same way that you need documentation to support your opinions of your clients.

Another factor to consider is that some social work programs require students to evaluate their practicum at the end of the term. Affiliation with the social work program through the practicum is important to the practicum setting and your field instructor does not want a negative evaluation any more than you do. You therefore have the same responsibility as she does to be frank during the supervisory conferences. The evaluation of the field instructor and your practicum is talked about in the last phase of the field education process—Chapter 9.

For example, it would not be fair for you to write in your evaluation that "you rarely received relevant feedback" if you had never mentioned the feedback problem to your instructor. In the same way, she would not write, for example, that "Joanne's attitude toward males is not appropriately professional," unless she had explored with you what she meant by your professional attitude toward males and in what ways you fell below her perceived standard, and unless she had provided you with a specific example from your practice assignments.

When your supervisory conference session is over, it is a good idea for you to look at your notes in relation to your preparatory material. Did you ask the questions you had intended to ask? If not, why not? If you did, were they dealt with to your satisfaction? Were you comfortable or uneasy with your field instructor's feedback? Was the feedback relevant and sufficient? Were examples given? Did you achieve what you had hoped for during the session? What additional topics were discussed? If you make a brief summary of all this at the end of each session, you may find that patterns begin to emerge.

For instance, you may have felt unhappy with the feedback once or twice because you were going through a difficult period with a difficult client. If you *always* feel unhappy with the feedback this may mean that you do not respond well to constructive criticism or that your field instructor is unable to make criticisms in a positive, meaningful way. You can then address this concern with your field instructor in your next supervisory conference. If you get useful responses about the feedback, this is definitely a beginning.

PROCESS RECORDINGS

As you will see from your practice methods book, process recordings are written accounts of interviews made after they have taken place. They are useful in addition to audiotape or videotape because they can include the interviewer's feelings and interpretations, which may not be the same thing at all as what the client *thinks* took place or what actually *did* take place.

Nevertheless, the process recording is almost as old as social work; it will probably be around for a long time and it has its advantages. For example, if you thought after the interview that you should have said something different to Mr. Gutman, you will be sorely tempted to include the different something in the process recording in place of what you really said. This does nothing to improve accuracy but it does indicate that learning has taken place. The very fact that you were able to critically analyze and improve on your responses says something for process recordings. Since the use of process recordings is to refine your practice skills, and since this book does not deal with skills, you are encouraged to read other books that cover process recordings in-depth and offer ways to organize the process recording.

TAPED RECORDINGS

If your interviews are taped, there will be no question of you inventing dialogue as you could do in a process recording. A videotape is obviously preferable to an audiotape because a lot of communication is nonverbal, but the videotape may also be initially threatening. At first, you may be delighted if the equipment is unavailable, the client refuses to be taped, or your field instructor fails to mention videotaping as a possibility. However, if you can survive the shock of seeing yourself as you are rather than as you imagine, you will come to rely on the videotape as an important analytical tool.

Your first task is to tell yourself firmly that this has to be done, you will survive it, you will benefit from it, and, more importantly, your increased awareness will benefit your clients. Once you have convinced yourself that all these things are true, your next task is to do it. The three points briefly outlined next may be of some help.

Asking Permission

In most instances, you must have the client's signed consent before you videotape an interview. If you wish that you could forget about the whole matter, your reluctance will readily transfer itself to the client and you will comfortably agree together that it is not a good idea. You may be even more reluctant with the next client, words will be heard from your field instructor, and a useful learning tool will have become an instrument of torture.

It is much more sensible, therefore, to beam affably upon the client, present the videotape as a normal part of interview procedures, and assume that the consent form will be signed. It will help your client if you say why you want it. You are a student and, to provide the client with the best possible service, you may need to be guided by your field instructor. The tape is to be used by her to guide you and by you to learn to serve the client better.

There is also the matter of who is to see it. You will see it, your field instructor will see it, your field liaison may see it, and the client is more than welcome to see it. No one else will see it unless you have first obtained explicit written consent from your client. At the end of your practicum, the tape will be erased unless your field instructor wants to keep it as a teaching tool to be used with other social work students. In that case, you will also need to ask for written consent from your client.

By now, your client will probably be quite happy with the idea. Contrary to popular belief, most clients do not object to being taped and some are even eager to see themselves on tape. You may want to use the tape later to point out to your client, Mr. Gutman, that he really mumbles, shuffles his feet, slouches, and stares at the floor all the time you were role-playing a job interview with him. A few role-plays later, when he has ceased to mumble, stare, and shuffle, you can show him on tape how far he has progressed.

If at the beginning he is still reluctant to use the tape, you might suggest a 5- or 10-minute trial run to see how it goes. If it bothers him after those first few minutes, shut it off. If, after all this, he still refuses written consent, you will just have to try again with the next client.

Using the Machine

If you do not want your client to stare at you doubtfully while you fiddle with buttons, give the machine a trial run in some quiet place where you can conceal your embarrassment and shout for help if necessary. Once you have learned how it works and run a preinterview test, do not hide it in a corner as though it were a diseased beast. Display it openly in a place where it will pick up you and your client, both visually and audibly. Obviously, you do not want to put the microphone next to the air conditioner or near an open window where the sound of large trucks will drown out most of the recording.

Analyzing the Tape

An interesting exercise is to critique your interview before you view the tape. You will learn from this how closely your memory parallels reality and subsequently you may be more effective when you have to analyze an interview without a tape.

When you view the tape, look for themes. Do you constantly allow your client to wander off the topic? Do you regularly have difficulty in persuading Mr. Gutman to express specific cognitions rather than vague and rambling feelings? Do you express feelings yourself or are you uncomfortable telling a client that you are uncomfortable? Do you hasten to fill in every conversational gap? Do you unconsciously pick at your teeth, play with your hair, or shuffle your feet?

If you watch the tape first without your field instructor, you will be able to select which parts to show her in case she does not have time to watch it all. These parts should obviously relate to any problems you are having with either your techniques or your client, but you need not restrict yourself to problems. If you did something well, particularly if it was something you did badly before, show her that part too. She needs to know your strengths as well as your weaknesses.

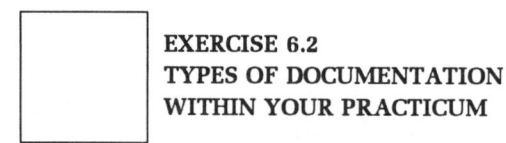

EXERCISE 6.2
TYPES OF DOCUMENTATION
WITHIN YOUR PRACTICUM

Various types of documentation are required for your practicum setting. The tasks and activities associated with writing, recording, documenting, and analyzing social work practice assist in achieving your learning goals and objectives.

List all the different types of documentation and recording you have completed in your practicum to date. For each type identify in what ways documentation or recording is assisting in the accomplishment of your learning goals and objectives. Write your responses in the spaces provided.

Type of Documentation or Recording   *Assisted in Learning*

**EXERCISE 6.3
INCREASING THE USEFULNESS
OF YOUR DOCUMENTATION**

List the steps you might take to more effectively use each type of documentation or recording outlined in Exercise 6.2 to achieve your learning goals and objectives.

**EXERCISE 6.4
ADDITIONAL TYPES OF DOCUMENTATION
AND RECORDING PROCEDURES**

What additional types of documentation or recording can you use to help prepare for your mid-term evaluation? Write your responses in the space provided below.

SUMMARY

Documenting your activities is an important learning tool and it evidences what you have accomplished. By the time you reach your mid-term evaluation, you will have accumulated a number of records, including your journal, notes in clients' files, notes on supervisory conferences, process recordings, and audiotapes or videotapes.

Your journal should be a record of your learning. Much of it will be narrative description, but you may want to record some items under two distinct headings: information obtained and interpretation of information. This two-column format is useful when you have observed an interview conducted by another social worker or when you are trying to integrate new information with material you already know.

Your journal should not contain every event that occurs during your practicum but only significant events. Often it is difficult to decide what counts as a significant event. Essentially, assume that all learning experiences count, including supervisory conferences with your field instructor and all events concerned with relationships or contentious issues. Your journal should not refer to clients by name because of confidentiality considerations.

Notes made in clients' files should be as accurate and objective as possible, because such notes can affect decisions made regarding the client. The material in clients' files is derived in part from interviews so it is also important that you keep accurate records of what occurred in your interviews. Note taking during client interviews is a delicate matter. You will probably need to write something, but the act of writing will also distract you from giving your concentrated attention to the client. If you plan to write up your interview as soon as possible after it has finished, you will need to write less while it is actually in progress.

Your notes on supervisory conferences with your field instructor will help you to determine the effectiveness of these sessions. You will know to what degree you achieved the learning objectives set for the session and you may be able to perceive patterns of communication or reaction running through the sessions. When you evaluate your field instructor and practicum (Chapter 9), you will have documented evidence on which to base your evaluations.

Process recordings are written accounts of interviews made after the interviews have taken place. They are less accurate and objective than tapes, but they may enable you to critically analyze your own responses to the client and substitute more appropriate responses as well as formulate assessments of the client. You will not have time to write a process recording after every interview, but you should write some at the beginning, middle, and end of your practicum. You can also use this type of recording as a learning tool if you have a difficult client system or feel a lack of progress.

A videotape will provide you with an accurate and objective record of your interview, but you may also find it somewhat intimidating. Because it is such an invaluable way of providing feedback to you, your field instructor, and your client, you will have to overcome your initial fears and reduce the same fears in your client. The client's written consent is necessary, and it is important that you are clear about what the tape is for, who will have access to it, and what will happen to it once your practicum is over.

Your strengths will be revealed through your documentation and remember, too, that the ability to document activities completely, coherently, and accurately is also a strength.

We will now turn to your mid-term evaluation: how to prepare for it, how to go through it, and how to use it as a guide to the remainder of your practicum and as a learning tool for your final evaluation.

SELECTED REFERENCES

Bogo, M., & Vayda, E. (1991). Developing a process model for field instruction. In D. Schneck, B. Grossman, & U. Glassman (Eds.), *Field education in social work: Contemporary issues and trends* (pp. 59–66). Dubuque, IA: Kendall/Hunt.

Collins, D., & Bogo, M. (1986). Competency-based field instruction: Bridging the gap between laboratory and field learning. *Clinical Supervisor, 4,* 39–52.

Cournoyer, B. (1991). *The social work skills workbook.* Belmont, CA: Wadsworth.

Johnston, N., Rooney, R., & Reitmeir, M.A. (1991). Sharing power: Student feedback to field supervisors. In D. Schneck, B. Grossman, & U. Glassman (Eds.), *Field education in social work: Contemporary issues and trends* (pp. 198–204). Dubuque, IA: Kendall/Hunt.

Raphael, F.B., & Rosenblum, A. (1991). The open expression of differences in the field practicum: Report of a pilot study. In D. Schneck, B. Grossman, & U. Glassman (Eds.), *Field education in social work: Contemporary issues and trends* (pp. 301–309). Dubuque, IA: Kendall/Hunt.

Schneck, D. (1991). Integration of learning in field education: Elusive goal and educational imperative. In D. Schneck, B. Grossman, & U. Glassman (Eds.), *Field education in social work: Contemporary issues and trends* (pp. 67–77). Dubuque, IA: Kendall/Hunt.

Urbanowski, M.L., & Dwyer, M.M. (1988). *Learning through field instruction.* Milwaukee, WI: Family Service of America.

Wijnberg, M.H., & Schwartz, M.C. (1977). Models of student supervision: The apprentice, growth, and role systems models. *Journal of Education for Social Work, 13,* 107–113.

CHAPTER 7

Mid-Term Evaluation

By now you have labored your way to the middle of your practicum, preparing diligently, performing zealously, and recording industriously. The time has come. The date and the hour have been set. Your field instructor awaits. It is time for your mid-term evaluation.

WHO IS AFFECTED?

Your evaluation may be a stressful experience for you. But it also affects the profession, your field instructor, and your social work program.

Evaluation as It Affects the Profession

During an observation of an interview with a couple, you may have heard the husband remark that the interviewer was a useless do-gooder. In a few cases, in fact, he may have been correct. A few social workers *are* useless do-gooders. Some proud individuals, who hold BSWs, MSWs, and PhDs, do not have any idea about what they are doing, what they should be doing, or why they should be doing it. In many cases, this is not their fault. They were not taught what to do and they were not corrected when they failed to do it. They moved passively through their practicums, obtaining "satisfactory" after "satisfactory," *relating* well to all the world, and *learning* minimal amounts in relation to concrete helping skills. They were then released to impart their nonlearning upon trusting clients, frustrated employers, doubting members of other professions, and innocent beginning social work students.

From an ethical point of view, it is the trusting clients and innocent students who suffer most. After all, a frustrated employer can always resort to termination. From the point of view of the social work profession, however, it is the doubt of other professional disciplines that is most problematic.

Tradespeople building a house assume that the carpenters, plumbers, electricians, and others will each do their respective jobs. A plumber who cannot plumb is not regarded with favor by the general contractor and the rest of the building team. If a number of plumbers appear to be unable to plumb, the whole of the plumbing trade falls into disrepute. In the same way, a multidisciplinary team of professionals caring for a client do not look with favor on an inadequate social worker. A number of inadequate social workers results in a general disrespect for the social work profession. A low-status profession tends to attract low-status students who become, in their turn, low-status workers and field instructors. And so the mess continues.

There are a number of ways out of this dilemma. First, the present coterie of inadequate social workers could be identified and fired. This is impractical. Second, incoming students could be subjected to a more stringent selection process in an attempt to improve the general standard. There are advocates for this approach. Third, the drift of an inadequate student from "satisfactory" to "satisfactory" to "graduation" could be stopped at the first "satisfactory." There are advocates for this approach too, but there are a number of barriers impeding its implementation. These barriers have to do with the component of social work that is defined as "art," and the various reactions of the student, the program, and the field instructor to an unsatisfactory practicum rating. For now, let us think for a moment about the feelings of your field instructor.

Evaluation as It Affects Your Field Instructor

A field instructor acts as one of the gatekeepers for the social work profession. She may have seen many students and many professional social workers. She knows, first hand, that inadequate social work practice can injure clients, produce negative feelings about the agency in the community, and have a damaging impact on other professionals. She also knows that most students admitted to your social work program have sufficient academic ability to pass their courses and most do pass. It is in the practicum setting that learning is turned into practice.

It is in the practicum that students who will become competent social workers can be most easily differentiated from those who will not; and it is the responsibility of the field instructor to make the differentiation. If she does not perform this task objectively and conscientiously, she is failing in her duty to our clients, our community, and our profession.

On the other hand, your field instructor understands the impact of a negative evaluation upon you. She has taught you. She has formed a relationship with you. She may personally like you very much. As a social worker, she is trained to be nonjudgmental. She spends her working life trying to be helpful, trying to be positive, giving the benefit of the doubt whenever possible, and being very careful to accept people for what they are and to avoid imposing her own values on them.

Yet now she is in a position where she is required to make a judgment. She is required to impose professional standards and values—which are her own values—upon you and may have to write that, in her opinion, you have failed to meet these standards. It is not surprising that many field instructors shrink from doing this. They agonize over the decision. They defend the student in their own minds by telling themselves that it might have been different with another field instructor in another practicum setting. Then they think about the student's future clients who will inevitably be hurt if the student is allowed to continue.

There is also the matter of the field instructor's responsibility as a teacher. Teachers of adults are only responsible for teaching; they are not also responsible for ensuring that students learn. Nevertheless, if the student fails to learn, there is always a nagging doubt in the field instructor's mind. Perhaps the material could have been presented differently. Perhaps there could have been more or different feedback, a different client, a different project.

Even when the field instructor knows she has done all she could for the student, there is still a lingering temptation to blame herself anyway, to let the student pass the first practicum in the hope that the next one will bring improvement.

Evaluation as It Affects Your Social Work Program

To complicate matters further, a negative evaluation can cause friction with your social work program. Most of the time the field instructor only recommends the grade; it is the program, via the field liaison, that assigns it and makes it official. Therefore, the field instructor must have the full support of your social work program if the evaluation is to have a real effect. In general, administrators of social work programs like to feel that they turn out competent social work students. They may be tempted to blame the field instructor for the failure, particularly if the student is academically bright, has an engaging personality, or has otherwise won favor with the social work faculty.

If the standards of the classroom courses are lower than those of the practicum, the field liaison may not agree that the student should be given an unsatisfactory mid-term evaluation. She may transfer the student to another practicum setting or bring pressure to bear on the field instructor to change her mind, perhaps through the field instructor's own supervisor or someone more senior in the agency's hierarchical structure. This is unusual. Rarely will a social work program not support the recommendation of a field instructor, especially if she can document her own teaching methods, the learning opportunities afforded to the student, and the student's performance in specific learning objectives.

Nevertheless, the very possibility of being blamed for friction between the program and the placement setting may be enough to persuade a less effective field instructor not to recommend an unsatisfactory rating.

Evaluation as It Affects the Student

Obviously, the person most affected by the evaluation is you. If there has been good communication between you and your field instructor, the written mid-term evaluation should hold no surprises. Nevertheless, there is a difference between being told that some area needs improvement and seeing a written comment such as, "Jim seems disorganized with regard to administrative matters and fails to meet deadlines."

What about those time sheets you failed to turn in? Your field instructor has explained the importance of time sheets on many occasions, far too often in fact. But to you they remain a nagging chore. You feel vaguely guilty about them and vaguely defiant. After all, you did the important client-related work. But, above all, you had hoped that they would not be mentioned.

Now that they have been mentioned, what does this mean in terms of your overall mid-term evaluation? The answer, of course, depends on a number of factors. First, how often were you late presenting your time sheets? Once, twice, or on a regular basis? Second, is the problem only time sheets or do the time sheets reflect a general negative attitude toward administrative duties? Perhaps you feel that writing reports, submitting statistics, and doing paperwork is a silly waste of time and you are not about to perform a task that you feel is a waste of time. Perhaps you have said so, or you think you have made your opinion clear by staring at the floor whenever your field instructor mentions time sheets.

One of the learning goals set by some social work programs is that students must be able to *function effectively within an organizational context.* This can mean a number of things. Remember, when goal setting was discussed, you were advised to look at your practicum evaluation form and derive your learning goals in part from your program's required minimum standards. For example, Appendix A sets out four objectives (2.1 through 2.4) which more precisely define functioning in an organizational context. Remember that objectives are more specific than goals.

Objective 2.1 on page 239 states that you should have "demonstrated the ability to work within and interpret [your] practicum setting policy, structure, and function to clientele and others." Working within agency policies means that required paperwork should be submitted when required. Similarly, Objective 2.3 on page 241 states that you should have "demonstrated the ability to describe and analyze the relationship between agency policies and service delivery." This means, in part, that you should understand *why* you have to do paperwork.

For example, an accumulation of time sheets might have provided long-term, documented evidence that staff members spend an average of 30% of their time on administrative duties and that this average has increased by 10% in the last five years. In other words, they are now spending 10% less time than they did five years ago on other duties, such as service to clients. Eventually, the agency's board of directors may address this problem by reducing the paperwork, hiring another secretary, updating the computer system, or reallocating responsibility for paperwork. But these decisions can only be made on the basis of documented evidence.

Failing to submit your time sheet before the deadline means that you have not met Objective 2.1. Staring sullenly at the floor when time sheets are mentioned means that you have not met Objective 2.3. All is not yet lost, however. There are two other objectives that you may have met perfectly. For example, you may have helped Mrs. Valoroso obtain subsidized day care for her son Leon; thus, you have "demonstrated [your] ability to identify and link available services, resources, and opportunities to meet the needs of the client system" (Objective 2.2 on page 240).

You may have written a brilliant report in which you linked a growing number of single, working parents in the community to inadequate day care facilities and to an increasing number of cases of child neglect. This report "demonstrated [your] ability to understand the broad social issues facing the organization and the community" (Objective 2.4 on page 242). In addition, you may have tactfully and sympathetically explained to Mrs. Valoroso that agency policy requires you to make a home visit and you cannot complete the necessary forms if she is out every time you call. This masterly interpretation of agency policy to a client refers to Objective 2.1 and may balance out your lack of performance with the time sheets.

The whole evaluation is a matter of balance. Your field instructor will note areas for improvement with regard to organizational functioning: time sheets and sullen staring. She will also note your accomplishments: the brilliant report, the provision of subsidized day care, and the tactful explanation to Mrs. Valoroso.

Social work programs differ in the way they define the various areas of functioning, in the way they assess them, and in the way they evaluate their social work students and practicum as a whole. Your program's evaluation form is more than likely different from that presented in Appendix A. The learning objectives may be assessed on a 1 to 5 scale, a 1 to 10 scale, as poor/satisfactory/excellent, or in some other way. The practicum as a whole may be rated on a point scale, on a pass/fail basis, or on a credit/no credit basis.

The only flaw in the evaluation system is that *subjectivity* is necessarily present in the whole affair. Your field instructor will have records, written and taped, to support her opinion of your performance in various areas, but nevertheless it is an opinion. Some field instructors' standards are higher than others; some practicum settings' requirements are more stringent than others. The same student turning in the same performance may be assessed as poor in one practicum setting and outstanding in another, or as poor and outstanding respectively by different field instructors in the same practicum setting.

You may think that this is not fair. In fact, you are quite right, but the unfairness is largely unavoidable given the present state of the profession. No agreement has been reached among social workers as to precisely what having a BSW or MSW degree means; that is, the body of knowledge that students must possess upon graduation is not clearly defined. Because the body of knowledge has not been defined, the phases on the road to acquiring it cannot be defined either.

The result is that the learning goals and objectives demanded of a social work student in the first practicum are decided independently by the various social work programs and are recorded in a way that is inexact and open to various interpretations. Anything that is open to interpretation will inevitably be interpreted differently by different field instructors according to their own standards of social work. Your mid-term and final evaluations are thus inherently subjective. This will remain so until our profession has developed standardized criteria by which social work students can be assessed. The profession's delineation of standardized criteria probably will not happen while you are in your practicum, so it may be a good idea to go with what your program currently uses.

The subjectivity will work in one of two ways: either you will receive a lower assessment than you might in a different situation or you will receive a higher assessment. If you receive a higher assessment rating, you will naturally be delighted, but the delight may be short-lived. In your next practicum, where the standards may be higher, the level of performance considered as "outstanding" in your previous practicum now may be considered "weak." You may complain that *this* field instructor is unfair; whereas, you really experienced the unfairness in your last practicum which failed to properly prepare you for the second one. In the event that both field instructors have the same low standards, your delight may last until you perform poorly in your first job or until your inadequate training allows you to injure your first unfortunate client.

If you receive a low assessment rating, you may get indignant. You may compare your assessment with that of another student who, in your opinion, did not work harder or achieve more than you yet she received an "excellent" rating and you received "satisfactory." There are two things to remember here. First, you are not in a position to *know* what learning assignments the other student had. You may think you know but you have not examined her work with the same attention or from the same knowledge base as has her field instructor. Second, you do not know what difficulties she had to contend with. Perhaps she dealt nonjudgmentally and effectively with an abusive, alcoholic mother when her own mother was also abusive and alcoholic.

The question of making allowances for the skills and backgrounds of different students is always a difficult one for the field instructor. A practicum assessment is supposed to reflect the actual level of skills attained, not the number of problems the student solved in order to get there. Nevertheless, the problem-solving process in itself says something about the student. A student who has had to overcome her own prejudices to attain a certain skill level has learned more than one who has not; moreover, she has demonstrated self-awareness, self-control, and an ability to use herself for the client's benefit.

All other things being equal, a student who has struggled to achieve will probably be given a slightly higher assessment rating than another student who has reached the same skill level without a struggle. If this does not seem fair, remember that most field instructors look for two things: evidence that learning has taken place and evidence that the student has the ability to learn.

You may resent your "satisfactory" rating because you have never before been a "satisfactory" student. You have always been an "outstanding" student, a joy to your field instructor and a source of assistance to other, less talented peers. The first obvious point here is that a student who is outstanding in the classroom is not necessarily outstanding in the field. Similarly, a social work instructor who is an "expert" in a particular subject may not teach it very well. The second point is that "satisfactory" is not to be despised. "Satisfactory" means *"completely* satisfactory." It means that you have reached the required basic learning goals and you are fully competent as a social worker at your level of training. If you never saw a client until two months ago, if you never worked in the field before or never worked at all before, attaining a "satisfactory" rating is no easy accomplishment. It should be a source of pride.

When all this is said, you may still be unhappy. If you can manage it, discuss your unhappiness with your field instructor during the mid-term evaluation conference.

THE EVALUATION CONFERENCE

An evaluation conference, like your other conferences, will be far more productive if you have prepared for it. You should have the same mid-term evaluation form that your field instructor has (see Appendix A). You know what areas you are to be evaluated on and what evidence is to be used to indicate if you have reached your learning objectives. You can therefore evaluate yourself. In what ways have you demonstrated that you can function effectively in a professional context (Goal 1), in an organizational context (Goal 2), in knowledge-directed practice (Goal 3), and within an evaluative context (Goal 4)? In what ways have you failed to demonstrate these capacities? What overall assessment rating would you give yourself and more importantly, why?

Next, to what degree have you achieved your learning objectives? To what degree have you not achieved them? How were your learning goals related to your program's and your practicum setting's required standards? How were your assignments related to your objectives? Which assignments did you do well and which did you do badly? What does this information tell you about what you still need to achieve? How can you revise your learning goals and objectives to reflect your progress to date and the progress yet to be made?

If you have processed all this data ahead of time and written down your reasons for rating yourself the way you did, you will be better prepared to assimilate the feedback given to you during the mid-term evaluation conference. You will also be in a position to ensure that all of your triumphs have been taken into account.

In the meeting itself, it may be made clearer to you as never before that your field instructor is the instructor and you are the student. This obvious power imbalance may be intensified if your field liaison is also present at the meeting. Now there are two of them, who you may feel are positioned at the other end of the room in hawk-eyed, silent judgment.

The first thing to remember is that the hawk-eyed judgment is an illusion, mainly brought about by your own level of stress. The primary purpose of an evaluation, particularly a mid-term evaluation, is to evaluate your growth to date and to facilitate your growth for the next half of your practicum experience. The idea is to summarize your achievements for the benefit of the agency, your social work program, and yourself so that you can all see clearly what remains to be achieved.

This summary of achievements is brought about by conversation with your field instructor. Now is your chance to register a concern if there is anything on the evaluation form that does not seem fair. You might, for example, bring to your instructor's attention a particularly brilliant interview which you do not think she took fully into account. Or you might mention that you have submitted your time sheets before the deadline on the last three occasions, thus demonstrating a capacity "to function in an organizational context" and a desire to improve.

Your concern must be reasoned, focused, and based on documented evidence and examples. Your instructor's response will then also be reasoned, focused, and based on documented evidence and examples. She may explain to you that your brilliant interview was balanced, in her opinion, by a series of other, not-so-brilliant interviews with examples and explanations provided in the practicum evaluation form. She may tell you that although you have improved in the matter of time sheets, you did not submit this or that report, or perhaps a statistical analysis.

You can respond to these critical appraisals in a number of ways. The easiest and least productive is to become defensive and angry, or defensive and silent, or just defensive. It may be hard for you to hear your work criticized, particularly in the presence of your field liaison and most particularly if you interpret the criticism as criticism of yourself. If you can avoid becoming defensive about the negatives, you might be able to hang on to the positives. There will be positives. Your instructor will know how to use your positive qualities to make you feel better about yourself, and thereby provide a balanced appraisal of your competencies.

If you can accept the positives and negatives as equally merited, you may then be able to approach the real purpose of the mid-term evaluation: to guide your future growth by revising your learning contract in the light of your present achievement. Some of the learning objectives you wrote down at the beginning of your practicum may now seem almost trivial. For example, you may have written as one of your learning objectives that you wanted to learn "how to engage clients." As it turns out, by now, engaging clients is almost second nature; your problem is to stop them from deluging you with their life histories and keep them focused on the issue at hand. You may agree with your field instructor that the engagement objective has been achieved. Your objective instead, for the second half of the practicum, may be "to learn to clarify purpose with clients and establish a mutual contract."

Some objectives may seem irrelevant or unattainable; others, obvious now in the light of experience, should have been omitted entirely. Your task, immediately after the mid-term evaluation, will be to revise your learning contract, indicating which objectives need to be pared down or supplemented, which have been achieved, and which have been newly formulated based on identified deficiencies. As before, you will need to discuss these learning objectives with your field instructor and get the revised contract approved, in writing, by both your field instructor and your field liaison.

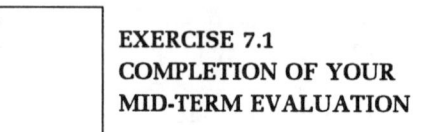

**EXERCISE 7.1
COMPLETION OF YOUR
MID-TERM EVALUATION**

Complete a mid-term evaluation of your performance in the practicum. As discussed, evaluation of your learning can take many forms. Use your journal, assignments, tasks, your program's mid-term evaluation form, and any previous exercises to assess your learning. Compare your program's mid-term evaluation form (if it has one) with the one provided in Appendix A. Although the completion of the evaluation is expected to be a cooperative effort, refer back to Exercise 1.2 on page 6 to determine whether you, your field instructor, or field liaison is ultimately responsible for evaluating, documenting, and summarizing your performance.

AN UNSATISFACTORY RATING

Even if you suffered some disappointment during your mid-term evaluation, the disappointment will soon pass. One exception is when an "unsatisfactory" assessment threatens your passing the practicum which, in turn, will threaten your social work career.

It is extremely rare that a student is rated "unsatisfactory" without a preliminary warning and a great deal of preliminary work on the part of the field instructor. In other words, you will not walk into the mid-term evaluation conference expecting a "satisfactory" and walk out having ignominiously "failed." An "unsatisfactory" should only follow from an identified and fairly major problem that has persisted despite efforts of your field instructor, your faculty liaison, and you to solve it. Such problems usually fall into one of the following six categories.

Resistant Attitude to Learning

Becoming defensive in the face of a disappointing evaluation is not productive or desirable, but it is perhaps excusable. However, if you are *habitually* defensive, if you *always* respond to criticism with denial or anger, it will be impossible for your field instructor to teach you. If she cannot teach you, it will be impossible for you to achieve your minimum learning goals and objectives that are required for you to pass your practicum.

Chronic Absenteeism

Your field instructor will always make allowances for a family crisis, an ailing automobile, or a life-threatening illness that keeps you away from the agency for a day or two. If the illness is really life-threatening, or if you have really suffered some personal disaster, arrangements may be made for you to make up the lost time, extend the practicum over a longer period of time, or even withdraw from the practicum with an "incomplete." An "incomplete" means that you can finish the practicum at a later date after you have coped with your personal disaster.

If you are absent habitually with flimsy excuses, if you are frequently late, or if you take two-hour lunch breaks, your field instructor will mention it to you. If you fail to mend your ways after repeated reminders, the result may very well be an "unsatisfactory" rating at your mid-term evaluation.

Personality Unsuited to Social Work

Not all people are cut out to be social workers. Some are naturally judgmental or abrupt in manner; some are overly businesslike or unapproachable; some are reserved to the point of coldness; some expect perfection from themselves and others. These kinds of personal characteristics are difficult to overcome and have a negative effect on relationships with clients. They are also problematic for the field instructor who has to advise her student, as tactfully as possible, to look for another career. She may point out gently to you that none of your clients have ever come back. She may point out, again gently, why she thinks this has occurred. She may try to help you develop different ways of relating to people.

Eventually, however, she will have to tell you that a different career might be more suitable and, if you will not voluntarily withdraw, she will have to recommend a failing grade to your field liaison.

Emotional Immaturity

Some of the most conscientious social work students are also very young. If you are still living at home, for example, and have always been financially supported by your parents, it may be hard for you to help a single mother balance her budget. If you are an immature 19-year-old, you may not be able to easily talk with an elderly man about death. If it seems to your field instructor that you have not yet developed the maturity required to be a social worker, she may advise you to withdraw for a year or two, gain some life experience and then come back.

Such advice is rarely well received because a student immature enough to need it will probably reject it. The only answer then for the field instructor is to assess the student as "unsatisfactory" and to document the reasons in writing to the field liaison.

The student who has emotional problems presents a particularly difficult dilemma for the instructor. Very rarely will a student in a practicum setting exhibit bizarre behavior or some other evidence of emotional upset. The field instructor, who is a trained and experienced social worker as well as a field instructor, cannot help but be aware that the student needs professional assistance. Normally, she will reach this conclusion long before the mid-term evaluation and will advise the student to obtain counseling outside the agency.

Unprofessional Behavior

Unprofessional behavior usually involves some breach of the *Code of Ethics* (presented in Figures 1.1 and 1.2), not out of ignorance but because the student does not seem to think the *Code* is important. For example, discussing the confidential affairs of clients in a loud voice in the local coffee shop may well earn you an "unsatisfactory." So may habitual failure to lock up client files, spreading client or agency tales with intent to harm, or other behaviors that demonstrate little regard for the client or the agency.

Inability to Speak English

Recent immigrants to the country may not yet have sufficient command of the English language to engage in a rapid discussion with a client, particularly if the client is upset and a little incoherent. These students may also have difficulty compiling reports and filling in necessary forms. Usually, the rating given under these circumstances will be "incomplete" rather than "unsatisfactory" since language skills will improve in time and, when they have improved, the student may become an excellent social worker.

GRIEVANCE PROCEDURES

If you are really unhappy with the results of the mid-term evaluation, the first obvious step is to discuss it with your field instructor and your field liaison. This process may possibly result in some form of a compromise. For example, you may agree to withdraw from the practicum rather than receive an "unsatisfactory." You then may have an opportunity to try a new practicum again at a later date in another setting, but your field instructor, your field liaison, and social work program must all agree that you be allowed to withdraw.

If the "unsatisfactory" has not resulted from a major problem but is more an accumulation of smaller things, your field instructor may allow you to finish the practicum, provided that you show a definite improvement in your activities in relation to specific learning objectives.

For a limited period, if she still hopes the problem can be resolved, your field instructor may even assume a therapeutic role during your supervisory conferences. Supervisory conferences are not therapy sessions. You are not a client, and your personal problems are your own business unless they are interfering with your work. If they are interfering, the field instructor may probe delicately in an effort to help you perform at a satisfactory level. As much as the field instructor might personally like to help you, though, the goal of her probing will be to increase your field performance and not the traditional goal of therapy. She may need to refer you for personal counseling.

If you cannot agree with your field instructor and field liaison to withdraw, seek counseling, accept a probationary practicum, or whatever is deemed appropriate, you may decide to appeal your field instructor's recommendation. The first step in this process is to determine your social work program's appeal procedures of mid-term grades. You may also consult your faculty advisor if one is assigned to you, or your practicum coordinator.

If their decision is that the assessment was justified and you are still unhappy, your only recourse is a formal university appeal. Appeal procedures vary considerably from one university to another and you should investigate the procedure at your university very carefully before you begin. We strongly urge you to think twice about appealing a failing grade in your practicum. It has been our experience that field instructors and field liaisons are very accurate in their judgments in reference to "weeding out" unsuitable social work students.

If it is the opinion of your field instructor, your field liaison, your faculty advisor, and the practicum coordinator that you should fail at mid-term, we suggest that you spare future clients of your inadequate practice skills by withdrawing from the social work program altogether.

Students rarely appeal a mid-term practicum rating. It is likely that your evaluation will pass without trauma and will fulfill its function of assessing and redirecting your growth.

SUMMARY

Your mid-term evaluation affects not only you but also your field instructor and your social work program. Your field instructor acts as one of the gatekeepers for the social work program. In this capacity, she is responsible for upholding social work standards and ensuring that students who are not yet competent do not pass the practicum until they have achieved the minimum standards (stated as learning goals) required by your social work program. Nevertheless, it may at times be difficult for her to assess a student as "unsatisfactory" because of the student's reaction, as well as the reactions of the field liaison and field coordinator.

Naturally, the person most affected by the evaluation is you. You should not be too worried at the prospect of the mid-term evaluation conference because you will be warned beforehand if any disaster is about to befall you. However, you should prepare for the meeting with the same care as you prepare for your supervisory conferences. Look over your program's practicum evaluation form (see Appendix A) and your learning contract (see Figures 4.1 through 4.4) and decide how well you have achieved on the basis of documented evidence, that is, on the basis of written reports, process recordings, videotapes, and so forth. You will then go into your evaluation conference prepared to absorb whatever feedback you receive. You will also be in a position to ensure that your mistakes have been properly balanced with your triumphs.

The primary purpose of a mid-term practicum evaluation is to assess your achievements to date in order to properly focus and direct your future growth. One of your major tasks after the evaluation will be to revise your learning contract by paring down or supplementing some learning objectives and adding or eliminating others.

It is very rare that students are assigned an unsatisfactory rating. "Unsatisfactory" will only follow from outrageous behavior or from some major problem that has persisted over time despite the efforts of the field instructor and student to solve it. In all likelihood your mid-term evaluation will prove to be nothing more than the completion of one more phase in your practicum experience.

We will now turn to some of the specific problem areas that you may encounter in your evaluation conference (Chapter 7) and practicum termination (Chapter 9). A few of them may already have arisen; some may not occur at all; and others may not appear until the second half of the practicum. You will probably not experience very many of them personally, but it is still useful for you to consider them.

SELECTED REFERENCES

Barnat, M.R. (1973). Student reactions to the first supervisory year: Relationship and resolutions. *Journal of Education for Social Work, 9,* 3-8.

Brennen, E.C. (1982). Evaluation of field teaching and learning. In B. W. Sheafor & L. E. Jenkins (Eds.), *Quality field instruction in social work* (pp. 76-97). White Plains, NY: Longman.

Collins, D., & Bogo, M. (1986). Competency-based field instruction: Bridging the gap between laboratory and field learning. *Clinical Supervisor, 4,* 39-52.

Dwyer, M., & Urbanowski, M. (1981). Field practice criteria: A valuable teaching/learning tool in undergraduate social work education. *Journal of Education for Social Work, 17,* 5-11.

Green, S.H. (1972). Educational assessments of student learning through practice in field instruction. *Social Work Education Reporter, 20,* 48-54.

Hartman, C., & Wills, R.M. (1991). The gatekeepers role in social work: A survey. In D. Schneck, B. Grossman, & U. Glassman (Eds.), *Field education in social work: Contemporary issues and trends* (pp. 310-319). Dubuque, IA: Kendall/Hunt.

Jenkins, L.E., & Sheafor, B.W. (1982). (Eds.). *Quality field instruction in social work.* White Plains, NY: Longman.

Larsen, J. (1980). Competency-based and task-centered practicum instruction. *Journal of Education for Social Work, 16,* 87-94.

Lemberger, J., & Marshack, E.F. (1991). Educational assessment in the field: An opportunity for teacher-learner mutuality. In D. Schneck, B. Grossman, & U. Glassman (Eds.), *Field education in social work: Contemporary issues and trends* (pp. 187-197). Dubuque, IA: Kendall/Hunt.

Schneck, D. (1991). Integration of learning in field education: Elusive goal and educational imperative. In D. Schneck, B. Grossman, & U. Glassman (Eds.), *Field education in social work: Contemporary issues and trends* (pp. 67-77). Dubuque, IA: Kendall/Hunt.

Sheafor, B.W., & Jenkins, L.E. (Eds.). (1982). *Quality field instruction in social work.* White Plains, NY: Longman.

Smith, S.L., & Baker, D.R. (1989). The relationship between educational background of field instructors and the quality of supervision. In M. Raskin (Ed.), *Empirical studies in field instruction* (pp. 257-270). New York: Haworth.

Tsang, N. (1989). Factors associated with fieldwork performance in a social work course in Hong Kong. In M. Raskin (Ed.), *Empirical studies in field instruction* (pp.337-358). New York: Haworth.

Waldfogel, D. (1983). Supervision of students and practitioners. In A. Rosenblatt & D. Waldfogel (Eds.), *Handbook of clinical social work* (pp. 319-344). San Francisco: Jossey-Bass.

CHAPTER 8

Dilemmas

MOST SOCIAL WORK STUDENTS sail cheerfully through their practicums without encountering any problems greater than missing the bus or forgetting to bring their lunch. A few stumble into difficulties with clients, field instructors, staff within the agency, or other students, sometimes through thoughtlessness or lack of guidance and sometimes through sheer misfortune. The following scenarios illustrate a few possible difficulties. Ideally, you will not encounter any of them. They are interesting to think about because they cover a wide range of situations.

CLIENT-RELATED ISSUES

Clients assigned to beginning students are carefully selected so that the student will have a good chance of success and will not be overwhelmed by the nature of the clients' problems. Clients selected in this way have usually approached the agency voluntarily, have a positive attitude toward social workers within the agency, and need a specific service that is easy to identify. Nevertheless, your field instructor may not be able to personally screen each of your clients and the occasional inappropriate client may slip through her protective net.

Suppose that your first interview with your first client goes something like this.

Scenario One

You (with a welcoming smile): "Hello, Mrs. Smith. My name is Martha Brown. I'm a social work student."

Mrs. Smith (glaring grimly): "I don't want a student. I want someone who knows what they're doing."

Mrs. Smith departs forthwith, ignoring your assurances, and you crawl away to find a place to hide. You relate the incident to your field instructor who soothes you, supports you, finds another social worker for Mrs. Smith and gives you Mrs. Brown instead. Mrs. Brown looks, if anything, grimmer than Mrs. Smith. After you have falteringly told her your name, you decide that you will not tell her you are a student until after you have established a rapport with her and demonstrated your ability to help. Somehow, a suitable time for declaring your studenthood never arrives but, apart from that, the interview goes well. You write a triumphant process recording, glossing over the student bit by writing simply that you introduced yourself, and your field instructor congratulates you on your developing interviewing and relationship skills.

A week or so later, you are present as an observer at a community support group session which your field instructor is facilitating. There, to your horror, sits Mrs. Brown. Your field instructor introduces you as a student. Mrs. Brown sits up straight, piercingly fixes her eyes on you, and remarks that you never said you were a student. Your field instructor also gives you the piercing eye, and you spend the session in acute misery, paying practically no attention to what is going on. After the session, your field instructor is gentle with you because she remembers the Mrs. Smith incident, but she also tells you quite definitely that your client had a right to know you were a student.

This said, she goes on to discuss the support group meeting, a discussion in which you are unable to participate intelligently because you were present only in body. You go home convinced that your field instructor thinks you are deceitful and naive and that Mrs. Brown thinks just about the same. The result of this conviction is that your relationship with your field instructor deteriorates and your next interview with Mrs. Brown is a bumbling disaster.

The moral here is that small deceits lead to larger ones. Be honest with your clients, your field instructor, and yourself. More examples of dilemmas are presented in Exercises 8.1 and 8.2. Dilemmas will occur in many relationships and contexts.

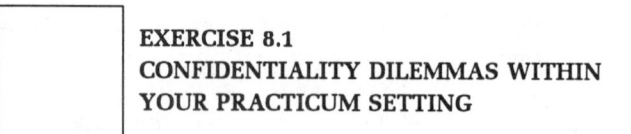

EXERCISE 8.1
CONFIDENTIALITY DILEMMAS WITHIN
YOUR PRACTICUM SETTING

Discuss the issue of confidentiality with your field instructor using each of the following case vignettes. Before the discussion, write your comments in the space provided following each exercise.

1. An adult client confides in you about a mutual genital exploration with an 11-year-old boy. There have been no complaints from the boy or from his parents. There is no evidence that such behavior was engaged in except for the information supplied by the client. Is there a need for you to document what the client told you? Remember, there is a possibility that someone else will be reading this file.

2. At a hospital setting, in a medical team conference, you are discussing a case of a 24-year-old woman who is undergoing tests to determine the cause and treatment for her inability to become pregnant. Prior to going back to school, you were employed in child protection services and knew the patient when she was 16 or 17 years old. You remember that at that time she had several VD infections. The patient recognizes you. She does not want her "past to be disclosed" and asks you to "maintain confidentiality." What can you do?

**EXERCISE 8.2
ETHICAL DILEMMAS WITHIN
YOUR PRACTICUM SETTING**

What ethical dilemmas have you had to deal with in your present practicum setting? How were they resolved? Write your comments in the space provided.

1. Client-related dilemmas:

2. Student-related dilemmas:

3. Instructor-related dilemmas:

Scenario Two

Having learned your lesson, you immediately inform your third client, Mr. Green, that you are a student. He seems a little reluctant to talk so you encourage him by giving your assurance that anything he says will be held in the strictest of confidence between the two of you. At the time, you believe this implicitly. Later, while you are talking to Doreen, the secretary, you realize that she is typing file records, including the information you obtained from Mr. Green. Later still, you learn that Mr. Green has asked for income assistance and your entry in his file has accordingly been shared with various government and law enforcement agencies. You think, with dismay, that you might as well have sent the record to the papers. Meanwhile, Mr. Green has discovered that what he said to you in the strictest confidence is now common knowledge in your local social service delivery system.

Filled with righteous indignation, he complains to your field instructor. Your instructor is still gentle as she explains to you that there is *absolute confidentiality*, where nothing your client says is shared with anyone in any form, and then there is *relative confidentiality*, where information is shared with colleagues as required. You will never be able to promise absolute confidentiality while you are still a student and, probably, you will never be able to promise it at all. Remember the *Code of Ethics* (Figures 1.1 and 1.2)?

Despite her gentleness, you feel that your field instructor is growing more and more convinced of your incompetence. You also feel vaguely resentful; she could have told you about relative confidentiality before. You look up confidentiality in your social work practice textbook to make sure and find the following principles:

1. Do not discuss your clients outside the helping setting (e.g., office, class, group, meeting) even if you change the names or details. Discussing clients with family or friends is not permitted. The social work profession is often very stressful and social workers sometimes need to "unwind" by talking about their feelings and the stress involved. Where such discussions involve clients, the discussion should take place at the office with supervisors and colleagues, not with family and friends who are not bound by the same rules of confidentiality as social workers. People may listen with interest to a social worker's story about her clients or her agency but, in the process, they may lose respect for the worker, the agency, or the profession. They may be thinking, "If I have a problem, I'll never go to her or any other social worker; it would get all over town."
2. If a client is not at home when you call, leave only your first name and say nothing about the nature of your business.
3. Do not become involved in formal discussions with colleagues over lunch or coffee. At a restaurant or other public place, there is obvious potential for your conversation to be overheard. Even when names are not mentioned, people might identify the client or think they have. If no identification is made, the nature of the discussion still gives others the impression that you are casual about confidentiality.
4. Make arrangements for your telephone calls to be taken by someone else when you are interviewing a client. Interruptions lead to a break in rapport and to inadvertent breaches of confidentiality. To the client, the message may be, "She has more important things to do than listen to me."

5. Ensure that your interview is private. It should be conducted in a private setting, not in the waiting room in view of other staff or clients.
6. Do not leave case records, telephone messages, or rough notes on your desk. Case records often have the name of the client prominently displayed on the file and they may catch the eye of someone passing by. Put your records away before you leave your desk and make sure that client files are locked up overnight. If a client observes that you are haphazard in managing your files, he may assume, with some justification, that you will be haphazard in protecting what he tells you.
7. Do not discuss clients at parties and other social activities. Colleagues often socialize together and, in such situations, it maybe very tempting to discuss a difficult case or talk about a case to illustrate a common problem.
8. Even if your client seems unconcerned about confidentiality, respect it anyway. Your client may want to begin the interview in the waiting room or initiate or continue a discussion in a public place. In such circumstances, gently defer the discussion until you can arrange a private setting.
9. The agency you work for is entitled to confidentiality regarding its internal operation. Your responsibility continues even after your practicum.

Scenario Three

Despite Mr. Green's indignation, your field instructor has decided that you should try to smooth matters over with him and continue to work with him. Your next contact with him is to be a home visit and another student at the agency has been assigned to go with you for moral support. On the morning of the visit, Tim, the other student tells you privately that he has urgent personal business to attend to and would you mind going by yourself. The field instructor need never know and it would help out Tim a lot.

You hesitate. You are away from home for the first time, living in a rural community when you are accustomed to city life. You selected a rural community because you had a theory that small towns were friendly, but this one seems to have closed its doors to outsiders. So far, you have not made many friends except for the other students, your field instructor does not seem particularly impressed, and your clients have not liked you much either. The last thing you want to do, at this point, is to alienate Tim.

You run into your field instructor as you are leaving the office. She looks at your three-inch heels, your short skirt and fitted shirt, your heavy makeup, sophisticated hairstyle, and dangling pieces of jewelry. Mr. Green, she points out tactfully, lives in a wooden frame house on a rutted dirt road in the middle of nowhere. Perhaps you would be more comfortable in different shoes and less restrictive clothes, and it would be a pity if you lost your jewelry. She adds that she thought Tim was going with you.

You tell her with some discomfort that Tim is meeting you in the parking lot and you will go home first to change your clothes. In fact, there is no time to change your clothes if you are not to be late for your appointment, and Tim is long gone looking after his personal affairs.

You are late anyway because road signs are few in the middle of nowhere and you had not believed that a road that bad would still be called a road. As you totter up the rickety steps to Mr. Green's front door, you notice that there is an outdoor toilet and a well with a hand pump a few hundred yards from the house. The implication strikes you slowly: no indoor bathroom, no running water in the house.

Mr. Green is more friendly toward you than you had expected. He ushers you into a room which appears to be carpeted with newspapers and dirty clothing. There is a wood stove in the corner with dangerous-looking pipes, a resident population of flies and roaches, and a smell whose origin you would rather not discover. Mr. Green removes a pile of something from an elderly sofa and invites you to take a seat.

He is far more communicative here than he was in the office. This house, he tells you with pride, has been in his family for four generations. He was born in it; he intends to die in it. You feebly try to follow why he introduced the thought of dying, Mr. Green, after all, is only 66 years old and he does not look suicidal. He appears, in fact, to be examining your legs.

You consider flight, telling yourself that you must have been mad to come here alone, in clothes so ill-designed for fleeing lecherous clutches. However, Mr. Green is not actively leering, he is merely looking; and he is talking while he looks, approaching the subject of your visit. As you listen to him talk, he seems less a potential rapist than a lonely, rather pathetic man. You are growing to understand him and his loneliness without family and friends.

You find yourself telling him about *your* lack of family and friends, enjoying his sympathy over your plight and his efforts to help you problem solve. In this same spirit of helpfulness, he offers you tea and homemade cake. You shudder inwardly but he would be very hurt if you refused and you are prepared to risk dysentery to preserve the relationship. You leave later than you had intended, basking in your new-found friendship and experiencing the first low twinges of indigestion.

There are several morals to this story. First, you were never in the slightest danger but you might have been. Mr. Green might have fallen on your legs with lustful cries. You might have run into trouble on that dreadful road. *Never go alone into a potentially dangerous situation.* If a situation might be dangerous—for example, if you are a child protection worker called to a case where the alleged offender has a history of violent behavior—*request an escort*, preferably a police escort. You will serve humankind far more effectively if you first pay attention to ensuring your own safety.

Second, your clothes should be appropriate to your task. You should not wear city clothes on a rural visit any more than you should go to a staff meeting dressed in a swimsuit. Third, there is the matter of your indigestion. Many of the homes you enter as a social worker will not be clean by your standards and in many of them you will be offered food and drink. If cleanliness is not an issue, you may be allergic to some foods, or doubtful about ethnic variations, or simply afloat on the proffered sea of coffee. You need to develop nonoffensive ways of refusing refreshments.

Fourth, your empathy with Mr. Green's friendless state led him to empathize with *your* friendless state so that your interview lost its focus and, before it was over, you had become the client. Sometimes it is helpful to divulge a little of your personal history to a client, but such a divulgence should be purposeful and focused on the client. It should never be used to gain an audience for a recital of your own woes. Neither should it reach the point where the client becomes the social worker and you become the client. Social workers have just as many woes as clients do—sometimes even the same woes—but the person to whom you can tell *your* tales of woe must be a relative, colleague or friend, or your own therapist, not an empathetic client.

Scenario Four

As well as continuing with Mr. Green, your field instructor has decided that you should continue with Mrs. Brown. Now that she knows you are a student, you are getting on extremely well with Mrs. Brown. She has a mother aged 84, she tells you, who is recovering in the hospital after a heart attack. Her mother does not want to go to a nursing home after being discharged, but neither can she live alone as she used to do. It would probably be best, Mrs. Brown says briskly, if she were to apply for legal guardianship of her mother and have her come to live with her. Touched by Mrs. Brown's obvious concern for her mother's welfare, you agree.

Further probing reveals that Mrs. Brown has a brother who is also prepared to look after their mother, but the brother's home would be totally unsuitable, Mrs. Brown says. The brother's wife, that Millie, has never gotten along with her. The brother's two boys are undisciplined horrors who would never give her a moment's peace. And anyway dear, Mrs. Brown finishes comfortably, you know how it is with men. Imagine being bathed by a man, dear, you at 84 and helpless in the tub. Imagine being diapered by your son.

Since you have never seen an adult in diapers, you display a suitable degree of horror. You agree, a little reluctantly, to go with Mrs. Brown to visit her mother and, if she consents, to appear in court on Mrs. Brown's behalf to obtain the legal guardianship. During your hospital visit, her mother consents quite cheerfully. You suspect that she would consent quite cheerfully to being dropped off the edge of a cliff, but this only reinforces in your mind the need for legal guardianship.

At this point, anxious about your impending court appearance, you approach your field instructor. Your field instructor draws a deep breath and clutches the edge of her desk. First, she says carefully, Mrs. Brown's mother is not your client. Discharge planning for Mrs. Brown's mother is the hospital's responsibility and you must not interfere with someone else's responsibility unless you are specifically asked. Second, there appears to be a dispute among Mrs. Brown, Mrs. Brown's brother, and their mother.

You must not take sides in a family dispute *ever*, whether the issue is property, custody, guardianship, or anything else. Last but not least, if the legal guardianship question proceeds any further, it is not unlikely that Mrs. Brown's brother will sue the agency, as well as you and/or your field instructor. You will not, therefore, appear in court. You will not see Mrs. Brown again or Mrs. Brown's mother or anyone having any connection at all with Mrs. Brown. And in the future, you will check with your field instructor before you promise any client so much as a second cup of coffee. Your field instructor releases her breath as you release yours. You had no idea that a simple promise, kindly meant, could have so many dangerous ramifications.

The moral here, of course, is that it is very easy to get in over your head through a sheer desire to be helpful. If you are not sure what you should promise to do for a client, promise nothing until you have asked your field instructor for advice.

Scenario Five

Mr. Green does not appear for his next appointment and you learn that he has been hospitalized with a stroke. You receive your field instructor's permission to visit him in the hospital and he seems pleased to see you and grateful for the visits. When he is due to be discharged, his social worker at the hospital asks for your input into the discharge planning. The medical staff is recommending a nursing home because Mr. Green is now partially paralyzed and can only walk with the help of a cane. Mr. Green, however, is mentally alert and has made it clear that he will not go into a nursing home. The next time you visit, he begs you to help him go home.

With Mrs. Brown vividly in mind, you do not make any promises. You relay the conversation precisely to your field instructor and she commends you on your restraint. Nevertheless, it is apparent that a value conflict exists regarding the recommendation you will make to the discharge planning team. Your field instructor believes that Mr. Green will deteriorate and possibly die if he is allowed to go home. You believe that Mr. Green understands this.

If he chooses to die in his own home rather than live in a nursing home, it is his decision to make. Your field instructor argues that he may adapt to the nursing home better than he imagines whereas, with all possible assistance, he would be unable to manage at home. It would be irresponsible, she says, to allow him to condemn himself without first giving the nursing home a try. You disagree. You think that he would never get out of the nursing home once he was in there and he would just die sooner and more miserably. Nevertheless, it is your field instructor's opinion that is relayed to the planning team and their decision is the nursing home for Mr. Green.

The moral here is that sometimes you will disagree with a decision made by a team on behalf of your client. This is always painful. You may feel the urge to protest angrily and loudly, to write bitter letters, to make a scene, to withdraw from your practicum in disgust. None of these behaviors will help your present client and they will certainly jeopardize your ability to help your future clients. You can only continue to function by learning to cope rationally with decisions you believe to be wrong.

STUDENT-RELATED ISSUES

You will not only run into client issues such as those just mentioned, but you may also run into dilemmas with other students as well. Consider the following scenario.

Scenario

Your costudent, Karen, is a very religious person. She makes no secret of the fact that she has been "born-again" and she wants others to share in her experience. One day she appears at work wearing a T-shirt with "Repent Your Sins" emblazoned on the back. She is called into the field instructor's office and emerges red-eyed and resentful because she has been told that her dress is inappropriate. She intends to protest to the instructor's supervisor and asks you, if you believe in religious freedom, to lend her your support.

First, suppose that you yourself are a born-again Christian. You agree with

Karen's views, you consider it her moral duty to express her beliefs, and you have only refrained from wearing such a shirt because you know your field instructor would disapprove and you have enough tension already. You therefore go with Karen to the supervisor's office. There you are told quite firmly that you are entitled to your own beliefs but so are other people. Some clients and some staff, too, may be offended by the shirt. Since social workers have a particular duty to avoid imposing their personal values on other people, Karen should not wear the shirt or any similar shirt again. If the behavior persists, further action will have to be taken.

You and Karen carry your complaint to your field liaison with similar results. Karen does not wear the shirt again and the incident passes. However, you are left with the feeling that it is now you and she against the world. Social work, you think, is definitely an environment that pays lip service to tolerance while accepting, in fact, only the most conventional of behaviors.

Now suppose that you are not a born-again Christian. You do not share Karen's views but you believe she has the right to express them and you go with her to the field instructor's office. You discover, once more, that a social worker's right to self-expression is limited. If you do not support Karen, for whatever reason, you may find the relationship strained. You stand to lose an important component of your practicum: the student support system.

The issue here, of course, is a social worker's right to express religious, political, or sexual beliefs that others may find deviant. Topics such as homosexuality, abortion, extramarital relationships, communism, fascism, separatism, and a whole variety of other "isms" are all potentially explosive. Issues that are not explosive at all to the majority culture may conjure sparks within minority groups. Social workers are not personally more or less tolerant than members of other professions.

Some social workers blithely accept just about everything; others hold deep-seated and sometimes rigid views about the moral acceptability of this or that. The difference between a social worker and a member of another profession is that the social worker is required to be nonjudgmental with clients. Social work is done within the client's belief system, from the client's point of view, towards the client's ends. If the social worker does not happen to agree with the client, it is not her place to say so. She must not impose her own views on the client; she must not disrupt the helping process with a statement of her own beliefs.

T-shirts bearing slogans, badges, buttons, crests, some types of clothing, and even some hairstyles carry a clear message about the wearer's own beliefs. Such messages may not be given by a social worker to a client; therefore, it follows that a social worker in the workplace is more limited than other people in the matter of dress and general freedom of expression. It is a strange paradox that increased tolerance for the client's freedom of expression leads to a reduced tolerance for the social worker's freedom of expression. It is odd that the social work world demands more conventional behavior from its inhabitants than do other worlds *because* of its need to be tolerant. However, that is the way it is. If you are to become a social worker, you must be prepared to accept the way it is.

INSTRUCTOR-RELATED ISSUES

You may also run into dilemmas with your field instructor. Consider the following two scenarios.

Scenario One

So far, your relationship with your field instructor has not been a bed of roses. To add to your problems, Tim was seen by a client in the shopping mall when he was supposed to have gone with you to visit Mr. Green. Somehow, the news reached your field instructor, who immediately confronted you. She noted the fact that you had told her a direct untruth and then she explained at length about solitary excursions turning into potentially dangerous situations. You do not know what she said to Tim but he was red-eyed for at least a couple of days.

When your field instructor tells you that she will be out of town for the following week, you breathe a soft sigh of relief. Another backup instructor whom you do not like very well has meanwhile been assigned to help you with any problems that may arise. You are determined that none will arise but, in fact, one does. You find yourself discussing this problem over lunch with a third worker whom you like much better than the one that was assigned to you. He gives you good advice and you do not bother to discuss the problem with your backup field instructor or with your regular field instructor when she returns.

A week later, when you have another minor problem, you wander into your mentor's office. Again, he gives you good advice and, again, you do not bother to take the problem to your field instructor. You continue asking him about your difficulties for another month until the situation comes to your field instructor's attention.

It is apparent at first glance that she is angry. She reminds you of the occasion when you accompanied Karen to her supervisor's office. You did not discuss the T-shirt issue with her first; you did not air your own feelings about it or give her the opportunity to explain why she thought that Karen's dress was inappropriate.

Instead, you went immediately to her supervisor. Now, you have established a habit of taking your difficulties to another staff member without also sharing them with your field instructor. Do you see that she cannot do her job as your field instructor unless she is aware of your problems and unless there is frank communication between the two of you? What are your feelings on this matter?

Your first feeling is bewilderment. You asked for advice, informally, from a person you liked; you did this in part because you had a desire to appear competent in the eyes of your field instructor. You wanted to appear to have solved your problems on your own, and you wanted to make up for past mistakes by coming up with a good performance. You see your field instructor's point of view but you privately think that she is overreacting.

There are two issues here. The first is the hierarchical structure of your practicum setting and the second is the continuity of your learning experience.

By now, you will have looked at your agency's organizational chart. In every agency, there are lines of authority, usually passing from the board of directors to the executive director to department heads to supervisors within the departments to front-line workers. Roles, responsibilities, and limits of decision-making authority are carefully defined. Formal lines of communication are set up to control and facilitate the passage of information. The importance of information should not be underestimated. By far, information is the most important tool/weapon that any administrator can possess, from the lowliest supervisor to the chairperson of the board.

When you went to your field instructor's supervisor without first consulting her, you were guilty of a double sin: flouting established lines of authority and depriving your field instructor of information. When you asked advice from another social worker without your field instructor's knowledge, you were guilty of the same two sins.

There are times when you will work quite legitimately with social workers other than your field instructor. On these occasions, however, your field instructor will *know*. She probably will have assigned the worker you are to work with; she will have planned the projects you are involved with; she will have discussed any problems with you and the other social worker. This way her authority is in no way undermined and her information system is left intact.

If you remember the two key words, *authority* and *information*, you should be able to avoid potential problems with your field instructor and other workers. Remember, too, that authority is particularly precious to those who have very little. Some social workers assigned to work with you may have no supervisees. They may want especially to be informed before the fact of anything you are going to discuss with your field instructor; and it is common courtesy to inform them.

The second issue has to do with the continuity of your learning. You should realize by now that learning in your practicum is not a random matter. It has been carefully planned by you and your field instructor so that your learning goals will be reached in phases, one experience building on another and leading on to a third. Furthermore, your planned practice experiences are designed to fit with the theoretical material you have learned in the classroom. The minimum standards set by your social work program underpin the material taught in the classroom. Your practicum learning goals, as well, are drawn from the program's minimum standards and in this way the connection between theory and practice is established.

Your field instructor is your guide on this planned path of learning. If she is not kept fully informed about your experiences, your problems, and your achievements, she cannot guide you and you cannot learn. Moreover, not all social workers are qualified to be field instructors. Your mentor, during the month or so you asked him for advice, did not mention to your field instructor that he was advising you. He, too, flouted the lines of authority and information. He was more guilty than you and he proved by his behavior that he is not yet ready to be a field instructor.

Scenario Two

Throughout your school life thus far, you have been supported by your parents. Recently, however, your father lost his job and his financial contribution to you has diminished by a substantial amount. You have been obliged to take a part-time job to make ends meet; you arrive at your practicum already tired with another endless day ahead. Your performance and even your interest in your performance have dropped to unsatisfactory levels.

Your field instructor confronts you with her perception of your failing efficiency. Do you agree with her estimate? Is anything wrong? Is there anything she can do to help? You agree wholeheartedly with her estimate but you do not want to discuss your personal problems with her. You feel your relationship is not good enough for that. Neither do you want to discuss them with your field liaison whom you do not know well, and there is no one else you feel you can approach. You drag helplessly on and you finish, as you suspected you might, with an "unsatisfactory" mid-term practicum assessment rating.

Many students have personal problems that interfere minimally with their practicum performance. Problems in the areas of money, transportation, failed romances, or family stresses are not uncommon. For some students, however, personal problems can prove to be overwhelming; they threaten their practicum and possibly their entire social work careers. Your field instructor is not in a position to intrude in your personal life. The most she can do is to point out your work deficiencies and stand ready to help you if she is asked. Your field liaison is in the same position; in fact, she is in a worse position because she is not present in your practicum setting to monitor the sequence of events.

However reluctant you may be to disclose your personal affairs, it may be better for you to do so than to risk an unsatisfactory rating. Neither your field instructor nor your field liaison want to see you fail. They will do everything in their power to help you out of your difficulty and arrange the practicum to suit your needs, without prying, with the very minimum of intrusion. Often, all you need to do is ask.

SUMMARY

Ideally, you will never encounter any of the situations we discussed, but reading about possibilities will enable you to be more sensitive to their possibility. Problems may arise around your clients, your field instructor, other staff, or other students in your practicum. There may also be personal difficulties that detract quite noticeably from your professional performance.

Some students do not like to admit that they are students. Perhaps, if you are older, you do not feel comfortable in the student role and avoid any mention of the fact out of sheer embarrassment. If age is not a factor, you may feel that a client who knows you are a student will not accept you, or a colleague will not believe you are competent. Skipping the "I am a student" part when you introduce yourself may not appear to be a major blunder. However, it is tantamount to misrepresentation and misrepresentation *is* a major blunder. It is illegal for you to make claims about yourself or your services that are inaccurate or cannot be substantiated. You make such a claim by omission when you fail to say you are a social work student and allow clients to assume that you are a qualified social worker.

Beginning social workers sometimes promise clients that "anything you say will never go beyond this room." In fact, information about clients is commonly typed by secretaries and is shared with agency staff, staff from other social service agencies, and various government and law enforcement bodies. It is therefore untrue and unethical to promise a client *absolute* confidentiality. The most you can do is to ensure *relative* confidentiality by guarding your files, watching your tongue, and giving out information only to those who need it to serve the client.

Courting danger in pursuit of providing service to clients is neither selfless nor noble—it is merely foolish. You should not go alone into any situation that is potentially dangerous. Whether the danger exists, of course, is a matter of judgment. Your field instructor may have a number of reasons for asking you to take a companion, none of which is connected with danger. Perhaps she wants another student or a worker to observe your interview; perhaps two students are to be involved with the same client. Nevertheless, if you are supposed to go with someone, go with someone. Do not go alone.

Social workers have the same needs as clients for sympathy and sharing. The helping relationship, by its very nature, involves an unusual degree of closeness and it is easy, in the midst of this closeness, to create a confusion between helper and client. Any sharing of your personal life with a client must be purposeful and intended for the benefit of the client.

Some clients are good at manipulating social workers, particularly beginning social workers who are inexperienced in the art of manipulation. You may be persuaded to involve yourself with another worker's client. You may find that you have inadvertently taken sides in a family dispute. Such situations can create conflicts between social workers, between agencies, and with clients. In the worst case, the client, or a relative of the client, may take legal action against the individual worker and/or the agency. It pays, therefore, to inform your field instructor about your involvement every step of the way.

Sometimes decisions regarding your client are not made by you alone, but by a team. You may be tempted to make an emotional protest if the team reaches a decision with which you do not agree. Such behavior will not help your present client and may jeopardize your ability to help future clients. The social work world is relatively rigid with regard to codes of behavior, dress, and even expression. The reason for this is not that social workers as a group are less tolerant than other people; rather, social workers must take particular care not to impose their values on their clients. Some forms of dress or behavior make a clear value statement and thus are discouraged in the social work environment.

If you are to maintain good relationships with your field instructor and other workers within your practicum setting, it is important for you to respect established lines of authority and communication. Respect for your field instructor's position will also help to ensure that your learning proceeds along a planned path. Practice goals based on theory will be achieved in easy stages, each experience designed to build on the one before it.

Occasionally, personal crises may disrupt the learning process. It may be difficult for you to disclose your personal problems to your field instructor or your field liaison, but, if you can bring yourself to do so, they will probably do everything in their power to help you and will intrude only minimally into your affairs.

We will now turn to the last phase of your field practicum experience—the termination process.

SELECTED REFERENCES

Barnat, M.R. (1973). Student reactions to the first supervisory year: Relationship and resolutions. *Journal of Education for Social Work, 9,* 3–8.

Barth, R., & Gambrill, E. (1984). Learning to interview: The quality of training opportunities. *Clinical Supervisor, 2,* 3–14.

Berengarten, S. (1961). Educational issues in field instruction in social work. *Social Service Review, 35,* 246–257.

Blake, R., & Peterman, P. (1985). *Social work field instruction: The undergraduate experience.* New York: University Press of America.

Dwyer, M., & Urbanowski, M. (1981). Field practice criteria: A valuable teaching/learning tool in undergraduate social work education. *Journal of Education for Social Work, 17,* 5–11.

Grossman, B., Levine-Jordano, N., & Shearer, P. (1991). Working with students—emotional reactions in the field: An educational framework. In D. Schneck, B. Grossman, & U. Glassman (Eds.), *Field education in social work: Contemporary issues and trends* (pp. 205–216). Dubuque, IA: Kendall/Hunt.

May, L.I., & Kilpatrick, A.C. (1989). Stress of self-awareness in clinical practice: Are students prepared? In M. Raskin (Ed.), *Empirical studies in field instruction* (pp. 303–320). New York: Haworth.

Waldfogel, D. (1983). Supervision of students and practitioners. In A. Rosenblatt & D. Waldfogel (Eds.), *Handbook of clinical social work* (pp. 319–344). San Francisco: Jossey-Bass.

Wijnberg, M.H., & Schwartz, M.C. (1977). Models of student supervision: The apprentice, growth, and role systems models. *Journal of Education for Social Work, 13*, 107–113.

Wilson, S. (1981). *Field instruction: Techniques for supervisors.* New York: Free Press.

CHAPTER 9

Termination

IN A SENSE, YOU have been preparing for termination from the first day you walked into your practicum setting. Everyone knew from the beginning that you would only be there for a specified period of time. You knew. Your clients were assigned to you on that understanding. Any projects you were involved in were designed so that they could be completed in the time available.

Nevertheless, there is a sadness to every ending, even if it is mingled with a feeling of relief. You are saying goodbye to people, a place, a phase of your life. The rituals that you must go through with regard to closure and evaluation are not only practically useful, they should also provide a sense of completion, of things having ended right.

TERMINATING WITH YOUR CLIENTS

Every session you have with a client involves a termination phase. About 10 minutes before the interview is due to end, you tell the client that 10 minutes remains, you deal with unfinished business, you summarize the session, and you make arrangements for the next session. Termination of the helping relationship follows the same process, except that there will be no following session. The client still has a life and may possibly still have a problem, however.

If client goals have not been achieved or additional problems have come to light, the client may need to be referred either to a different agency or to another worker in your agency. In either case, you will need to summarize the client's progress to date so that the new worker will understand the situation and can assess whether the referral is appropriate. It is also courteous to speak personally with the worker to whom you have made the referral. Even if there is no referral, you will need to prepare a closing summary to share with the client and to enter in the client's file.

For example, Mrs. Smith's elusive problem may finally have been defined as an inability to manage her budget, compounded by a tendency to spend the rent money on marijuana. At your suggestion, Mrs. Smith enrolled in a drug rehabilitation program. For a month or two, all seemed well. Mrs. Smith arrived at every interview with a lined sheet of paper ruled neatly into "income" and "outgo," accompanied by receipts, none of them for the purchase of marijuana.

Then, a chance remark by Jane, her 7-year-old daughter, revealed the fact that Mrs. Smith had recently acquired a number of boyfriends. Confronted, Mrs. Smith agreed that a friend she met in the drug rehabilitation group had shown her how to supplement her income. The budget was balanced, Mrs. Smith said cheerily. She was happy; Jane, properly fed and clothed for the first time in years, was also happy; the boyfriends were especially happy.

You are not as happy, but by now you have developed an affection for Mrs. Smith, with her toothy beam and her balanced budget. She, on her part, regards you as the only person in her life who knows she is a prostitute, knows she does drugs, and still recognizes her as a concerned mother and a worthwhile person. She does not perceive that she has a problem any more, but she still likes to come and talk. When you leave, she says, she will probably stop coming; it would not be the same with anyone else.

You think that she probably will stop coming even though you have referred her to another social worker. In your care, she has progressed from supporting her habit with the rent money to supporting it through prostitution but you are still reluctant to let her go. You like her—you will miss her. In a strange way you are almost as dependent on her as she is on you.

An experienced worker will usually be able to prevent a client from becoming dependent on a helping relationship and will certainly be able to avoid becoming dependent on a client. A beginning worker, anxious to establish empathy, is more likely to slide into a comfortable though unproductive mutually dependent relationship. It is just as well that your relationship with Mrs. Smith will end because you are leaving; but the termination of any long-term helping relationship will always have difficult elements.

One of the things you can do is warn your clients well beforehand, to give them plenty of time to adjust to the idea and gradually reduce the frequency of their visits. For example, instead of seeing Mrs. Smith weekly, you might see her once every two weeks and then once every three weeks. During the last session, you can summarize with her how far she has come and what problems remain to be resolved, and introduce her to her new social worker. If she is to terminate with the agency, you can tell her that she is welcome to return if the need arises. Few agencies conduct follow-up interviews with clients because of limited resources but, ideally, a contact several weeks after official termination and another a few months later is a good idea.

TERMINATING WITH YOUR FIELD INSTRUCTOR

Terminating with your field instructor formally begins with your final evaluation conference. It is very similar to the preliminary and mid-term evaluations discussed in previous chapters of this book. Complete Exercises 9.1, 9.2, and 9.3 as a part of the formal ending phase in your practicum setting.

Your relationship with your field instructor may have been excellent, indifferent, or relatively poor depending on the circumstances and you and your field instructor's individual qualities. Whatever the relationship, you owe it to your field instructor to sit down with her at the end of your practicum and review with her what went right and what went wrong, and what would have been a helpful alternative. When you leave she will probably have another social work student. She will be able to teach this student more effectively if she receives feedback from you about how well you thought she functioned in her teaching role. Some social work programs require a formal evaluation of your field instructor's performance and your practicum experience as part of the termination process. Others assume, more informally, that you will provide feedback in the same way that feedback was provided to you. Exercise 9.1 on pages 205–213 is useful to you in reference to your evaluation of your field instructor.

Availability of Field Instructor

The first item in Exercise 9.1 has to do with the availability of your field instructor. Did she schedule, and keep, regular conference meetings with you? Were these sessions frequent enough and long enough to adequately monitor your progress? Was she there between supervision sessions to give advice, support, and direction if you encountered an unexpected problem? Did she assign another worker to take over as your field instructor if she had to be away for any period? Of course, your expectations will take into account the fact that she had other things to do. You will not rate her as ineffective because she failed to run to your aid every time you thought you needed assistance.

An important element of availability is approachability. She may have been physically there when you had a problem, but was she there in the sense that you were comfortable in asking your questions? Did she encourage contact or did she make you feel that you were a nuisance, a burden, an unwanted interruption? If you did feel like a nuisance, try to decide objectively whether you *were* a nuisance. Was your anxiety level so high at the beginning that you asked about *everything*, even things you could have figured out for yourself? Did you lie in wait for her in corridors, trap her at coffee breaks, cling helplessly to her through every minor problem? Even if you did those things, she should have been able to manage your dependence without injuring your self-esteem. Nevertheless, you should make allowances. When you rate her on availability, rate her on whether she was *reasonably* there and *reasonably* approachable.

If you were a nuisance and you are now in a position to see that you were, consider your realization an indication of how far you have come. You are now more confident, more able to handle routine problems. You will probably be confident enough to sit down with your field instructor and discuss the various ways in which she effectively or ineffectively dealt with an anxious and dependent beginning social work student. You will probably also need to produce examples of what would have been helpful to you in those situations where she was ineffective. The next anxious and beginning student will certainly benefit if you do this.

Knowledge Base

The second item in Exercise 9.1 refers to your field instructor's knowledge base. How much does she know about the type of clients the agency serves, the community resources, the organizational system, and the peculiarities and policies within the system? Certainly she will know more than you do in these areas but there may be other areas in which your knowledge is greater.

It is sometimes difficult for a field instructor to keep up with the pressures of her own work and also to keep abreast of innovations in the field. You as a student, newly emerged from your textbooks, are in a position to bring information into the agency about the latest social work theories and techniques. The pearls of wisdom provided to you by your classroom teachers can be shared with your field instructor and other agency staff. Sharing these pearls is a matter requiring discretion. Your field instructor may feel threatened by you. She may feel that her own knowledge and skills are indirectly being questioned. Nevertheless, one of the hallmarks of a knowledgeable person is the willingness to acquire new knowledge.

Was your field instructor willing to learn from you—provided, of course, that you expressed your knowledge with a suitable regard for her sensibilities? Was she willing to consider new approaches? Did she ever admit, openly and honestly, that she did not know but she was interested in finding out? Did she ever suggest that another social worker knew more than she did in a certain area and would be better able to answer your question?

When it comes to evaluation, you probably will not be able to judge the strength of your field instructor's knowledge base very accurately, apart from a general feeling that she knows, or does not know, what she is doing. You should, however, have some sense of her openness to learning. If she is receptive and not defensive and if she is willing to admit, without embarrassment, that she does not know everything, you can rate her fairly high on knowledge.

Ability to Direct Learning

The third item in Exercise 9.1 is your field instructor's ability to direct your learning. Did she work with you on understanding your practicum's learning goals and objectives? Did she then assign you to projects relevant to those objectives and clients who would challenge but not overwhelm you? Did she suggest added activities to expand your indirect learning such as sitting in on a committee meeting or paying a visit to a different community setting? Did she discuss your suggested activities with you to see if they would help you meet your learning objectives? Was the focus of your learning directed only to case management and agency-specific procedures, or did she link theory and practice to events and the dynamics of your assignments? Your field instructor's ability to help you integrate classroom and practice is a very important aspect of your practicum learning experience.

You are expected to take primary responsibility for your learning experience but your field instructor is supposed to guide you, especially at the beginning. If a situation worked well for you, it may have done so because your field instructor selected it carefully, with regard to its level of difficulty and your skill level. If you were bored or in over your head, your field instructor may have made a misjudgment.

From the privileged pinnacle of hindsight, you are now in a position to evaluate your field instructor's ability to place you in appropriate situations. Are there any situations you remember where the work was too difficult, too easy, or just about right? You might mention these to your field instructor and give reasons why they were difficult, easy, or about right. She will then have a better idea of which assignments are appropriate and which may be problematic for her next student.

Use of Self to Impact Knowledge

The fourth item in Exercise 9.1 is evaluating her ability to impact *your* knowledge. How well did she teach you? Did she help you understand your own habitual patterns or themes of interaction? Did she point out your emerging interviewing styles? Did she create links for you between what you did and what you might have done in a way that enabled you to do it better next time?

As a beginning social work student, it is likely that you have a natural affinity for people. In the stress of conducting a first interview, you may remember little of what you were taught in school. Theories about engaging and focusing, active listening, and summarizing may be lost in the general confusion. Nevertheless, your natural talents will carry you through. Empathy and warmth may be instinctive for you; interest may be genuine; caring may be easy. It is your field instructor's task to mold this natural ability into a conscious technique. She must make you aware of your strengths so that you can use them purposefully to benefit your clients.

For example, she may have asked you to videotape your first interview or to make a detailed process recording. She may have then pointed out to you that you were using reflection of content when you repeated to Mrs. Smith something she had just said. When you rephrased Mrs. Smith's words to give them a slightly different meaning, you were using interpretation. The silence you were worried about in the middle of the interview was, in fact, a positive use of silence. One of your questions resulted in clarification; another was an appropriate use of confrontation; a third was an inappropriate change of topic, which allowed the client to evade the issue at hand.

Through this kind of analysis, your field instructor can help you to be aware of techniques you may have used by chance. Her comments are specific and constructive. Her criticisms are directed at your practice, your struggle to become a professional social worker, and not at you personally. She should have used your initial efforts as a teaching tool to reinforce your strengths and point to areas that need improvement.

When you come to evaluate her field instruction ability, look first at how far you have progressed since the beginning of the practicum. Were you sufficiently challenged by your practice assignments? Compare your first process recording or tape with one you have just completed. Probably, the improvement will be apparent and will give you a measure of just how much you have learned. You can also evaluate your improvement in other areas. How much have you learned about how your practicum setting functions?

Do you know what resources are available in your community and how to access them? What knowledge have you acquired about the types of clients your agency serves and the special problems that may confront them? Did you learn anything about research, about management, about group process, about interpersonal relations?

Of course, it was you who did all of this learning; but you must still give your field instructor part of the credit. Try to remember what techniques she used to help you learn. Perhaps she made you a temporary member of a research committee or took you with her to an interdisciplinary meeting or asked you to help her balance a budget. Perhaps she assigned you a statistical project involving time sheets or showed you how to design a newsletter using graphics.

Which of her teaching techniques were effective? Which were less effective?

Why? If you can review with her what teaching methods were best for you in getting across specific material, she will be able to relate the method and assignments to your personal qualities. This will guide her with future students when she is trying to teach the same thing.

Evaluation Process

The fifth item in Exercise 9.1 has to do with your field instructor's evaluation of you as a student. You received a preliminary evaluation at the beginning and a comprehensive one at mid-term. You will receive a final evaluation before you leave; it should follow exactly the same format as the mid-term. However, as we mentioned in Chapter 7, a formal evaluation should not hold any surprises. Evaluation is an ongoing process; it begins on the first day and continues with every contact between you and your field instructor. Its purpose is to provide you with relevant, timely, and specific feedback so that you can use each learning experience as a stepping-stone to the next. The first question, therefore, asks you if evaluation was ongoing as opposed to periodic.

The second question asks you if the evaluation was fair. A fair evaluation is one that points out your strengths and weaknesses in a specific manner on the basis of objective evidence. For example, your field instructor may say in your final evaluation, "Betty has greatly improved her interviewing skills this semester." You would not complain that this is unfair, although it is unfair, because it is positive. However, if your field instructor says instead, "Betty's interviewing skills need work," you might complain, and with some justification.

The remark that your interviewing skills need work is obviously true, everyone's interviewing skills need work, but it is neither fair nor useful. To be useful, it has to be specific. For example, "Betty has difficulty obtaining social histories," points to a clearly defined interviewing skill that needs improvement. To be fair, it has to be documented. Your field instructor may document it by adding, "Betty needed two or three additional contacts with all her clients before she could obtain a complete social history."

In short, the question, "Was it fair?" is not asking whether it was negative. Unfair evaluations may be positively glowing; fair evaluations may be glowing or disastrous. When you answer the question about the fairness of your field instructor's evaluation of your progress within your practicum, you should ask yourself whether her comments were specific enough to be useful and whether they were documented with reference to your work.

The fourth part of evaluation explores the extent to which you agreed with your field instructor's evaluation. However objective your field instructor tries to be and however much documentary evidence she tries to produce, some parts of your practicum evaluation will still rest on her own perception. For example, she may say, "Betty feels she is not accepted by agency staff, whereas, in reality, staff members both like and accept her."

Unless you can accurately survey the attitudes of agency staff, you cannot know objectively which is the correct perception. There should not be many remarks on your formal evaluation that are purely a matter of perception, particularly if they are negative remarks. During your supervisory conference sessions your field instructor may have voiced some perceptions that you did not agree with. It is probably not worth mentioning these unless the difference of opinion led to a particular conflict or a deterioration in the relationship.

Expectations

The sixth item in Exercise 9.1 deals with your field instructor's expectations about your performance. In general, did you feel that she expected too much of you or too little, or were her expectations just about in line with your own? One of the problems facing you as a beginning practicum student is that you are usually not sure what the expectations are.

A problem facing the social work profession is that there is little agreement about what the expectations ought to be. For example, everyone agrees that you should be able to "identify and select appropriate helping strategies." However, the *degree* to which you should be able to identify and select appropriate helping strategies by the end of your first practicum is open to question.

You will probably conclude that your field instructor's expectations were too high if you found difficulty in meeting them, too low if you met them very easily, and about right if they gave you a satisfying challenge. You might also compare your field instructor's standards with the standards imposed on other students by other field instructors.

In the long run, your judgment must be subjective, but there are still ways in which a subjective judgment can be useful. For example, if every student remarks that a particular field instructor's expectations are low, it is likely that her expectations *are* low relative to those of other instructors. She may pick up on this herself or be advised by your field liaison to raise her standards.

Feedback

The seventh item in Exercise 9.1 refers to feedback: its continuity, depth, and quality. The ongoing nature of feedback has already been discussed. The distinction between quality and depth mostly has to do with whether the feedback is correctly focused at the listener's level. For example, feedback given to a MSW student may be expected to probe a topic to a greater depth than feedback given to a BSW student. From the point of view of the graduate student, feedback that does not attain the required depth would not be quality feedback. However, the more involved feedback provided to a student, the greater the possibility of confusion.

"Quality" feedback may, therefore, be viewed as feedback that provides sufficient information to meet the needs of the recipient. When you are trying to decide whether your field instructor gave you quality feedback, all you need to ask yourself is, "Was it clear and useful?"

Conflict

The eighth item in Exercise 9.1 deals with the level of conflict. You will have had a very dull and unusual practicum if you have not disagreed at all with your field instructor. Disagreements in some areas are normal, almost inevitable, and often productive. Disagreement, though, is not the same as conflict. The word *conflict* implies a sharper disagreement in which the differing opinions held by the combatants are very deeply felt. For example, in the last chapter, you thought that Mr.

Green should be allowed to return to his own home after his stroke and your field instructor thought that he should go to a nursing home. Earlier in your practicum you may have found it difficult to disagree with your field instructor—the power balance, after all, is unequal—but this time, on Mr. Green's behalf, you were prepared to stand your ground. You argued rationally, logically, and sometimes passionately; your field instructor countered; and in the end it was her opinion that prevailed.

Whether or not this conflict was resolved depends on how you felt about losing. Resolution does not necessarily mean that one of you must change sides and agree with the other; there are many conflicts which, in this sense, can never be resolved. Resolution does mean that, if you cannot agree, you can amicably agree to disagree. You can live and let live. Your relationship can survive the difference of opinion. For example, if you still felt, after the heat of the argument had cooled, that your field instructor was blind, unfair, insensitive, and obstructive, and if you resented her and her decision and possibly the entire discharge planning system, then the conflict was not resolved. On the other hand, if you understood that she genuinely believed in what she said and had sound reasoning to back it up, then the conflict was resolved.

Decisions affecting people's lives are made regularly in social work, often around contentious issues. Conflicts arise frequently because most social workers are prepared to go to battle for their clients. For all agencies not to become hotbeds of constant strife, social workers must be skilled in resolving conflict. One of your tasks during your practicum is to learn to disagree without resentment, and one of your field instructor's tasks is to help you learn this. When you answer the question about resolution of conflict, you should not be looking for areas of agreement; you should be looking, instead, for the presence of resentment.

Teaching Style

The ninth item in Exercise 9.1 asks you whether your field instructor's teaching methods made allowance for your learning styles. Learning styles have already been discussed in Chapter 5. If you learn best through active experimentation, for example, and your field instructor expected you to learn through reading and talking things out, you may have experienced frustration.

Remember, when answering the question, that your field instructor could not take your learning style into account if you did not tell her what it was. If you did tell her, and she was still unable to provide you with appropriate learning experiences, this fact is worthy of note.

Level of Autonomy

The tenth item in Exercise 9.1 has to do with autonomy and independent learning. Naturally, you will need more guidance during the first practicum than you will during subsequent ones. You can expect your independence at the beginning to be limited. Your field instructor must find a reasonable balance between dogging your every step and allowing you complete autonomy. The optimum balance will vary with the individual, depending on each student's inclinations and abilities. Essentially, you must give a subjective estimate of how comfortable you felt with the degree of freedom you were allowed.

Did you feel suffocated or rootless or free within secure limits? Did your field instructor assign you every task, ignoring your attempts to find tasks for yourself? Did she welcome or stifle your bids for independence? Was she responsive to your suggestions? Was she overcontrolling and anxious or uncomfortably permissive?

Overall Effectiveness and Recommendations

When you come to integrate all the different parts of your evaluation into an overall rating (the eleventh item in Exercise 9.1), you will appreciate the difficulty your field instructor has in assessing your performance. Your evaluation will be taken seriously by your field liaison, your field instructor, the practicum coordinator, and the agency. Negative comments will pierce your field instructor's heart; positive comments will boost her self-esteem.

All comments, if reinforced by other students over time, will have an eventual effect on whether your field instructor continues as a field instructor and, possibly, on whether the practicum setting continues to have students. More students may be assigned, or fewer, or none, or a different type of student. You have a responsibility to your program, your practicum setting, and your field instructor to give as honest an evaluation as possible. An honest evaluation should also be constructive. If you have a negative comment to make, add recommendations (item twelve) as to how the situation might be improved and balance the negatives with positives. Finally, do you have recommendations about this practicum setting for your field instructor, your field liaison, your integrative seminar instructor, your social work program, and future students?

**EXERCISE 9.1
EVALUATION OF YOUR
FIELD INSTRUCTOR**

1. Availability of field instructor

   Regularly scheduled conferences:

   Informal consultation:

Reasonably approachable:

2. Field instructor's knowledge base

    Describe:

    Willingness to acquire new knowledge:

3. Ability to direct learning

   Assisted in development of learning objectives:

   Degree to which others directed your learning:

   Linked knowledge or theory to practice situations:

   Assigned projects relevant to learning experiences:

4. Ability to impact knowledge

   Reinforced your strengths:

   Identified areas for your improvement:

   Challenged you by assignments:

   Used appropriate teaching techniques:

5. Evaluation process

   Was it ongoing?

   Was it fair?

   Was it specific?

   Extent of agreement:

6. Field instructor's expectations

   Realistic?

   In relation to other social work student expectations:

7. Ability to provide feedback

   Continuity:

   Depth:

   Quality:

8. Level of conflict

   How resolved:

   Tolerated differences of opinions?

9. Learning and teaching style

   Describe:

   Goodness-of-fit:

10. Encouragement of independent learning and autonomy

    Balance between freedom and guidance:

    Responsive to suggestions:

11. Overall effectiveness of the field instructor

    Quality of supervision:

12. Recommendations for

   Field instructor:

   Field liaison and practicum coordinator:

   Integrative seminar instructor:

   Agency/practicum setting:

   Future students:

TERMINATING WITH THE AGENCY

Before you leave your practicum, you will say your goodbyes to people you have met, particularly those whom you have worked with closely. You should not automatically assume that it is goodbye forever. Social work is a small world and it is likely that you will meet these people again, very soon or in future years. If you part on a positive note, you will not only feel better about your practicum experience, you will have made an investment in your social work career.

You will be asked to evaluate your practicum setting in the same way you were asked to evaluate your field instructor (Exercise 9.1). Exercise 9.2 is an example of an evaluation form that you can use to evaluate your practicum setting.

Attitude of Agency

The first question in Exercise 9.2 asks about the attitude of the social workers and staff toward social work students. Did they accept you, want you, like you, or did you feel rejected? If you did feel rejected, make a particular effort to decide whether it was a real rejection or if it was due, at least in part, to your imagination. Many beginning students are anxious to be accepted by agency staff, so anxious that they see rejection where it is not intended.

Factors other than acceptance should also be taken into account. Did other social workers cheerfully use you like a workhorse, assuming you were there to do whatever no one else had time for? If they did, that is flattering in its way. At least they thought you were competent. But it also shows a lack of understanding of your student role. If they did understand that you were there to learn, did they contribute to your learning? Did they willingly answer your questions, offering information and adding explanations? Did they suggest that you accompany them to noon lectures, special presentations, or other events approved by your field instructor? Did they appear to mind if you sat in a corner reading?

Your assessment of the social workers' attitudes will necessarily be subjective. You should accordingly be very careful that you have not read into a look or a gesture something that was never there. Reading in a practicum setting seems sometimes to be associated with a certain amount of guilt. Other social workers are not reading; they are not even sitting; they are dashing hither and thither in a flurry of activity. You may have felt that it was lazy to sit down with a book, but reading is a way to learn, and learning is why you were there. It will be important for you to clear with your field instructor if it is all right to read at your practicum and what reading material is appropriate. Sometimes students read for their classroom courses while they are at their practicums. This may or may not be acceptable to the field instructor. Some do not mind if the reading materials are directly related to the practicum setting or the client's problem, but they do not approve of reading general classroom assignments.

Available Assistance

The second item in Exercise 9.2 asks if assistance was available in times of a crisis. The definition of a crisis depends on who is doing the defining. You may have thought you were in a crisis and resented the fact that nobody ran to your aid. On the other hand, your perception of crisis is still a crisis and it is not unreasonable to expect that someone will take the time to explain to you why things are not as bad as you thought. Occasionally, of course, you may have been involved in a genuine crisis and then you certainly had a right to expect assistance.

When you answer the question about assistance in crisis, consider three things. First, did you know whom to ask, failing the presence of your field instructor? Second, did the person you asked respond to your satisfaction at the time? Third, looking back at the situation, do you think that the response was adequate given the actual nature of the crisis? If you did not know where to go for help or if you received inadequate help, these things are worthy of mention.

Learning Opportunities

The next item asks you to evaluate the range of learning opportunities in your practicum setting. In terms of quantity and quality of learning opportunities, did the available assignments and projects provide you with different types of learning? You were only involved with those cases particularly relevant to your learning needs. Other students, with different needs, may have been given other kinds of cases. Assignments can provide direct and indirect learning. If you are not sure what variation the agency has available, this is a good question to ask your field instructor.

In this question you are essentially evaluating the practicum setting as an environment for field education learning. What learning opportunities were available to you in terms of number and type of cases and exposure to different situations? You can give the number of cases you were involved with and describe briefly the kinds of problems they presented; be careful not to give client names or other identifying information. Nonclinical experiences will also be of interest, particularly less usual ones. For example, if your agency has recently introduced a nonsmoking policy, you may have been involved in a survey of staff reactions. Or perhaps a special event was being planned and you were a member of an interagency committee.

Physical Layout

The fourth item in Exercise 9.2 refers to the physical layout provided to students. Your evaluation here should take into account the practicum setting's facilities. Perhaps there was only one interviewing room equipped with a one-way mirror and you only interviewed one client there because it was in much demand by other staff. Perhaps there was a limited number of video or audio machines.

Perhaps you did not observe a social worker doing play therapy or art therapy with children as you had hoped because facilities were not available. Note points that seemed important. For example, the one-way mirror may have been helpful to you because, although you only interviewed once in front of it, you observed on a number of occasions from behind it.

Orientation Procedures

Orientation procedures, the next item, should be quite straightforward. You can state whether you attended a formal orientation meeting, were given a guided tour, received a student manual, and so forth, or whether your orientation was more informal, consisting of introductions and a tour by your field instructor. You might also note whether your orientation was adequate. Were you still confused about the filing system? Did you know where to find a pen? Were you given material containing agency policies and procedures to read so that you knew at least where to go for information in case you had a question?

Workload

The next question asks you whether your caseload was heavy, light, or satisfactory. The optimum size of a caseload depends on a number of factors. First, how many other activities were you involved in? If casework was only a part of your total learning experience, two or three cases may well have been a satisfactory load.

Second, how complex were the cases assigned? Some cases demand a great deal of attention, both in terms of analyzing and planning and in terms of the number of contacts required. Other cases need only a few contacts and involve fairly routine provision of material assistance.

Third, at what level were you required to explore and document your cases? For example, you may have been asked to prepare a treatment plan for each one, listing key facts, the projected feelings of all significant persons, possible behavioral manifestations of feelings, desired goals including time frames, measurements for goal achievement, intervention strategies, and conditions of intervention. You may have been asked to incorporate a single-subject research design into each case, with an analysis of results and a final report. You may have been asked for a written analysis of each taped interview and a process recording for each interview that was not taped. Of course, all this is highly unlikely. Nevertheless, some field instructors prefer that you study a few cases thoroughly rather than work with a number at a more superficial level.

Your estimate of your caseload will depend on how well you were able to cope with it. If you had difficulty, you will probably say it was heavy; if you were comfortably occupied, you will say it was satisfactory. This is as good a way to do it as any, but you should also take into account the speed at which you work. Do you think, for example, that you work faster than average and that another student, given your satisfactory caseload, might have found it too heavy? Perhaps you had an integrative seminar or group conference that gave you some basis for comparison of yourself with other students in field education.

Learning Environment

The seventh item in Exercise 9.2 asks whether the practicum setting's environment was conducive to learning. The focus here is on the environment of your practicum setting, not on your home environment or other personal factors affecting your performance. Were you comfortable at the agency? Were there stresses such as fear of evaluation or interpersonal tensions?

Accomplishment of Learning Goals

The next question asks whether you were able to accomplish your learning goals and objectives. Your responses here will probably be that you accomplished some goals and objectives fully and others to a certain extent. If there are definite reasons why you were not able to accomplish some goals and objectives to the degree you would have liked, you can note these reasons.

For example, the ninth question asks whether your practicum set any blocks or barriers to learning. You may have been blocked in your desire to learn about work with children because the practicum setting did not have the facilities to provide a playroom. You may have been blocked in your desire to practice couple counseling because it was your field instructor's policy to assign only individual clients to beginning students.

All practicum settings have limitations and you should have been aware of most of them before you accepted the practicum setting, and certainly before you set your learning goals and objectives. For example, if you had a strong desire to observe work with children and you had a practicum setting which did not provide such interventions, you can hardly blame the setting for blocking the achievement of your objective. On the other hand, some limitations are not apparent until you are actually in the setting. Perhaps you carefully established that the practicum setting provided couple counseling but you did not know that, as a beginning social work student, you would not be allowed to practice it. You can note in your evaluation those limitations that affected your learning and that you were unlikely to have known about before entering the setting.

Finally, add a comment regarding whether your practicum setting was your first choice. Even if it was not, did it turn out to be better, worse, or as you expected? To what degree were you satisfied with the overall learning experienced? Would you recommend this practicum setting to future social work students? Why or why not? Is it more suitable for some types of students than others?

Evaluating your practicum setting is important information as you terminate the experience and begin to plan for future learning. In addition, evaluation provides important information that both the practicum setting and the practicum coordinator need for ongoing planning, development, and monitoring of practicums for student learning.

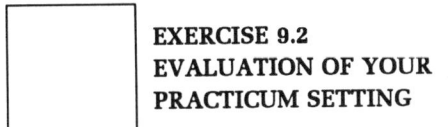

**EXERCISE 9.2
EVALUATION OF YOUR
PRACTICUM SETTING**

1. Evaluate the attitude of agency social workers toward social work students.

   Understanding of student role:

Contribution to your learning:

2. Was assistance available in times of crisis?

   Nature of help available and response:

   Designated alternative field instructor:

   Degree of satisfaction:

   Adequacy of response given the nature of the crisis:

3. Evaluate the range of learning opportunities.

   Availability of learning opportunities:

   Exposure to different situations:

4. Evaluate the physical layout for students—space, facilities, etc.

5. Evaluate the agency's orientation process.

6. Evaluate the workload.

    Quantity of work:

    Complexity of assignments:

    Nature of documentation requirements:

7. Was the agency environment conducive to learning? (Specify.)

8. Were you able to accomplish your learning goals? (If not for what reasons?)

9. What practicum limitations affected your learning which you were unlikely to have known about before entering the setting? (Specify.)

10. Was this practicum your first choice? (Why or why not?)

   Degree of satisfaction:

11. Would you recommend this practicum setting for future social work students? (Why or why not?)

EXERCISE 9.3
YOUR FINAL EVALUATION

Generally, it is the social work student who assumes major responsibility for the task of writing the evaluation. The final comments are then negotiated with your field instructor and field liaison. It is very important to determine whether it will be you, your field instructor, or your field liaison who will take responsibility for documenting and recording your final evaluation. Check to verify the responsibilities of each member of the practicum team and record them in the spaces provided. Check your responses to Exercise 1.2 on page 6. Have any of these responsibilities changed over the semester? If so, why?

1. Your responsibilities:

2. Your field instructor's responsibilities:

3. Your field liaison's responsibilities:

Complete your final practicum evaluation. Use the same evaluation form you used at mid-term (see Appendix A). Remember to refer to your learning contract, assignments, journal recordings, tapings, and other types of documentation to substantiate your performance.

PREPARING FOR YOUR NEXT PRACTICUM

At the beginning of this chapter, when we discussed termination with clients, we mentioned that the termination phase normally includes making arrangements for the following session. In the same way, termination of the first practicum involves making plans for the second one (if appropriate).

If your social work program has a second practicum, it will be different from the first in that you will not be starting from the very beginning. You now have some skills, some practical knowledge, and a clearer idea of where you are going. In a way, you pose a greater challenge to your second field instructor as a higher-level student since she cannot now assume that you know nothing. She must assess your existing skills and knowledge before she can know what assignments will be appropriate for you.

You can help your next field instructor in this task if you complete your own self-evaluation at the end of your practicum. You will have to do this anyway to prepare yourself for your final evaluation but now you can take it one step further. You can write down not just what you have achieved in this first practicum but what you would like to achieve in the second. In other words, you can start to tentatively formulate your learning goals and objectives and begin to write your second learning contract.

Review the examples of various learning contracts in Figures 4.1 through 4.4 (pages 115–118) and your own learning contract, Exercise 4.1, as a basis for the next one. Now write down some tentative goals and objectives that emerged from your final evaluation for your next practicum. Use Exercise 9.4 on the following page to develop your list.

Of course, these goals and objectives will have to be revised to conform to the nature of the second practicum setting; however, you will have a guide. You will have written down, while still fresh in your mind, the learning goals and objectives you have reached and the goals you have not yet reached, your strengths, your weaknesses, and your preferred methods of learning. You will have prepared a beginning map to your overall professional career. In fact, you may already have some thoughts about the type of practicum setting that may best meet your educational needs. In this regard, Exercise 9.5 on page 226 asks you to list potential future practicum settings. Unlike your first practicum, many agencies and services are now familiar to you; so you have a head start in the selection process. Ideas can then be put into a plan of action that is ready when you start the next practicum process.

You have now survived your first practicum. A tremendous amount of learning has occurred. Congratulations. You deserve a pat on the back! The outcome of this process is, of course, that you are now very well prepared to have a second successful practicum. You can be sure that surviving in your next practicum, or starting work, will be second nature to you.

**EXERCISE 9.4
GETTING READY FOR YOUR
NEXT PRACTICUM SETTING**

Based on your experience in this practicum setting and your final practicum evaluation, write a list of learning needs for your next practicum. Identify your needs in the space provided below.

**EXERCISE 9.5
POSSIBILITIES OF FUTURE
PRACTICUM SETTINGS**

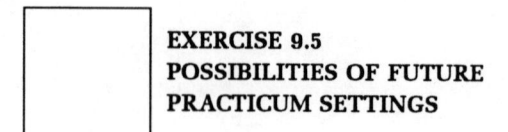

List potential future settings for your next practicum. What steps might you take to begin planning for it? Write names of agencies and your plans in the spaces provided. Keep focused. This process may help put your ideas into action when you begin your next practicum.

SUMMARY

Ending your practicum involves terminating with your clients, your field instructor, and the agency as a whole.

Tell your clients well in advance that you will be leaving to give them time to prepare psychologically. It is sometimes advisable to reduce the frequency of your contacts toward the end, seeing them once every three or four weeks, for example, instead of every week. During the last session, you can summarize how far the client has come and what problems remain to be solved. You can also introduce the new worker if the client is to remain with the agency or discuss the transfer to a new agency if the client has been referred.

You owe it to your field instructor to sit down with her at the end of the practicum to review the field instruction process. You may be required to fill out a field instructor evaluation form and she, like you, will not want any surprises. The form will generally cover areas pertinent to learning and her instruction, although the form you are given will more than likely be different from Exercise 9.1.

A good field instructor should be available and approachable. She should also have a sound knowledge base and be able to direct your learning in ways that will facilitate the achievement of your goals. She should know what teaching methods are likely to be effective in light of your preferred learning styles and she should be able to evaluate fairly how much you have learned. Evaluation is ongoing and should be provided in the form of quality feedback at each supervisory conference session. The mid-term and final evaluations will then be only a formal summary of what has been said before.

Disagreement between you and your field instructor in some areas is normal and often productive. However, conflicts involving deeply felt opinions must be resolved if the relationship is to be preserved. In some cases, it will not be possible to reach agreement and resolution will only come through an agreement to disagree.

A good field instructor will allow you as much independence as possible, taking into account your abilities and the vulnerability of the client system. Expectations of your performance will be set at a level that is generally consistent with the standards of other field instructors.

When you have evaluated your field instructor and overcome the difficulty of integrating all the various elements into an overall rating, you will next be asked to evaluate your practicum setting along the guidelines contained in Exercise 9.2. Pertinent areas with regard to the practicum will generally include the attitude of the social work staff, assistance in times of crisis, available case assignments, orientation procedures, learning opportunities, caseload level, agency limitations, and the provision of a physically and emotionally sound learning environment.

Preparation for your final evaluation will include completing a self-evaluation. You can use this self-evaluation to formulate tentative goals for your second practicum period or for a work experience. These goals will obviously have to be revised when you begin the practicum in order to accommodate the nature of the setting, but at least you will have given yourself a guideline.

As well as a tentative list of learning goals, you will have the advantage next time of knowing a little more about what you want from a practicum. You will be a little less anxious because you have been through it all before. You will have the skills and practical knowledge to enable you to move on to a more challenging practicum setting. We hope you have truly enjoyed your first practicum experience and hope this book contributed to that enjoyment. Good luck with your next learning experience!

SELECTED REFERENCES

Barnat, M.R. (1973). Student reactions to the first supervisory year: Relationships and resolutions. *Journal of Education for Social Work, 9,* 3–8.

Brennen, E.C. (1982). Evaluation of field teaching and learning. In B. W. Sheafor & L. E. Jenkins (Eds.), *Quality field instruction in social work* (pp. 76–97). White Plains, NY: Longman.

Collins, D., & Bogo, M. (1986). Competency-based field instruction: Bridging the gap between laboratory and field learning. *Clinical Supervisor, 4,* 39–52.

Dwyer, M., & Urbanowski, M. (1981). Field practice criteria: A valuable teaching/learning tool in undergraduate social work education. *Journal of Education for Social Work, 17,* 5–11.

Fine Holtzman, R., & Raskin, M. (1989). Why field placements fail: Study results. In M. Raskin (Ed.), *Empirical studies in field instruction* (pp. 77–88). New York: Haworth.

Fortune, A.E., Feathers, C.E., Rook, S.R., Scrimenti, R.M., Smollen, P., Stemerman, B., & Tucker, E.L. (1989). Student satisfaction with field placement. In M. Raskin (Ed.), *Empirical studies in field instruction* (pp. 359–381). New York: Haworth.

Green, S.H. (1972). Educational assessments of student learning through practice in field instruction. *Social Work Education Reporter, 20,* 48–54.

Grossman, B., Levine-Jordano, N., & Shearer, P. (1991). Working with students' emotional reactions in the field: An educational framework. In D. Schneck, B. Grossman, & U. Glassman (Eds.), *Field education in social work: Contemporary issues and trends* (pp. 205–216). Dubuque, IA: Kendall/Hunt.

Johnston, N., Rooney, R., & Reitmeir, M.A. (1991). Sharing power: Student feedback to field supervisors. In D. Schneck, B. Grossman, & U. Glassman (Eds.), *Field education in social work: Contemporary issues and trends* (pp. 198–204). Dubuque, IA: Kendall/Hunt.

Larsen, J., & Hepworth, D. (1980). Enhancing the effectiveness of practicum instruction: An empirical study. *Journal of Education for Social Work, 18,* 50–58.

Lemberger, J., & Marshack, E.F. (1991). Educational assessment in the field: An opportunity for teacher-learner mutuality. In D. Schneck, B. Grossman, & U. Glassman (Eds.), *Field education in social work: Contemporary issues and trends* (pp. 187–197). Dubuque, IA: Kendall/Hunt.

Raskin, M. (1989). Factors associated with student satisfaction in undergraduate social work field placements. In M. Raskin (Ed.), *Empirical studies in field instruction* (pp. 321–336). New York: Haworth.

Schneck, D. (1991). Integration of learning in field education: Elusive goal and educational imperative. In D. Schneck, B. Grossman, & U. Glassman (Eds.), *Field education in social work: Contemporary issues and trends* (pp. 67–77). Dubuque, IA: Kendall/Hunt.

Wijnberg, M.H., & Schwartz, M.C. (1977). Models of student supervision: The apprentice, growth, and role systems models. *Journal of Education for Social Work, 13,* 107–113.

Wilson, S. (1981). *Field instruction: Techniques for supervisors.* New York: Free Press.

APPENDIX A

Practicum Evaluation Form
(Mid-Term and Final)

Student name: _____

Practicum setting: _____

Field instructor: _____

Field liaison: _____

Integrative seminar instructor: _____

Mid-term *or* final evaluation (circle one)

Date: _____

Semester: Fall _____   Winter _____   Other _____

Appendix A

INTRODUCTION

This generic practicum evaluation form has been devised to provide a guide for the mid-term and final evaluation of student practice in the practicum. The following four learning goals have been selected for the evaluation:

1. Functions effectively within a professional context
2. Functions effectively within an organizational context
3. Functions effectively utilizing knowledge-directed practice skills
4. Functions effectively within an evaluative context

It is intended that this form will serve as an evaluation guide for students in the practicum. The student should have a copy of this form at the outset of the practicum and should be encouraged to use it for self-evaluation throughout the entire course.

In addition, it is expected that the field instructor and field liaison will use this evaluation form for ongoing assessment as well as for mid-term and final evaluations of the student's performance in the practicum.

Although the completion of the evaluation form is expected to be a cooperative effort between the student and field instructor, the field instructor is ultimately responsible for rating, documenting, and summarizing the student's performance.

Feedback

The field instructor, field liaison, and student are requested to conjointly discuss and examine each learning objective and provide an example of how the objective was achieved and an example of how it was not achieved (if appropriate).

LEARNING GOAL 1: FUNCTIONS EFFECTIVELY WITHIN A PROFESSIONAL CONTEXT

The student will develop an understanding of the profession of social work and will demonstrate both professional development and an ability to function within a professional framework. This includes articulating and applying knowledge and values within a generalist social work framework.

Learning Objectives:

1.1 Has demonstrated an understanding of the "person-in-environment" concept from a social work perspective.

How demonstrated:

How not demonstrated:

Specific areas that need improvement:

On the scale below, rate the practicum student in relation to this specific learning objective from 1 to 10 where 1 means "complete failure" and 10 means "complete success."

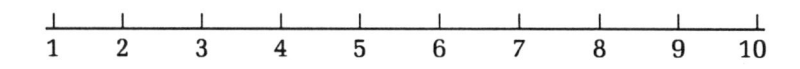

```
1   2   3   4   5   6   7   8   9   10
```

What specific tasks and/or behaviors need to be demonstrated to raise the above rating on the next practicum evaluation? Explain in detail below.

1.2 Has demonstrated values consistent with those of the profession and an understanding of and commitment to ethical standards.

How demonstrated:

How not demonstrated:

Specific areas that need improvement:

On the scale below, rate the practicum student in relation to this specific learning objective from 1 to 10 where 1 means "complete failure" and 10 means "complete success."

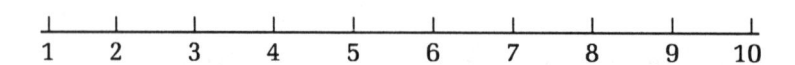

```
 |   |   |   |   |   |   |   |   |
 1   2   3   4   5   6   7   8   9   10
```

What specific tasks and/or behaviors need to be demonstrated to raise the above rating on the next practicum evaluation? Explain in detail below.

1.3 Has demonstrated the ability to engage in a variety of social work roles.

How demonstrated:

How not demonstrated:

Specific areas that need improvement:

On the scale below, rate the practicum student in relation to this specific learning objective from 1 to 10 where 1 means "complete failure" and 10 means "complete success."

```
|____|____|____|____|____|____|____|____|____|
1    2    3    4    5    6    7    8    9    10
```

What specific tasks and/or behaviors need to be demonstrated to raise the above rating on the next practicum evaluation? Explain in detail below.

234 *Appendix A*

1.4 Has demonstrated the ability to recognize the impact of personal behaviors and values on others.

How demonstrated:

How not demonstrated:

Specific areas that need improvement:

On the scale below, rate the practicum student in relation to this specific learning objective from 1 to 10 where 1 means "complete failure" and 10 means "complete success."

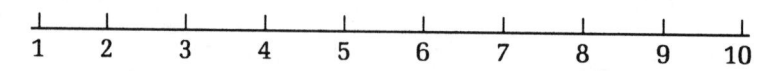

```
|----|----|----|----|----|----|----|----|----|
1    2    3    4    5    6    7    8    9    10
```

What specific tasks and/or behaviors need to be demonstrated to raise the above rating on the next practicum evaluation? Explain in detail below.

1.5 Has demonstrated the ability to take initiative toward increasing knowledge and skills relevant to performance demands.

How demonstrated:

How not demonstrated:

Specific areas that need improvement:

On the scale below, rate the practicum student in relation to this specific learning objective from 1 to 10 where 1 means "complete failure" and 10 means "complete success."

```
|----|----|----|----|----|----|----|----|----|
1    2    3    4    5    6    7    8    9    10
```

What specific tasks and/or behaviors need to be demonstrated to raise the above rating on the next practicum evaluation? Explain in detail below.

A

1.6 Has demonstrated the ability to utilize field instruction appropriately by active participation and preparation.

How demonstrated:

How not demonstrated:

Specific areas that need improvement:

On the scale below, rate the practicum student in relation to this specific learning objective from 1 to 10 where 1 means "complete failure" and 10 means "complete success."

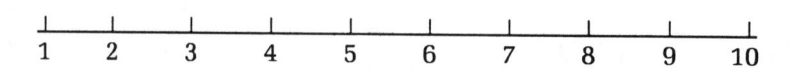

```
|----|----|----|----|----|----|----|----|----|
1    2    3    4    5    6    7    8    9    10
```

What specific tasks and/or behaviors need to be demonstrated to raise the above rating on the next practicum evaluation? Explain in detail below.

1.7 Has demonstrated the ability to meet work performance requirements in the practicum including punctuality and productivity.

How demonstrated:

How not demonstrated:

Specific areas that need improvement:

On the scale below, rate the practicum student in relation to this specific learning objective from 1 to 10 where 1 means "complete failure" and 10 means "complete success."

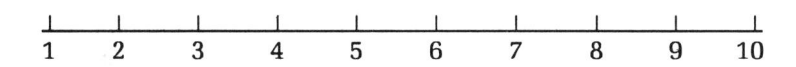

```
|----|----|----|----|----|----|----|----|----|
1    2    3    4    5    6    7    8    9    10
```

What specific tasks and/or behaviors need to be demonstrated to raise the above rating on the next practicum evaluation? Explain in detail below.

A

1.8 Other_____

How demonstrated:

How not demonstrated:

Specific areas that need improvement:

On the scale below, rate the practicum student in relation to this specific learning objective from 1 to 10 where 1 means "complete failure" and 10 means "complete success."

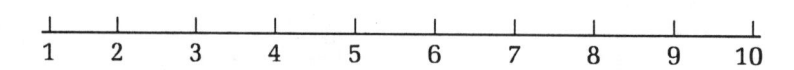

```
|___|___|___|___|___|___|___|___|___|
1   2   3   4   5   6   7   8   9   10
```

What specific tasks and/or behaviors need to be demonstrated to raise the above rating on the next practicum evaluation? Explain in detail below.

LEARNING GOAL 2:
FUNCTIONS EFFECTIVELY WITHIN AN ORGANIZATIONAL CONTEXT

The student will articulate an understanding of, and an ability to work within, a social service organization according to its purpose, structure, and constraints and to analyze the relationship to the community served.

Learning Objectives:

2.1 Has demonstrated the ability to work within and interpret practicum setting policy, structure, and function to clientele and others.

How demonstrated:

How not demonstrated:

Specific areas that need improvement:

On the scale below, rate the practicum student in relation to this specific learning objective from 1 to 10 where 1 means "complete failure" and 10 means "complete success."

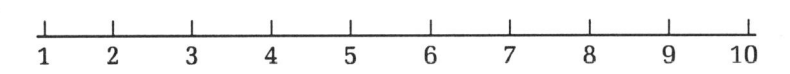

```
|----|----|----|----|----|----|----|----|----|
1    2    3    4    5    6    7    8    9    10
```

What specific tasks and/or behaviors need to be demonstrated to raise the above rating on the next practicum evaluation? Explain in detail below.

A

240 *Appendix A*

2.2 Has demonstrated the ability to identify and link available services, resources, and opportunities to meet the needs of the client system.

How demonstrated:

How not demonstrated:

Specific areas that need improvement:

On the scale below, rate the practicum student in relation to this specific learning objective from 1 to 10 where 1 means "complete failure" and 10 means "complete success."

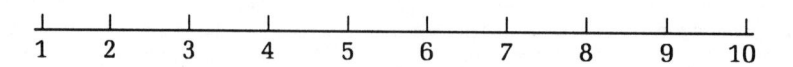

```
|----|----|----|----|----|----|----|----|----|
1    2    3    4    5    6    7    8    9    10
```

What specific tasks and/or behaviors need to be demonstrated to raise the above rating on the next practicum evaluation? Explain in detail below.

2.3 Has demonstrated the ability to describe and analyze the relationship between agency policies and service delivery.

How demonstrated:

How not demonstrated:

Specific areas that need improvement:

On the scale below, rate the practicum student in relation to this specific learning objective from 1 to 10 where 1 means "complete failure" and 10 means "complete success."

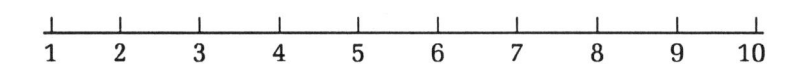

```
|----|----|----|----|----|----|----|----|----|----|
 1    2    3    4    5    6    7    8    9    10
```

What specific tasks and/or behaviors need to be demonstrated to raise the above rating on the next practicum evaluation? Explain in detail below.

2.4 Has demonstrated the ability to understand the broad social issues facing the organization and the community.

How demonstrated:

How not demonstrated:

Specific areas that need improvement:

On the scale below, rate the practicum student in relation to this specific learning objective from 1 to 10 where 1 means "complete failure" and 10 means "complete success."

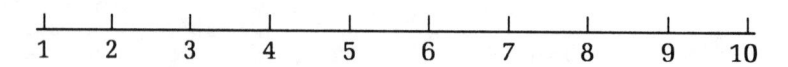

```
1   2   3   4   5   6   7   8   9   10
```

What specific tasks and/or behaviors need to be demonstrated to raise the above rating on the next practicum evaluation? Explain in detail below.

2.5 Other_____

How demonstrated:

How not demonstrated:

Specific areas that need improvement:

On the scale below, rate the practicum student in relation to this specific learning objective from 1 to 10 where 1 means "complete failure" and 10 means "complete success."

```
|____|____|____|____|____|____|____|____|____|
 1    2    3    4    5    6    7    8    9   10
```

What specific tasks and/or behaviors need to be demonstrated to raise the above rating on the next practicum evaluation? Explain in detail below.

LEARNING GOAL 3:
FUNCTIONS EFFECTIVELY UTILIZING
KNOWLEDGE-DIRECTED PRACTICE SKILLS

The student will apply knowledge to practice situations and develop competence in applying the general method of social work.

Engagement

Learning Objectives:

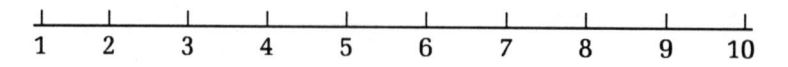

3.1 Has demonstrated the ability to engage others and identify problems or concerns.

How demonstrated:

How not demonstrated:

Specific areas that need improvement:

On the scale below, rate the practicum student in relation to this specific learning objective from 1 to 10 where 1 means "complete failure" and 10 means "complete success."

```
|___|___|___|___|___|___|___|___|___|
 1   2   3   4   5   6   7   8   9   10
```

What specific tasks and/or behaviors need to be demonstrated to raise the above rating on the next practicum evaluation? Explain in detail below.

3.2 Has demonstrated the ability to clarify purpose, role, and establish a mutual contract.

How demonstrated:

How not demonstrated:

Specific areas that need improvement:

On the scale below, rate the practicum student in relation to this specific learning objective from 1 to 10 where 1 means "complete failure" and 10 means "complete success."

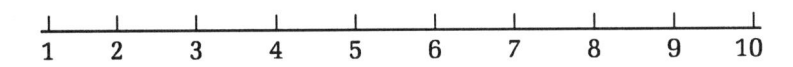

```
|----|----|----|----|----|----|----|----|----|----|
 1    2    3    4    5    6    7    8    9   10
```

What specific tasks and/or behaviors need to be demonstrated to raise the above rating on the next practicum evaluation? Explain in detail below.

Appendix A

3.3 Other_____

How demonstrated:

How not demonstrated:

Specific areas that need improvement:

On the scale below, rate the practicum student in relation to this specific learning objective from 1 to 10 where 1 means "complete failure" and 10 means "complete success."

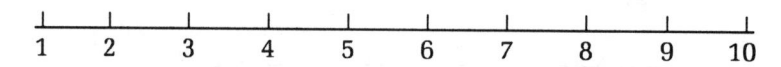

```
|----|----|----|----|----|----|----|----|----|
1    2    3    4    5    6    7    8    9   10
```

What specific tasks and/or behaviors need to be demonstrated to raise the above rating on the next practicum evaluation? Explain in detail below.

Assessment

Learning Objectives:

3.4 Has demonstrated the ability to identify the necessary data required and obtain it from appropriate sources.

How demonstrated:

How not demonstrated:

Specific areas that need improvement:

On the scale below, rate the practicum student in relation to this specific learning objective from 1 to 10 where 1 means "complete failure" and 10 means "complete success."

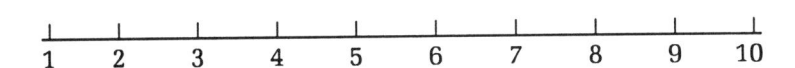

```
|----|----|----|----|----|----|----|----|----|
1    2    3    4    5    6    7    8    9    10
```

What specific tasks and/or behaviors need to be demonstrated to raise the above rating on the next practicum evaluation? Explain in detail below.

A

Appendix A

3.5 Has demonstrated the ability to articulate a comprehensive assessment.

How demonstrated:

How not demonstrated:

Specific areas that need improvement:

On the scale below, rate the practicum student in relation to this specific learning objective from 1 to 10 where 1 means "complete failure" and 10 means "complete success."

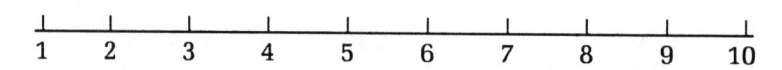

```
|----|----|----|----|----|----|----|----|----|----|
 1    2    3    4    5    6    7    8    9    10
```

What specific tasks and/or behaviors need to be demonstrated to raise the above rating on the next practicum evaluation? Explain in detail below.

3.6   Other_____

How demonstrated:

How not demonstrated:

Specific areas that need improvement:

On the scale below, rate the practicum student in relation to this specific learning objective from 1 to 10 where 1 means "complete failure" and 10 means "complete success."

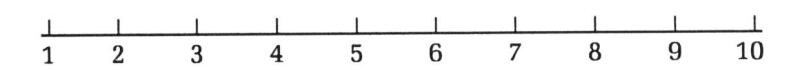

```
 |    |    |    |    |    |    |    |    |    |
 1    2    3    4    5    6    7    8    9   10
```

What specific tasks and/or behaviors need to be demonstrated to raise the above rating on the next practicum evaluation? Explain in detail below.

A

Planning

Learning Objectives:

3.7   Has demonstrated the ability to develop a social work plan based on the assessment.

How demonstrated:

How not demonstrated:

Specific areas that need improvement:

On the scale below, rate the practicum student in relation to this specific learning objective from 1 to 10 where 1 means "complete failure" and 10 means "complete success."

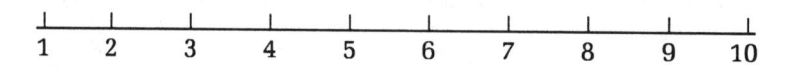

```
|----|----|----|----|----|----|----|----|----|
1    2    3    4    5    6    7    8    9    10
```

What specific tasks and/or behaviors need to be demonstrated to raise the above rating on the next practicum evaluation? Explain in detail below.

3.8   Other_____

How demonstrated:

How not demonstrated:

Specific areas that need improvement:

On the scale below, rate the practicum student in relation to this specific learning objective from 1 to 10 where 1 means "complete failure" and 10 means "complete success."

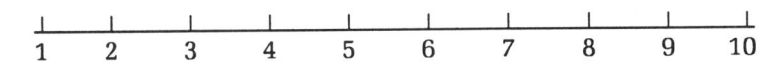

```
|----|----|----|----|----|----|----|----|----|
1    2    3    4    5    6    7    8    9    10
```

What specific tasks and/or behaviors need to be demonstrated to raise the above rating on the next practicum evaluation? Explain in detail below.

Implementation

Learning Objectives:

3.9 Has demonstrated the ability to identify and select appropriate helping strategies.

How demonstrated:

How not demonstrated:

Specific areas that need improvement:

On the scale below, rate the practicum student in relation to this specific learning objective from 1 to 10 where 1 means "complete failure" and 10 means "complete success."

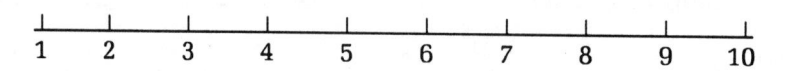

```
|   |   |   |   |   |   |   |   |   |
1   2   3   4   5   6   7   8   9   10
```

What specific tasks and/or behaviors need to be demonstrated to raise the above rating on the next practicum evaluation? Explain in detail below.

3.10 Has demonstrated an understanding of the complexities and difficulties in change.

How demonstrated:

How not demonstrated:

Specific areas that need improvement:

On the scale below, rate the practicum student in relation to this specific learning objective from 1 to 10 where 1 means "complete failure" and 10 means "complete success."

```
|----|----|----|----|----|----|----|----|----|----|
1    2    3    4    5    6    7    8    9    10
```

What specific tasks and/or behaviors need to be demonstrated to raise the above rating on the next practicum evaluation? Explain in detail below.

A

3.11 Other_____

How demonstrated:

How not demonstrated:

Specific areas that need improvement:

On the scale below, rate the practicum student in relation to this specific learning objective from 1 to 10 where 1 means "complete failure" and 10 means "complete success."

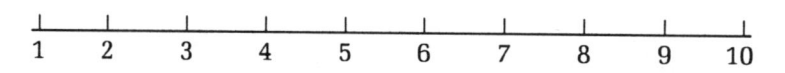

```
|---|---|---|---|---|---|---|---|---|
1   2   3   4   5   6   7   8   9   10
```

What specific tasks and/or behaviors need to be demonstrated to raise the above rating on the next practicum evaluation? Explain in detail below.

Evaluation

Learning Objectives:

3.12 Has demonstrated the ability to analyze and describe different phases of the helping process.

How demonstrated:

How not demonstrated:

Specific areas that need improvement:

On the scale below, rate the practicum student in relation to this specific learning objective from 1 to 10 where 1 means "complete failure" and 10 means "complete success."

```
 1  2  3  4  5  6  7  8  9  10
```

What specific tasks and/or behaviors need to be demonstrated to raise the above rating on the next practicum evaluation? Explain in detail below.

3.13 Has demonstrated the ability to involve the clients in evaluating the extent to which the objectives are being accomplished.

How demonstrated:

How not demonstrated:

Specific areas that need improvement:

On the scale below, rate the practicum student in relation to this specific learning objective from 1 to 10 where 1 means "complete failure" and 10 means "complete success."

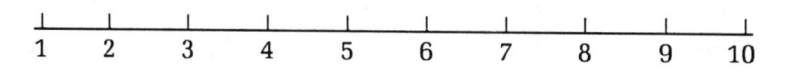

```
|----|----|----|----|----|----|----|----|----|----|
 1    2    3    4    5    6    7    8    9    10
```

What specific tasks and/or behaviors need to be demonstrated to raise the above rating on the next practicum evaluation? Explain in detail below.

3.14 Other_____

How demonstrated:

How not demonstrated:

Specific areas that need improvement:

On the scale below, rate the practicum student in relation to this specific learning objective from 1 to 10 where 1 means "complete failure" and 10 means "complete success."

```
|----|----|----|----|----|----|----|----|----|
1    2    3    4    5    6    7    8    9    10
```

What specific tasks and/or behaviors need to be demonstrated to raise the above rating on the next practicum evaluation? Explain in detail below.

Termination

Learning Objectives:

3.15 Has demonstrated the ability to terminate constructively with appropriate follow-up or referral.

How demonstrated:

How not demonstrated:

Specific areas that need improvement:

On the scale below, rate the practicum student in relation to this specific learning objective from 1 to 10 where 1 means "complete failure" and 10 means "complete success."

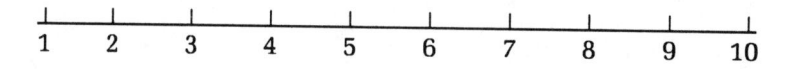

```
|----|----|----|----|----|----|----|----|----|
1    2    3    4    5    6    7    8    9    10
```

What specific tasks and/or behaviors need to be demonstrated to raise the above rating on the next practicum evaluation? Explain in detail below.

3.16 Other_____

How demonstrated:

How not demonstrated:

Specific areas that need improvement:

On the scale below, rate the practicum student in relation to this specific learning objective from 1 to 10 where 1 means "complete failure" and 10 means "complete success."

```
|----|----|----|----|----|----|----|----|----|
1    2    3    4    5    6    7    8    9    10
```

What specific tasks and/or behaviors need to be demonstrated to raise the above rating on the next practicum evaluation? Explain in detail below.

LEARNING GOAL 4: FUNCTIONS EFFECTIVELY WITHIN AN EVALUATIVE CONTEXT

The student will contribute to the improvement of service delivery by evaluating professional development, effectiveness as a social work practitioner, and the practicum setting.

Learning Objectives:

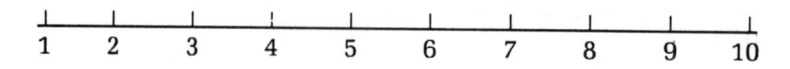

4.1 Has demonstrated the ability to evaluate accurately a level of competence and effectiveness in practice.

How demonstrated:

How not demonstrated:

Specific areas that need improvement:

On the scale below, rate the practicum student in relation to this specific learning objective from 1 to 10 where 1 means "complete failure" and 10 means "complete success."

```
|____|____|____|____|____|____|____|____|____|
1    2    3    4    5    6    7    8    9   10
```

What specific tasks and/or behaviors need to be demonstrated to raise the above rating on the next practicum evaluation? Explain in detail below.

4.2 Has demonstrated the ability to receive, understand, and consider feedback.

How demonstrated:

How not demonstrated:

Specific areas that need improvement:

On the scale below, rate the practicum student in relation to this specific learning objective from 1 to 10 where 1 means "complete failure" and 10 means "complete success."

```
|----|----|----|----|----|----|----|----|----|----|
 1    2    3    4    5    6    7    8    9    10
```

What specific tasks and/or behaviors need to be demonstrated to raise the above rating on the next practicum evaluation? Explain in detail below.

4.3 Has demonstrated the ability to evaluate the practicum experience.

How demonstrated:

How not demonstrated:

Specific areas that need improvement:

On the scale below, rate the practicum student in relation to this specific learning objective from 1 to 10 where 1 means "complete failure" and 10 means "complete success."

```
|----|----|----|----|----|----|----|----|----|----|
 1    2    3    4    5    6    7    8    9    10
```

What specific tasks and/or behaviors need to be demonstrated to raise the above rating on the next practicum evaluation? Explain in detail below.

4.4 Other_____

How demonstrated:

How not demonstrated:

Specific areas that need improvement:

On the scale below, rate the practicum student in relation to this specific learning objective from 1 to 10 where 1 means "complete failure" and 10 means "complete success."

```
|____|____|____|____|____|____|____|____|____|
1    2    3    4    5    6    7    8    9    10
```

What specific tasks and/or behaviors need to be demonstrated to raise the above rating on the next practicum evaluation? Explain in detail below.

Grade recommended or assessment:

Summary comments by field instructor—include areas of strength, any concerns, and focus for continued learning:

Summary comments by student—include areas of strength, any concerns, and focus for continued learning:

Summary comments by field liaison—include areas of strength, any concerns, and focus for continued learning:

Field Instructor's Signature	Student's Signature	Field Liaison's Signature
_____	_____	_____

Index

Agency:
    as a social system, 97–102
    clientele of an, 78
    crises of an, 76–77
    definition of, 28
    evaluation of, 214–223
    philosophy of an, 77
    resources of an, 79
    structure of an, 77
    theoretical orientation of an, 78
American *Code of Ethics*, 13–16
Apprenticeship, a practicum as an, 1

Canadian *Code of Ethics*, 16–26
Code of Ethics:
    American, 13–16
    Canadian, 16–26
Community, getting to know your, 103–107
Compromise, the practice of, 86

Dilemmas:
    client-related practicum, 181–190
    instructor-related practicum, 191–194
    student-related practicum, 190–191
Documentation, the use of, 152–166

Ethical decision making, 41

Field education manual, definition of, 28
Field instructor, 2, 29, 75, 124–125, 198–213
Field liaison, 2, 29, 125
Field placement, see practicum
Field supervisor, see field instructor
Files, the use of client, 160–161
Final practicum evaluation, 223–264

Grading process, practicum, 6
Grievance procedures, 178–179
Group supervisory conferences, 144

Humility, the practice of, 86

Integrative seminars, 7, 30
Interviews, preparing for the first, 152
Interviews, preplacement, 64–71, 80

Journal, keeping a, 90, 155–160

Learning contracts, 111-124
Learning objectives, defining, 114
Learning styles, using your, 126-128

Mid-term evaluation conferences, 174-178

Observing others, 87-88

Portfolio, creating a student, 54-57
Practice methods course, definition of, 30
Practicum:
    definition of a, 31
    perceptions of a, 10
    preparing for a second, 224
    rating of a, 62-63, 71-74
    selection of a, 58-61
Practicum coordinator, 2, 31
Practicum evaluation forms, interpretation of, 113
Practicum instructor, see field instructor
Practicum setting, 32, 91-95
Practicum student, definition of, 32
Preliminary practicum evaluation, 128-132
Preplacement interviews, 64-71, 80
Preplacement students, 8, 32
Process recordings, 162

Recordings:
    process, 162
    taped, 162

Self-profile, creating a, 48-51
Seminars, integrative, 7
Social work, the profession of, 9
Social work program, definition of a, 33, 54
Students, preplacement, 8, 32
Supervisory conferences:
    definition of, 33
    evaluating, 146-151
    keeping notes from, 161
    planning for, 145
    preparing for, 108
    use of, 136-144
Support systems, finding, 88

Taped recordings, 162
Termination:
    with the agency, 214-222
    with the client, 197-198
    with the field instructor, 198-213
Thank you letter, writing of a, 81-82

Values, student, 38

THE BOOK'S MANUFACTURE

The Social Work Practicum: A Student Guide
was typeset by Andrukow Compositors,
Calgary, Alberta, Canada.
Text and display type is Melior.
Printing and binding were done by
Arcata Graphics, Kingsport, Tennessee.
Cover design and internal design by John B. Goetz,
Design & Production Services, Co., Chicago.